David Willis McCullough

THE
UNENDING
MYSTERY

David Willis McCullough's previous books include
Brooklyn . . . and How It Got That Way, several mysteries, and, as editor, a number of anthologies, most
recently *Wars of the Irish Kings*. For many years he
was a member of the Book-of-the-Month Club Editorial Board. He lives in Hastings-on-Hudson, New York.

THE
UNENDING
MYSTERY

A JOURNEY THROUGH
LABYRINTHS AND MAZES

David Willis McCullough

ANCHOR BOOKS
A DIVISION OF RANDOM HOUSE, INC.
NEW YORK

FOR

ROSS FERLITO

AND

PETER HEIDTMANN

FIRST ANCHOR BOOKS EDITION, NOVEMBER 2005

The Library of Congress has cataloged the Pantheon edition as follows:
McCullough, David W.
The unending mystery: a journey through labyrinths and mazes /
David Willis McCullough.
p.   cm.
Includes biographical references and index.
1. Labyrinths.   2. Maze gardens.   3. Maze puzzles.   I. Title.
BL325.L3M33 2004
306.4'8—dc21
20040349867

Anchor ISBN-10: 1-4000-3164-8
Anchor ISBN-13: 978-1-4000-3164-1

Author photograph © John Maggioto
Book design by M. Kristen Bearse

www.anchorbooks.com

Printed in the United States of America
10   9   8   7   6   5   4   3   2   1

CONTENTS

THE
UNENDING
MYSTERY

INTRODUCTION

"Be Like the Fox . . ."

EVEN THE NEWEST LABYRINTH HAS A PAST. Labyrinths are painted on the walls of ancient caves and carved onto Neolithic rock out-croppings. They appear in some of the oldest legends in lands as different as the Greek Isles and the American Southwest, but were also the stuff of myths even older than the stories as we now know them. They have represented the birth of a single child and the annual rebirth of an entire season, even of the earth itself. They have at different times symbolized the descent into hell and the fiery underworld, the ascent to the heavenly City of God and the more mundane route to Jerusalem. They have served as the hallmark of architects and may have been used as mathematical devices to calibrate a working lunar calendar.

The labyrinth has played a role in divine worship in cathedrals, and its more worldly cousin, the high-walled maze, has provided effective trysting spots for lovers in many a garden. The semantic difference between the words *labyrinth* and *maze* is a new one. For most of their histories the terms have been interchangeable. But the new distinction—which has yet to make it into some dictionaries—is useful. Nowadays, a labyrinth is a single circuitous path that leads uninterrupted to a center, while a maze is a puzzle with many forks in the road that demand choices. More detailed distinctions will emerge later on in this book, but for now it is good enough to think in terms of the single-path, nonjudgmental labyrinth versus the tricky, perhaps entrapping maze. A labyrinth appears on one of the oldest minted coins, and it might be useful to think of the labyrinth and the maze as the heads and tails of a coin, the rather solemn labyrinth (heads, of course) and the raffish, devil-may-care maze. It would be a mistake not to consider them together. To maintain, as some have, that the maze is a frivolous distraction from a more serious subject is to miss the complexity—and the ambiguity—of a labyrinth. And it seems equally fruitless to debate whether the maze, as it is now defined, is a subdivision of labyrinths or if the labyrinth is actually just an especially tidy maze.

The names themselves, divorced from any particular image, play active roles in our everyday vocabulary as synonyms for chaos, disorder and confusion. The New York Public Library computer lists 344 titles that contain the word *labyrinth*, 204 with *maze*. (The cautious librarian who so helpfully provided these figures, however, insisted that I warn you that some may be different editions of the same books.) Almost none of them deal with the subject of this book; they range, instead, from modern political history (*The Turkish Labyrinth*) to medical studies of the inner ear. Mountain climbers call alpine ice fields labyrinths. A cab driver threading his way to a midtown railroad station complains about the maze of one-way streets. A *New York Times* headline reads, "The Labyrinthine Morass of Spying in the Cold War." What editorial writer commenting on cities or city government could survive without the words, usually accompanied by the adjective *bureaucratic*? Everyone knows what those words mean, even when they are wrong.

But the labyrinth is one of mankind's oldest artistic creations, an image drawn or carved or scratched by a human hand that does not copy something seen in nature. It is one of the first images—

maybe *the* first—to be inspired by the human imagination. And very early in its history, the image and the name both became closely associated with that most human of creations, the city. Throughout its long history, the labyrinth (and later the maze) has been associated either symbolically or actually with many different ideas or concepts, but the connection with the city is almost always there.

Over the centuries, the seductive image of the labyrinth has become a glorious magpie's nest that can be stolen or borrowed or adapted for almost any purpose. The claims are staggering. A labyrinth can induce pregnancy, revive virility, ease childbirth, cure cancer, restore eyesight, heal the lame, free souls from purgatory. You can win the hand of a beautiful girl by running the path faster than any other boy in town. You can learn the wisdom of King Solomon by decoding its meaning. It's an athletic field. It's a dance floor, a place to thresh grain, a sacrificial site. The diameter of the labyrinth in Chartres Cathedral is one-millionth the diameter of the earth exactly (or is it one-billionth?), and in its geometry are hidden the secrets of the universe's building blocks. All this is worth hearing because it has all been so devoutly believed. We can only ask, What is there about this image that inspires such belief?

The end of the twentieth century saw a great revival of interest in labyrinths and mazes. (Jeff Saward, a British labyrinth expert, has pointed out that the same thing happened at the end of the nineteenth.) On a practical level, the maze craze—the building of puzzle mazes as tourist attractions and the carving of cornfields into maize mazes—has saved many stately homes in England and family farms in North America from falling into financial ruin. Spiritually, the discovery, or rediscovery, of the labyrinth as an aid to meditation has had a profound effect. Religious institutions from the so-called New Age to the profoundly conservative have installed permanent or temporary labyrinths for their worshippers. And like the stately homes that added a maze or two to draw a paying crowd, churches are finding new visitors (some of whom join as members) walking their paths. Medical facilities are the new growth sectors, with hospitals and clinics adding labyrinths for their patients, their patients' families and the medical staff itself. Lap-sized labyrinths made of wood, plastic or just an image printed on cloth or a piece of paper are now common sights at bedsides, where patients follow the ancient pathways with their fingers to seek the peace and comfort some walkers find. And the trendiest health spas now often have labyrinths on their well-manicured grounds.

I should make a personal statement concerning how I feel about labyrinths. I have walked hundreds of them in France, Britain and the United States, ones in cathedrals, fields, public parks, woods, playgrounds, Renaissance fairs, backyards, just about anywhere. They have been made of stone or turf or brick or canvas, been lined with hedges or marked out with chalk, flags, seashells, tree stumps, masking tape or—once—Christmas tree lights. I have never had a profound flash of insight or a Saul-on-the-road-to-Damascus revelation, as some have reported. I have never been cured of any medical affliction. Yet I believe that walking a full-sized medieval or Chartres Cathedral–style labyrinth can be a deeply moving experience, that it can have a truly calming effect and that every now and then, it can be an occasion of joy. The happy moments need not be profound. I once found myself happily remembering the stations not of the cross, but of stops on a suburban railway line. I have sensed that the way to the center can be introspective and the way out as upbeat as what I imagine the way back from the cemetery must be like at a New Orleans jazz funeral. Sometimes, that is, not always. With me, what is triggered most often by walking those twisting, curving paths is memory, good memories and bad ones, and now and then a sense of moving through a design as old as the human imagination, one that's blessedly free of dogma and judgment.

At the conclusion of "Little Gidding," the last of his "Four Quartets," T. S. Eliot writes:

> *We shall not cease from exploration*
> *And the end of all our exploring*
> *Will be to arrive where we started*
> *And know the place for the first time.*

It is a popular quotation with labyrinth enthusiasts in that it suggests a feeling they know well. Apt as Eliot is, I prefer the concluding lines of Wendell Berry's "Manifesto: The Mad Farmer Liberation Front":

> *Be like the fox*
> *who makes more tracks than necessary,*
> *some in the wrong direction.*
> *Practice resurrection.*

But perhaps it's best to consider the words of a working labyrinth builder. Ariane Burgess is a Scot who now lives in New York City and continues to rally children of the Mott Haven section of the South Bronx to help her construct labyrinths in the shadows of their neighborhood's high-rise housing projects. She says, "When volunteers look at a labyrinth and say, 'Nothing's in the center,' I say, 'You are.' "

One

THE IMAGE

THE DESIGN MAY LOOK COMPLICATED, but with a little practice a child could scratch it on a wall in seconds: the long arcs to the left and right, the sudden reversals in direction, a path that leads back and forth, inward and outward, until it finally reaches the center. It seems complex, with each side mirroring the other, but you can trace it freehand in the bare earth or on a sandy beach in just the time it takes to drag a stick across the ground. Or you could use a trick, a mnemonic device. Draw a plus sign, and put a dot in each of the four corners. Different people might see this image differently, as basic geometry or a magical device or an emblematic representation of the cross of Christ defended by the apostles Matthew, Mark, Luke and John. Or perhaps it is a compass rose, indicating north, south, east and west as well as the four corners of the earth. Now, starting at the top of the upright arm of the plus sign, draw a curving line to the dot on the left. Then, from the dot on the upper right, draw a curving line to the end of the arm on the left. Continue on around the image—connecting arm to dot, dot to arm—until it is complete, the simplest possible labyrinth.*

---

*See Appendix: How to Draw a Labyrinth.

The labyrinth design is far older than most of the myths and stories about it that we now remember. An image cut into the wall of a tomb in Sardinia may date back to 2500 B.C. Another, in the Val Camonica, near Brescia on the Italian mainland, may date to 1800 B.C. Some think a labyrinth painted in red on the roof of a small cave near Trapani in Sicily may even have been made in 3000 B.C. And although all these dates can be challenged (as indeed they have been), similar designs are found on Neolithic and Bronze Age remains in Spain, Ireland and North Africa and on ancient rock faces in the American Southwest. Sometimes square or rectangular, sometimes round, oval or simply lopsided, the image is always basically the same. Never a simple, elegant spiral sweeping steadily inward, it is always a single meandering path with no branches or dead ends that weaves and circles— usually seven times—before reaching the center. Now usually called the classic, or Cretan, design (from the labyrinth's later association with the Minotaur legend and with coins imprinted with a similar labyrinth design minted in fourth- and fifth- century B.C. Crete), it is self-contained, complex and built around an undeniable center.

Its meaning is one of our oldest mysteries, but clues to the origins of the labyrinth design can be seen in Neolithic and Bronze Age rock carvings on rugged hillsides throughout Europe. One of the best examples is in Argyll, on the west coast of Scotland, at a place called Achnabreck ("Rock of the Host" in Gaelic). It is a

cluster of three large, curved outcroppings covered with man-made Stone Age markings. As with the sites of similar markings in northern England and Spain, the setting is spectacular, a high, wooded ridge between the Sound of Jura and Loch Fyne, with the glint of light reflecting off water far in the distance and a steep hillside dropping through stands of trees and open fields to the valley far below. Although visible in full daylight, the carvings are best seen during the hour or so before sunset as the receding light catches the grooves and incisions to cast deepening patterns of shadows. Observers over the centuries have suspected the carving to be a map either of the landscape below or the heavens overhead. The gray rocks are marked with round, hollowed-out depressions the size of halved golf and tennis balls. Archaeologists call them "cups" and most—but not all—are surrounded by concentric circles, or "rings," often as many as seven of them, just as there are seven circuits to the Cretan labyrinth. There are also targetlike clusters of concentric rings without cups, and many of the cup-and-rings are joined together by straight lines that resemble gutters. Also carved into the rocks are spirals, even double and triple spirals that resemble smaller versions of the much-photographed spirals at Newgrange, the fourth-millennium B.C. passage grave in the Boyne Valley of Ireland.

Four or five millennia after the fact, it is impossible for us to know what those seemingly random designs may have meant to their carvers. But this—luckily—has not stopped anyone from trying to guess. Over the years the map theories have been the most popular, partially because the same images appear on outcroppings hundreds, even thousands of miles apart, as though Neolithic travelers had common symbols to guide them from place to place or to orient them under the stars. One of the earliest nineteenth-century theories was that the cup-and-rings were models of the circular hill forts that stood close by many of the carvings. Other suggestions have been that they were molds for making weapons and arti-

facts, or that they were grooves in which sticks were placed to ground tents or larger structures, or that they were primitive artistic expressions or "Kilroy Was Here" signatures. A particularly melodramatic theory—and one that reflects the popular notion that our ancestors were very gory folk indeed—was that the outcroppings marked sacrificial sites and that the cups, rings and spirals were to catch and display blood, even though most sites slope far too much to hold blood—or support tents—for long.

Alexander Thom has contributed much to modern understanding of Stone Age archaeology, astronomy and architecture with his contention that the builders of Stonehenge and other prehistoric monuments used a basic unit of measure called the megalithic yard (2.72 feet). His calculations show that straight lines in many of these carvings can be sighted along to make astronomical observations. In fact, he suggested that the carved spirals might encode information on the proper astronomic use of standing stones and circles. But, then, Professor Thom's critics have noted his uncanny ability to line up just about any megalithic site with something in the night sky.

Whatever their purpose or meaning, circles and spirals were clearly the basic elements of these early inscriptions. Throughout history (and before), circles and spirals have been attributed considerable power, be it in geometry, theology or magic. The circle, without beginning or end, has symbolized infinity or perfection in many cultures, and the spiral—a coiled serpent that renews itself by shedding its skin—has been a common and reoccurring sign of rebirth and regeneration. A vivid representation of the link between spiral and snake can be seen in a petroglyph at Gila Bend, Arizona. Much of the carving would not look out of place at Achnabreck. A ring-and-cup-like target of concentric circles is linked by a straight line to a tightly wound spiral. Next to the spiral is carved a fairly realistic snake.

Separated by thousands of years, two different sacred sanctuaries in the British Isles, for surely very different reasons, saw fit to honor the spiral. In the megalithic circle called Temple Wood, just a few miles north of Achnabreck, a carved spiral unwinds on one side of a standing stone, turns the corner to the broader front and rewinds there. The stone may have been carved where it stands or may have been brought from an even older monument. Having endured millennia of foul Scottish weather, the double spiral is difficult to see, but it survives. Hundreds of miles south in Llanbedr, a small seacoast town in Wales, is another ancient rock spiral. The village, once famous for its seashells, contains two ancient dolmens and several standing stones, and in a place of honor in the local church is a granite stone with spiral ornamentation that someone found years ago up in the hills and, recognizing it as something sacred, brought it into the church. A coiling spiral venerated in a Christian sanctuary, in spite of God's curse on Eden's serpent? Clearly it evokes a faith older than the current creed.

A labyrinth, of course, is not made of concentric circles with a cup at its heart, and it is not a graceful spiral. But if those two basic petroglyphic images—the circles and the spiral—are placed one on top of the other, the result is something that with very little modification looks a lot like a labyrinth, a complex, self-contained image that is not found in nature. That the labyrinth is a created and not a natural shape is important. The circles, spiral, lines and dots that cover the outcroppings at Achnabreck are all shapes observable in the world around the stone outcropping, either in the landscape or the sky or the bones and entrails of slaughtered animals. At times the line between what was man-made and what was natural on the carved stones is downright confusing. One of the memorable flaps in modern paleontology came when geologists pointed out that some of the markings being studied and interpreted (sometimes quite fancifully) were in fact natural pockmarks. A particularly memorable case was when what had been interpreted as scenes of a battle between two warring tribes chipped onto a boulder at Clonfinlough in Ireland turned out to be a matter of ordinary weathering. A turning point in the evolution of culture came at the moment when somewhere an anonymous rock carver or wall painter combined and elaborated on the simple images he—or maybe it was a she—saw in nature to create a new, unique and utterly human-made image, a labyrinth.

Part of the appeal of the cathedral at Chartres, home of one of the oldest church labyrinths in Europe, is the tension—amidst the beauty of the medieval stained-glass windows—in the some-times bizarre jumble of rounded Romanesque and pointed Gothic arches. The Gothic spirit prevails, but there is the excitement of observing the moment in history when the rounded arch reaches up to become an arrow pointed toward heaven. There is some-thing of the same tension at Achnabreck—a place that may be no less sacred than Chartres—as the cup-and-rings sometimes over-lap one another and the multiarmed spirals curve to comply with the irregularity of the stone. Sometimes they almost—but never quite—become labyrinths. Among the similar carvings at Bally-gowan, a much smaller and less spectacular outcropping a few miles away, the historian Nigel Pennick has identified an image that might, charitably, be called labyrinthine, but few others have seen it that way. Some cup-and-rings turning into labyrinths can be found in more recent (900–500 B.C.) petroglyphs at Pontevedra, in Galicia, Spain, but the time is not quite right at Achnabreck. The final step to the invented image is yet to come.

No one knows what tongue these early rock carvers spoke, but whatever it was no one was calling their images labyrinths. *Lab-yrintus* is a Roman word, although no one is confident about its origin. The multivolume *Oxford English Dictionary*, the great arbiter of English word origins, throws up its hands and even in the most recent updating sticks to "unknown" when it comes to the word's roots, although it does add that they were probably non-Hellenic. Sir Arthur Evans, the turn-of-the-twentieth-century excavator (and rebuilder) of the ruins at Knossos, came up with a very tidy solution that—for a time, at least—enjoyed considerable popularity. He observed that one of the most common decorations in the palace, either as sculpture or as wall painting, was the image of the double-headed ax called *labrys*. Early Greek visitors to the ruins, he reasoned, saw the ax images, which were much more obvious than they were when Evans unearthed them, and called the site a *labyrinth*, a place of the double-headed axes, and the word then became confused with the legend of the imprisoned Minotaur and the maze. Most etymologists no longer accept this, but they have yet to advance a more convenient solution. In any case, *labyrinth* seems to have entered the English language in the late fourteenth century, referring to a confusing structure with many hallways (a reference from 1387 mentions "wyndyngs and wrynkelyngs"). Nearly fifty years later the word appeared in French, meaning an intricate wooden palisade used for military defense. Later, the French would also adopt *le dédale* (after Daedalus, the legendary maze maker) as a synonym.

If *labyrinth* has its murky roots in the classical world, *maze* is a thoroughly northern word. As an abbreviation of *amaze*, from its very beginnings in Old English it meant to "confuse," "confound" or "astonish." It also came to refer to a trick, as when, in *Troilus and Criseyde*, Chaucer wrote, "All this was but a mase." Variations of the same word with the same meaning pop up in many of the Scandinavian languages, although oddly enough in one Norwegian dialect it came to mean not "to confuse" but "to lose consciousness."

Throughout most of their histories, the words *labyrinth* and *maze* have been synonyms, but in the last twenty-five years or so an effort has been made to reduce confusion and see them as two distinct concepts. Accordingly, a labyrinth is now said to have a single path that weaves its way around a central point until it reaches its goal in the center. There are no forks in the road, no dead ends, no choices to be made. It is unicursal, one course, one-way. A maze is multicursal. There are many possible ways to go, but only one that will reach the center. It is a puzzle and—as it was with Chaucer—a trick in which there are many choices to be made, many incorrect possibilities and dead ends to avoid before reaching the goal. As an actual design, however, the puzzle maze is far younger than the labyrinth, appearing first in sixteenth-century books and gardens.

But in other parts of the world there are other names for the almost identical classical seven-circuit labyrinth image. In the American Southwest, the Hopi have the *tapu'at* (or "mother and child"). In Wales, there is *caerdroia* (probably a variation of the Welsh *caer y troiau*, "City of Turnings," which some read as "City of Troy"). In India, it is *kota* ("fort" or "city" in Hindi). As for Scandinavia, the Swedish labyrinth expert John Kraft has noted that many of the stone labyrinths there are named for cities famous as ruins: Troy (the most frequently used name), Jericho, Nineveh, Babylon, even Lisbon (destroyed, as readers of *Candide* know, by an earthquake in 1755).

The archaeologist Colin Renfrew has written about the phenomenon of nearly identical features of prehistoric architecture appearing in different cultures in different parts of the world. Corbeling, for instance, in which each upward course of stone extends out a little farther until it forms half of an arch or, even more complexly, part of a dome, is a common Stone Age building technique. Since it is found both at Newgrange, in Ireland, and in the Greek islands, popular belief once held that an ancient Mycenaean (or perhaps Irish) master builder had traveled about the known world constructing—Daedalus-like—stone wonders as he went. Proof of this was seen in a mark thought to be an image of a double-headed ax carved onto one of the megaliths at Stonehenge. Perhaps the ax—if indeed it was an ax—was even the master's signature. Renfrew and others have a far simpler explanation. They argue that no matter where they live, people will solve technical problems the same way if they have the same—or similar—

building materials to work with. If you have flat stones at hand and need to build an arch, corbeling (to use that example again) is the easiest, most obvious solution.

It is more difficult to account for the universality of the labyrinth image. The common building material here is not flat stone but the human imagination. What is hidden in its well-ordered, seemingly chaotic convolutions? What is there about it that was appealing even before there was a myth to accompany it? What made it both one of *Homo sapiens'* first complex designs and an enduring puzzle that still flickers across computer screens? One thing seems clear: like the corbel arch, it seems to emerge naturally and not as the result of a mystical Johnny Appleseed or an itinerant evangelist.

The ability to dash one off could have been nothing more than a child's trick of dexterity, a feat much like making a cat's cradle out of string. But perhaps the ability to make the sign of the labyrinth was taken as a manifestation of a deeper, more mystical, more magical knowledge. Its sinuous symmetry reminds some of the coils from entrails of sacrifices studied and poked over by ancient mystics to predict the future. It reminds others of the convolutions of the brain. Indeed a medieval Indian manuscript about the brain is illustrated not with an anatomical drawing but with a sketch of a labyrinth. To some, the folds and passages have a more gynecological symbolism. The Hopi Mother Earth drawings certainly suggests as much. In parts of Hindu India, pregnant women were once—and perhaps still are—given a design almost identical to the classic Cretan labyrinth to study. Called the *chakra vyuha*, it was intended to concentrate the woman's mind and ease the labor of childbirth as she followed the path out from the center with her eyes or fingers. The critic Lucy R. Lippard has written of another Hindu birth ritual in which a labyrinth design is traced in saffron on a bronze plate, then washed away with water that is drunk by the woman about to give birth. Similarly, some anecdotal evidence—but no more than that—suggests that in some parts of Cornwall, England, pregnant women studied, and perhaps traced with their fingers, labyrinth patterns cut into slate, much like the one exhibited in the Witchcraft Museum in Boscastle. And Ariadne's string, leading Theseus out of the mythic labyrinth on Crete, can easily be seen as an umbilicus. In its ambiguous universality, the labyrinth image becomes, as the poet Gerard Manley Hopkins once described night, the "womb-of-all, home-of-all, hearse-of-all."

The traditional interpretation of the Cretan labyrinth is that it represents a tortuous, all but inescapable maze. This doesn't make sense, because the "escape" is too easy. A reasonably competent laboratory monkey could find its way into the center and out again even without the promise of a banana. There is nothing in the least bit forbidding about it. It has been suggested that the design is in fact simply the correct route—perhaps it could be called a Minoan AAA road map—through a truly daunting, but unrecorded puzzle. But this idea, too, defies logic.

To understand the simplicity of the Cretan labyrinth image, it is helpful to consider the tidy, symmetrical design that is all but universally accepted as the symbol of the human heart. As a decoration on a Valentine's Day card, it bears little resemblance to the messy, ungainly organ that pulses away inside the rib cage. Yet millions who could never identify a real heart have no trouble knowing what that little symbol means. At some point very early in human history, sometime before the fifth century B.C., when the Cretan labyrinth image first appeared on coins minted in Knossos, the neat, elegant, easy-to-draw design became accepted as a symbol for something—both a place and a concept—far less comprehensible.

The ease with which the seven-circuit classical labyrinth can be drawn is surely one reason for its universality. It is a graffiti scrawler's dream come true. The same cannot be said for its descendant, the eleven-circuit medieval version. The original labyrinth is inspired folk art. The medieval one is a mathematical masterpiece. Although some believe the design was brought back from the Holy Land by returning crusaders, it in fact seems to have emerged in the late twelfth century from illustrations on manuscript pages in monastery libraries. Glorified in stone on the floors of France's great cathedrals, the image is the work of a geometrician, a sacred geometrician no doubt, but first and foremost a man who knew his numbers. The hand that drew it used a compass and a ruler.

He could also have been a mapmaker. For centuries, perhaps ever since it was drawn and painted in the thirteenth century, the *Mappa Mundi*, a giant map of the world, has been housed at the cathedral in Hereford, England. It is a little larger than five feet tall and four feet wide, with Jerusalem at its center. As with most medieval maps, east is at the top and west at the bottom. India is located the farthest east, just below the Garden of Eden and a scene of the Last Judgment in which an enthroned Jesus is dispatching sinners into, literally, the open-mouthed jaws of hell. Ireland is the western frontier. The *Mappa Mundi* depicts and locates the major churches of Christendom. There are also biblical scenes (Noah's ark, the Tower of Babel), natural landmarks (Etna's fiery volcanic cone), exotic animals (an elephant) and a few mythological figures, including a rather demure Minotaur—with

his tail draped elegantly over his arm— who stands, oddly enough, near the shore of the Caspian Sea. Two tiny holes can be found amidst the scars and scrapes on the map's single sheet of oversized parchment. They are not signs of age, however, but marks made by the point of the sharp arm of the mapmaker's compass and are in the center of two places represented

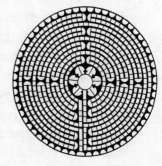

as perfect circles. One is walled and fortified Jerusalem. The other, just about as prominent as the Holy City, is the labyrinth on Crete. It is not, however, the traditional Cretan labyrinth, but an almost exact replica of the one that can still be seen at Chartres, and the details of its design could not have been drawn without a compass. This crowded map with its—to modern eyes— delightfully cartoonish sketches of men and beasts is hardly precise. It makes no effort to reproduce geographic shapes accurately (with rare exceptions, such as Sicily's distinctive triangular coastline) or draw historical buildings as they actually looked. Yet the labyrinth is eye-catching in its stark precision. There is nothing sketchy about it.

Perhaps another reason for this prominent display of geometry can be found on the lower left-hand corner of the *Mappa*, beyond the edge of the map itself. The Roman emperor Augustus is seen instructing (with a Latin caption) three surveyors, who are named, to go forth, "describe" every continent and report back. The geometrically exact labyrinth in a work that is otherwise drawn almost completely by freehand may be a testament to the surveyors'—and by extension the cartographer's—professionalism. After all, according to legend, both the labyrinth and the compass were inventions of Daedalus's.

The medieval, or Chartres-style, labyrinth is nothing if not precise. There are eleven circuits, or rings, surrounding the center, and the pathway turns thirty-four times en route from the entrance to the center, alternating left turns with right turns. As the path progresses, it journeys either a half or a quarter of the available circumference of each particular circuit it enters before it turns and reverses its direction again. The pattern of quarter and half distances is not consistent, as the alternating left and right turns are. But it is uniform, and it reverses itself halfway along the path to the center to repeat the sequence of quarters and halves in reverse order. The end of the reversed pattern is the center, and the way out, of course, repeats the whole sequence and reversal.

This pattern (which has been written about at length by Craig Wright), and even the rhythm of movement along the pathway of the labyrinth, may be clearer if the sequence of moving along the circuit is written out. Again, notice that after the half-circuit sweep at the midpoint on the way in, the sequence is reversed.

The walker enters the medieval labyrinth moving straight ahead until the pathway reaches the fifth of the eleven circuits and then makes a sharp (ninety degree) turn to the left. The pattern begins:

QUARTER of the way along the circuit, then turning toward the center, it reverses direction and goes a

QUARTER of the way back, makes a sharp left turn and goes straight toward the center and again passes four circuits and turns left on the fifth. Then, a

HALF way along the next circuit, reverses, a

HALF way along the next, reverses, then a

QUARTER

QUARTER

HALF

QUARTER

HALF

QUARTER

HALF

QUARTER

QUARTER

HALF

QUARTER

HALF: the midpoint on the way in; the pattern reverses.

QUARTER

HALF

QUARTER

QUARTER

HALF

QUARTER

HALF

QUARTER

HALF

QUARTER

QUARTER

HALF

HALF, then a sharp right turn toward the center, passing four circuits and making a right turn on the fifth

QUARTER

QUARTER, then a sharp right turn, passing four more circuits and
going directly into the Center.

No one walking the path is likely to notice all this, but it cre-
ates an unconscious rhythm. You can feel it simply by reading
the sequence aloud. The walker may, however, sense that on the
way to the center more time is spent walking away from the goal
than heading toward it. That is because the path from the outside
does not begin at the eleventh—or farthest—ring but goes immediately to the fifth circuit, then quickly makes its switchback
way inward to the very edge of the center before winding slowly
out to the farthest rings. Finally, surprisingly quickly, it rushes
back to enter the goal. Willem Kuipers, a modern Dutch labyrinth designer, has assembled an impressive array of charts and
graphs to demonstrate what generations of walkers have known
in their hearts, that the Chartres labyrinth's distinctive length
and cadence promote introspection and reflection. As for the long
arcs in the pathway of the Cretan labyrinth, Kuipers thinks they
better satisfy a sense of "quest."

The change from the Cretan labyrinth to the labyrinth of

Chartres is more than an advancement in geometry. The labyrinth became Christianized. Scenes of Theseus battling the Minotaur may decorate the centers of some medieval labyrinths, where the "cup" of the cup-and-rings once was, but now it is understood as a parable of Christ defeating the devil. Even more basically, the very pattern of the pathway's turns and reversals of direction form the shape and imprint of the cross upon the ancient image. The monks who, beginning in the ninth century, sketched the new, evolving design, did their work well. Even if in time they needed a ruler and a compass to do the job, the labyrinth had become a Christian icon.

Great claims have been made for the labyrinth. In the 1970s, before such books were popular, Jill Purce published a provocative study of the meaning (or meanings) of the spiral. In it she writes that the labyrinth is "at once the cosmos, the world, the individual life, the temple, the town, man, the womb—or the intestines—of the Mother (earth), the convolutions of the brain, the consciousness, the heart, the pilgrimage, the journey, and the Way."

Today, it is difficult to look at a labyrinth and not think of a path. But in the long and rich history of the labyrinth, seeing the image as a pathway to be walked is a new development, dating back a relatively recent eight hundred years or so. The chapters that follow will deal with the ways men and women have used the image for inspiration and contemplation, for decoration or for just plain fun. Whatever the labyrinth meant, it was abstract. It was also a work of inspired creation. We can see it now as one of our ancestors' first intellectual and artistic accomplishments, a transformation of one of their earliest marks on the face of the earth: a path leading somewhere else.

Two

THE MYTH

IT IS UNLIKELY THAT ANYONE in fifth or fourth century B.C. Crete had ever seen a real labyrinth, but heavy silver coins minted then at Knossos show what labyrinths looked like. On some coins they are round, on others square, but in all of them a single pathway twists and turns seven times as it circles its way to the center. Some of the coins' flip sides also show a crouching, perhaps prancing, figure of a man with a bull's head, his arms and legs contorted at sharp right angles. As an example of trumped-up local piety, the coins are the equal of the modern Roman manhole covers that Mussolini emblazoned with the old imperial initials S.P.Q.R. In both cases everyday objects—a coin, a manhole cover—were glorified to recall a grander, earlier time now embodied—if embodied at all—only by ruins. For the ancient Greeks and Cretans who traded with those silver coins, the story of King Minos's labyrinth at Knossos and the Minotaur—the half man, half bull—it imprisoned were as long gone as Julius Caesar was to Mussolini's Blackshirts.

The myth of the labyrinth—far older than the siege of Troy—was popular in the ancient world. In describing the shield of Achilles, Homer refers to it as something long in the past. The earliest classical travelers—there was still no Greek word for "tourist"—were well aware of it. Herodotus might not have been

familiar with the details of the Minotaur's prison, but when he came across ruins of a confusing structure in the Egyptian desert, something he thought "greater than the pyramids," he knew it was a labyrinth. And a historic, not a mythic one. Knossos was his point of reference.

Whether it is myth or history, the basic story is simple enough. Minos, like ancient heroes of Ireland and many other cultures, owned a spectacularly handsome bull. It had been given to him by the sea god Poseidon, with the understanding that the king would offer it up as a sacrifice. But the white bull from the sea was so handsome Minos could not bear to part with it and instead offered up an inferior beast from his herd. Poseidon got his revenge. He saw to it that the king's wife, Pasiphaë, fell in love with the white bull, which on Crete at that time was not unheard of. Pasiphaë's own mother-in-law, Europa, had fallen in love with a bull (Zeus, in disguise, playing one of his little tricks) and the result was the birth of Minos, who appeared fully human. The queen commissioned Daedalus, a master inventor and architect hiding out in Crete because of a murder charge against him back in Athens, to build a seductive imitation cow that she could hide inside. But Pasiphaë was not as lucky as Europa. After the mating (one version makes a point of saying the discreet Daedalus left the pasture and tactfully avoided witnessing the successful deception), a hideous offspring was born, half man, half bull. Minos became either so enraged or so embarrassed that he had the ever-inventive Daedalus build a labyrinthine enclosure for the Minotaur (and some said Pasiphaë as well) so complex that anyone who got in could never find a way out.

All this was happening at a time when Crete dominated the world and Athens, far from being what it would become, was something of a backwater community ruled over by King Aegeus. There are several versions of how it happened, but one of Minos's

sons was either accidentally killed or murdered in Athens, and as
retribution, the more powerful king demanded that every nine
years seven virgins and seven young men from Athens be deliv-
ered to the labyrinth and take their chances against the Minotaur. Two sets of hostages had been sent to Knossos, and no one
had ever returned. When it was time for the third offering, Theseus, Aegeus's son, accompanied them to Crete. The moment
Ariadne, Minos's daughter, saw Theseus it was love at first sight,
and to lead him back out alive, she gave him a ball of string to
unravel as he made his way through the labyrinth. (In British
English, the word for a ball of yarn was *clew*, which over the
years modified into *clue*, an aid in solving a mystery.) With the
Minotaur slain, the hostages escaped to Athens, although Theseus abandoned Ariadne on the island of Naxos en route. He also
forgot to raise the white sail that he had promised his father he
would use if he survived the labyrinth, and when King Aegeus
saw the ship returning with its black sails billowing, his grief was
so great he killed himself by jumping into the sea that would bear
his name.

That is the basic legend, although as it spread it grew many
variations. In one, the hostages were not seven boys and seven
girls but five girls and nine boys, two of whom were disguised as
girls. In some Ariadne had Theseus promise to marry her. In others she also gave him a magical ball to throw at the Minotaur and
weaken him. Or she also gave Theseus a special sword to slaughter the beast. Patrick Conty's maverick reading of the myth
makes Ariadne's clew more than a simple ball of yarn. Instead it
is a complex knot, a forerunner of the Gordian knot, which
promised that whoever untied it would rule the world. Alexander
the Great solved that riddle simply by cutting it with his sword.
Theseus did untie it, in this version, and the pattern he saw in
the knotted string was a map that led him to the center. In some
versions Theseus did not abandon Ariadne but lost her in a storm
at sea. In another, he forgot to raise the white sail because of a

curse put upon him by the jilted Ariadne, while the twentieth-century French novelist André Gide has suggested that the "forgetfulness" was simply a ploy by an ambitious heir to the crown, who, suspecting his father's reaction to news of his death, used it to come into his kingdom at the moment of his greatest triumph. As for Ariadne, in many versions, the abandoned princess literally took to drink by marrying Bacchus, the god of wine. Yet, five virgins or seven, absentmindedness or revenge, the story is basically the same.

But Theseus was not the only man to escape the labyrinth. Daedalus—the architect, master builder and inventor of such basic items as the handsaw and the plumb line—also escaped with his son, Icarus. Daedalus, of course, had built the labyrinth as well as the hollow imitation cow so lifelike it fooled a rutting bull. Minos was so enraged that Daedalus had conspired with his wife that he imprisoned him in the labyrinth as well. (Or could the reason have been something else? There is an ancient tradition of royal clients killing or maiming their architects so that their wonderful buildings would not be duplicated in another kingdom. Many centuries later—it was said—the shah who commissioned the Taj Mahal as a tomb for his wife had its builder blinded so he could not create another.) But lacking Ariadne's clew, not even Daedalus could find his way out of his own building. Instead, ever inventive, he created wings for himself and his son and they flew away, out over the walls—perhaps the labyrinth was roofless after all—and across the sea. In one version of the story, workers in the fields saw the escape but thought nothing unusual was going on: gods were simply flying past. Daedalus had warned the boy not to fly too high because the heat of the sun would melt the wax in the wings. But enjoying the wonders of flight, Icarus forgot or didn't care to obey, flew too high and fell into the sea. Although no one noticed, it was, as the poet W. H. Auden wrote, "Something amazing, a boy falling out of the sky."

Daedalus swooped down and retrieved the body and buried his

son on an island later called Icaria. Then he flew on and eventually came to Cumae, near Naples, where he built a temple to
Apollo, the god of the sun who had killed his son. It included
scenes of what had happened on Crete, although, as Virgil wrote,
Daedalus could not bear to show the death of Icarus. Later, a
revengeful Minos heard that Daedalus had come to live in Sicily
and set a trap to catch him. He offered a rich reward to anyone
who could find a way to work a thread through the spiraling—
need we say labyrinthine?—internal path of a triton shell. Daedalus, unable to resist the challenge, tied the thread to an ant
with a piece of gossamer, drilled a hole in the point of the shell,
inserted a dollop of honey and freed the ant, which made its way
to the goal. The triton was thus threaded with a string that can't
help but remind us of Ariadne's.

Minos, though, did not get to kill Daedalus, who learned in
time that he was in danger. It all came down to an ending—at
least in many versions of the story—worthy of a particularly
macabre Tom and Jerry cartoon. Daedalus, aided by two daughters of the local king whose loyalty he had won by making them
beautiful toys, waited until Minos was soaking in a nice hot tub.
Then they scalded him to death by pouring boiling water—some
say burning pitch—on him through a pipe they'd cut into the
ceiling of the bath. Daedalus went on to die a peaceful death
of old age in Sardinia, where, coincidentally enough, one of the
oldest known rock carvings of a labyrinth—dating probably to
1500 B.C.—was found on the wall of a tomb near Luzzanas. It is
a seven-circuit classic Cretan design, just like the ones on the
Knossos coins.

What these early mythic accounts do not include, however,
are detailed descriptions of the labyrinth. There are not even very
many good hints. What we get are suggestions that it was dark
and confusing, that it was enclosed within a huge building. Was it
open to the sky? Was the floor littered with the bones and awful

remains of earlier victims? Did hot winds from Africa blow through the fetid corridors? Modern readers probably picture the sort of maze laboratory rats and fairgoers in fun houses try to make their way through, a confused pathway marked with constant choices and dead ends. But that sort of puzzle labyrinth was not to emerge until the Middle Ages blended into the Renaissance. All the early drawings and carvings of labyrinths show only that single meandering way offering the walker no opportunity for choice or chance. As mentioned earlier, it was a simplified symbol—like a Saint Valentine's Day heart—for a more complex reality.

But there are a few hints, most of which turn up late in Roman retellings of the tale. Plutarch (ca. A.D. 46–120) mentions that after escaping Crete, Theseus and the hostages landed on the island of Delos, where they celebrated their victory with a dance "which consists of a series of serpentine figures danced in regular time and representing the winding passages of the Labyrinth." The poet Catullus (ca. 84–54 B.C.), whose version of the Cretan adventure is more one of a woman wronged than a hero triumphant, has the abandoned Ariadne call out to Theseus that it was she who had saved him when he was trapped in "the very whirl of death." The Latin is *versantem turbine leti*, which a more unorthodox translator has rendered as "the whirly whirl of death"—about as dizzying a suggestion of the twisting labyrinth as we would get for many centuries.

There were, however, actual, substantial buildings called labyrinths for hardy travelers to visit. Most modern Egyptian guidebooks don't have much to say about Hawaya, near El Faiyum. There is nothing much there, anymore, but a small pyramid and a lot of wasteland. But its "labyrinth," built by the pharaoh now known as Amenemhet III, was a center of early tourism visited (or at least described) by such writers as Herodotus, Strabo, Diodorus Siculus and Pliny the Elder. Herodotus (ca. 484–424 B.C.) set

down one of the earliest eyewitness descriptions of what passed
for a labyrinth.

The Egyptian pyramids, he wrote with unusual modesty, were
beyond description.

> Yet the labyrinth surpasses even the pyramids, for it has twelve
> courts enclosed with walls, with doors opposite each other, with six
> facing the north and six the south contiguous to one another and the
> same exterior wall encloses them. It contains two kinds of rooms,
> some under ground and some above ground over them to the number
> of three thousand fifteen hundred of each. The rooms above ground,
> I myself went through and saw, and relate from personal impression.
> But the rooms under ground I only know from report, for the Egyp-
> tians who have charge of the building would on no account show
> me them, saying that there were the sepulchres of the kings who
> originally built the labyrinth and the sacred crocodiles. . . . But the
> upper ones, which surpass all human works, I saw. For the passages
> through the corridors and the windings through the courts, from
> their great variety, presented a thousand occasions of wonder as I
> passed from a court to the rooms, from the rooms to halls, to other
> corridors from the halls and to other courts from the rooms. The
> roofs of all these are of stone, as also are the walls; but the walls are
> full of sculptured figures. Each court is surrounded with a colonnade
> of white stone closely fitted; and adjoining the extremity of the lab-
> yrinth is a pyramid . . . and a way to it is made under ground.

For Herodotus, a man of boundless curiosity, it had just the right
mixture of oddity, mystery and danger.

Pliny the Elder (A.D. 23–79), a Roman, visited the same site
about five hundred years later and found it—in greater ruin—an
even more sinister place. He wrote about it and other labyrinths
he had only heard stories of (one on the Greek island of Lemnos,
another—an Etruscan tomb—near Chiusi in Italy) in his *Natural*

History. Labyrinths were no longer wondrous curiosities. They were, he wrote, "quite the most abnormal achievement on which man has spent his resources." Pliny saw it as something monstrous, but he was also aware of the difference between the labyrinth image and the Egyptian reality. He contrasted the labyrinth he visited with both the beautiful labyrinthine mosaic designs on the floors of Roman villas and the "ceremonial" labyrinth game Roman boys on horseback played on specially marked fields, and found the Egyptian labyrinth to be a complex of grim, dark, confusing buildings. Daedalus, he wrote, had copied it for the lost labyrinth on Crete, but had built only "a hundredth part" of its passages that "wind, advance and retreat in a bewilderingly intricate manner." And it was real, he writes, not something made up by an ancient storyteller.

He goes on to say that "doors are set into the walls at frequent intervals to suggest deceptively the way ahead and to force the visitor to go back upon the very same tracks he had already followed in his wanderings." The entrance and some of the columns were made of marble, but "the rest of the structure is of Aswan granite, the great blocks of which have been laid in such a way that even the great lapse of centuries cannot destroy them." Like Herodotus, he writes that the complex, with its halls, pyramids and ornate sculpture, cannot be fully described and then warns, "It is when he is already exhausted with walking that the visitor reaches the bewildering maze of passages. Moreover, there are rooms in lofty upper stories reached by inclines and porches from which flights of 90 stairs lead down to the ground." Inside there are columns carved with images of gods, kings and monsters. "Some of the halls are laid out in such a way that when the doors open there is a terrifying rumble of thunder therein: incidentally, most of the building has to be traversed in darkness."

The Egyptian labyrinth, then, was dark and confusing, full of frightening noises and grotesque images older than memory, and crisscrossed with passages that could lead to great heights or dive underground. And everything said about it, Pliny wrote, was just as true for the Cretan labyrinth. Looking at it, the first-century Greco-Roman geographer Strabo noticed something that would be discovered by labyrinth observers for centuries to come: that what seems chaotic up close, when seen from a distance or above becomes understandable and logical.

Writing in the fourteenth century, Boccaccio (1313–1375) recognized that the idea of labyrinths had changed over the centuries: "This labyrinth was not made as we design ours, that is with circles and windings of the walls, through which anyone who goes without turning round infallibly arrives at the middle, and then following the winding without turning, comes outside; but, there was . . . a mountain all excavated within, made with square chambers, so that each chamber has four doors, one in each side, each door leading to a similar room, so that a man who enters grows bewildered and does not know how to get out." He could be describing a M. C. Escher print.

Most classical travelers who came to Crete in search of Minos's labyrinth left disappointed, usually having been shown only empty fields, piles of rubble or deserted caves. There is, though, one account by a Greek writer named Flavius Philostratus of a group of tourists in A.D. 66 being shown a labyrinth that "once on a time housed the Minotaur." Perhaps this was a traveler's tall tale, or maybe some canny Cretan promoter had simply arranged to give the public what it wanted to see. In the centuries to come, many sites on Crete would be pointed out as the labyrinth. In 1609, an Englishman named William Lithgow was shown a dangerous-looking place near Mount Ida (probably a Roman stone quarry) with, he wrote, "many doors and pillars." He dared not enter, "for there are many hollow places within it, so that [if] a man stumble or fall he can hardly be rescued." Later in the same century another traveler, Bernard Randolph, wrote that he refused to enter what he was told to be the labyrinth because he didn't believe his guide. Also, "the noisome smells are enough to stifle one." The poet and artist Edward Lear had a more pleasant time in 1864 when he was shown a place with trees, nightingales and "scattered masses of brickwork." All in all, when it comes to labyrinth tourism on Crete, travelers might well remember the words of St. Paul in his "Epistle to Titus." Claiming to be quoting "one of their countrymen" he wrote, "Cretans are ever liars."

In his biography of Theseus, hero of the labyrinth, Plutarch treats the prince as though he were a historical figure, but from time to time interrupts the traditional story (which he tells with surprisingly little drama) with second opinions. The tale of the Minotaur, he says, is one everybody knew, but there are other versions worth hearing. Plutarch is sometimes droll with these alternative accounts. Earlier in the history of Theseus's pre-Cretan adventures he tells how the young prince heroically killed the ferocious Phaea, "the wild sow of Crommyon." Then, as something of an afterthought, he adds that some said the "sow" was not actually a monster, just the nickname of a "depraved" woman with murderous habits whom Theseus happened to kill along his way to Athens. With the labyrinth, he simply adds what he says is the Cretan side of the story. And it should be remembered that the myths about Crete came from the mainland, not the island itself.

The Cretans claimed that Minos's queen, Pasiphaë, did not fall in love with a prize bull, although she may well have been "too intimate" with the king's brutal general Taurus, whose name could be translated as "bull." And there was no Minotaur either. In this version, Taurus seems to play the roles of both bull and Minotaur. But there was a labyrinth. Youths and maidens from submissive Athens were indeed sent to powerful Crete as hostages and were imprisoned in a building called the Labyrinth presided over by the cruel Taurus. The young Athenians were not devoured by a monster but awarded as prizes at funeral games

Minos staged in memory of his son who had died in Athens. Rather than subduing the Minotaur, Theseus defeated Taurus at the games and won back the Athenians. It was also at the games that the beautiful Ariadne first saw and fell in love with Theseus. Plutarch points out that one of Crete's unusual customs was allowing women to attend such events. It is not mentioned, but perhaps Ariadne's ball of yarn was a token she gave the handsome Athenian, much as medieval women were later said to give ribbons to favored knights before jousts.

In *The Golden Bough*, the pioneering Scottish anthropologist James Frazer suggests that the Minotaur may actually have been a hollow bronze statue of a man with a bull's head in which human sacrifices were placed and roasted alive. Or, Frazer adds, perhaps—as with the worship of Moloch at Carthage—the young sacrifices were placed in the sloping arms of the idol, from which they rolled down into a burning pit, as the onlookers played flutes and timbrels "to drown out the screams" and danced in celebration. By inference, the labyrinth is that sacrificial dance floor.

Frazer published the first version of his book in 1890, not long after Sir Arthur Evans unearthed at Knossos what many people thought was King Minos's labyrinth. Evans (1851–1941), a wealthy, well-connected Oxford archaeologist, went to Crete in the 1880s with an interest in engraved Minoan gems, but became fascinated with Knossos. He actually bought the site in 1898, hired a huge work crew and began digging. Evans had not "discovered" the palace. At least eight teams of archaeologists had dug there before him, and it must always be remembered that he was not an explorer. He knew what he wanted to find, and he found it even if it meant re-creating (or even creating) it on the spot. In the process, he more or less invented an advanced prehistoric society he called Minoan, a name neither that society nor the Greeks had ever used.

By the time he finished in 1935, Evans had unearthed a vast complex of palaces, grand staircases, amazingly well-preserved frescos (some said suspiciously well preserved), residential districts and warehouse areas that he declared—in a mammoth multivolume study published over a number of years—was the Palace of Minos. Although the complex had been devastated by earthquakes at least three times, he believed parts of the structure dated back to 3000 B.C., while other sections were as recent as 1250 B.C. And when he finished digging and analyzing, he rebuilt the palace as he thought it once was, using (ever mindful of those earthquakes) artfully disguised cement and structural steel.

After all those centuries of searching, tourists finally had something to look at. The hillside at Knossos became the island's principal attraction, and while eager local guides today may still say it is the very spot where Theseus slew the Minotaur, that is not what Evans ever claimed. He took credit for the palace being Minos's (many scholars believe "Minos, son of Zeus" was simply the generic title for any ruler of Knossos). In his fund-raising publications, he may have traded on the appeal of the labyrinth myth and hinted about finding the source ("this huge building with its maze of corridors and tortuous passages . . . was in fact the Labyrinth of later tradition"), but he claimed to have very little patience with stories of the Minotaur and a maze. In fact, he said the frequent retelling of the gory tale in the ancient world was a plot on the part of chauvinistic Athenians to "exaggerate the tyrannical side" of the early Minoan society in order "to convert the Palace of a long series of great rulers into an ogres' den." The only labyrinth whose authenticity he ever claimed was one he designed himself for the front hall of the lavish mansion, now demolished, he built outside Oxford, a place with a curious iron structure on its roof that reminded many visitors of the Eiffel Tower.

"The preconceived idea that the Palace ... was itself of a labyrinthine nature dies hard," he wrote. The notion was seemingly supported by the twisted subterranean passages through which "a stooping man might make his way, but are really great stone-built drains," by a dramatic fresco showing "girl performers grappling with a charging bull" and by mazelike wall decorations borrowed, Evans believed, from the Egyptians. "Mysterious forms and features such as these," he wrote, "seen in the twilight of early saga may well have called up the vision of the 'Greek Labyrinth' together with the monster that abode within its innermost lair." In the palace itself, "there was nothing of these baffling involutions and tortuously secretive approaches." Though vast, the building was built foursquare around a central court, with symmetrical north and south entrances.

The mistaken belief, he felt, came from ancient Greeks'—perhaps willful—misunderstanding of the ruins they found on Crete, an "afterwork of Hellenic days," to use Evans's phrase. A fine visual example of this confusion was found on that mazelike Egyptian design. (The proper name for its repeated series of right-angle turns is *meander*, and it is not a labyrinth since there is no center to the design, simply endlessly repeated turnings.) At some point after it had become a ruin, but long before Evans rediscovered it, some ancient hand had drawn in crude figures lost in what seemed to be a maze.

Evans, however, did not help reduce the confusion when he himself applied the word *labyrinth* to the ruined palace, even though he had his own definition of the word. Without there ever being an actual maze, he wrote, the name *labyrinth* was nevertheless proper for the building. "From the old Cretan analogies it simply defines it as the sanctuary of the *labrys* or the double[-headed] axe, the symbolic weapon of Minoan divinity, worshiped so often in the Palace shrines and repeated [in designs] on its blocks and pillars." History, though, has not been kind to this interpretation of the meaning and importance of the double ax, and as we saw in

chapter 1, most scholars now think the connection between *labrys* and *labyrinth*—popular as it once was—existed only in Evans's imagination.

Although Theseus and the Minotaur receive scant attention in Evans's exhaustive five-volume analysis of the ruins, dance is given a fair amount of attention. There is even a photograph of contemporary turn-of-the-twentieth-century Cretan folk dancers. But, then, beginning with the *Iliad*, dancers appear in just about every version of what happened in King Minos's royal court. In a lyrical description of the scenes of everyday life that adorn Achilles' wondrous shield, Homer mentions the "dancing floor" that Daedalus built for Ariadne. Could this floor be the labyrinth? There's no mention of hostages or the slaughter of a bull-man, but there is a dynamic description of the kind of dancing that went on there. In Robert Fitzgerald's translation:

> *Here young men and the most desired young girls*
> *were dancing, linked, touching each other's wrists*
> *the girls in linen, in soft gowns, the men*
> *in well-knit khitons given a gloss with oil,*
> *the girls wore garlands, and the men had daggers,*
> *golden-hilted, hung on silver lanyards.*
> *Trained and adept they circled there with ease*
> *the way a potter sitting at his wheel*
> *will give it a practice twirl between his palms*
> *to see it run; or else, again, in lines*
> *as though in ranks, they moved on one another:*
> *magical dancing!*

Some of the most vivid descriptions of dance in most versions of the story appear when Theseus and the freed hostages stop at

Delos, the smallest of the Greek islands, on the way back to Athens. There, they celebrate by dancing, imitating the twists and turns they had taken in the labyrinth, a pattern that seems also to have resembled the mating ritual of cranes. It became known as the *geranos*, or crane dance, and was performed there and on Crete into the twentieth century. In some versions, dancers even link themselves together by holding handkerchiefs, suggesting Ariadne's thread.

Intentionally paraphrasing Homer, Evans describes some of the dances he saw his workers and their partners performing as fast-moving and athletic chain dances "turning forwards and backwards as a potter turns a wheel." In some dances, he writes, the leader at the head of the line often took dramatic leaps into the air, adding that it was not uncommon for him to land with one foot in the hands of the second person in line, be flipped into the air, turn a somersault and land on his feet. On a circa 665 B.C. black-figured Greek krater now called the François vase, the dance at Delos appears as a chain of sedate, well-dressed couples—each identified by name—holding hands and being led by a lute-strumming Theseus. Most of the dancers are the former Athenian hostages, although a few members of the ship's crew also seem to be joining in.

Could the image of the labyrinth be the footprint of a dance stamped out on a dirt floor, an imprint that was later preserved as a permanent design? It seems altogether possible that the labyrinth, at its very beginning, had not been a search through a puzzling maze. Think of it as a ritual dance performed on a floor specially marked to help the dancers move through the intricate pattern, much as ballroom-dance schools used to paint the steps of waltzes and fox-trots on their floors.

Some of the curious details of the Theseus story make more sense when thought of in terms of dance. The mention that both men and women attended the games at Knossos, for instance, may be a remnant explanation that men and women danced together on Crete rather than separately as they did in some Greek societies. (Homer, too, makes a point of the fact that the couples described on Achilles' shield danced together and actually touched.) Might the suggestion in one version that the hostages were not seven girls and seven boys but five girls, seven obvious boys and two cross-dressers indicate the corps de ballet of a forgotten ceremony?

The poet, novelist and sometimes classicist Robert Graves (1895–1985)—who is not always treated seriously by more academic classicists—believed the whole labyrinth myth might have had its origins as a mosaic dance floor in front of the palace at Knossos, a floor "with a maze pattern used to guide performers in an erotic spring dance." The inspiration for the design was, he suggests, the brushwood traps used to catch partridges, birds that according to Graves perform an "ecstatic hobbling love dance" similar perhaps to the cranes'. At the center of the mazelike trap was a caged male who sent out love calls to decoy mates into the snare, where "they would be knocked on the head by the hunter." Presumably in the dance, the prize at the center was a good deal more pleasant than a knock on the head.

A partridge, though, does make a brief appearance in the labyrinth myth. In his *Metamorphosis*, Ovid tells how Daedalus rescues the corpse of Icarus from the sea and buries it while "a noisy partridge from a muddy ditch looks out and drums her wings with loud approval." It is a reference to the nephew Daedalus murdered back in Athens, the whole reason he had come to King Minos's court in the first place. Daedalus had become jealous of his sister's son, his apprentice, because he gave every promise of being more inventive than Daedalus himself. He'd created a compass to draw circles, and had even boasted about how he had been inspired by the sharp bones of a fish skeleton to invent a handsaw. That was the last straw for Daedalus, who claimed to have already invented that tool, and he threw his nephew from the roof of a temple. Although Daedalus tried to hide the body, the gods turned the boy's soul into a partridge. The bird celebrating the death of Daedalus's son might have been simply a literary touch, another metamorphosis, but it may also reflect a vestigial memory of the origins of Ariadne's dancing floor.

Seeing the labyrinth myth rooted not in the slaughter of a monster but as an erotic dance on a specially marked floor certainly makes it easier to come up with a possible explanation for the enigmatic design scratched rather crudely onto what at first appears to be a drab little seventh-century B.C. Etruscan wine jug in the Capitoline Museum in Rome. Called the Tragliatella jar for the place in Italy where it was discovered—in a tomb—in 1878, the pitcher is one of the most hotly debated items in labyrinth studies.

Reading its design from left to right as though it were a comic strip, one sees first a scene with a woman holding a ball in her hand facing a man. (Is the ball the "clew" or perhaps a golden apple? Does the scene depict Ariadne and Theseus or is it Aphrodite and Paris and the "judgment" that in time led to the Trojan War?) Then come seven young men on foot bearing shields emblazoned with the insignia of a wild boar, followed by two men on horseback carrying shields with bird designs. There's also what may be a monkey, although some say it is a hunchbacked dwarf. What comes next—after a graffiti-like sketch of a labyrinth that bears the perhaps misleading label "Troia"—is a romantic interlude often skipped over in discussions of the vase. There, at the conclusion of what might be a procession or a dance or even an athletic competition, two long-haired couples—or is it just one couple seen in two different positions?—copulate enthusiastically next to a labyrinth that looks a good deal like the ones on the Knossos coins.

More will be said about this mysterious scene on an Etruscan jug in the next chapter. But—frivolous or not—reading it as a provocative, erotic dance "whirly-whirling" inward down a pathway toward its climax might explain a lot about the origins of the labyrinth.

Three

THE CITY

OVER THE CENTURIES, THESEUS THE MINOTAUR KILLER has been many different people. In the ancient world, his muscular exploits as a hero and adventurer were the equal of his cousin Heracles' (Hercules to the Romans) celebrated labors. In feudal times, he was seen as a hero king much like King Arthur. Indeed, his first feat, the one that marked the end of his childhood, in many ways prefigures the first feat of Arthur Pendragon's. Young Arthur had to remove a sword from a stone as a sign that he would be king. Young Theseus—in the rural village where he was brought up by his mother—had to be able to lift a giant rock and find a sword (and, perhaps more practically, a pair of sandals) before he could take the road to Athens and be acknowledged as a prince. The sword and the sandals had been put there by his father, King Aegeus, before Theseus was born as part of a ploy to hide—and protect—his heir. In medieval times, when parables, religious analogies and allegories lurked in everything from numbers to the symbolic significance of common animals, Theseus was honored in Christian churches because one of his deeds prefigured Christ's. Both had descended into the underworld to face the devil to free lost souls. Theseus went there late in his life to reclaim Persephone, just as Jesus would between the crucifixion and the resurrection. Be it called Tartarus or hell, both emerged heroically, even if Theseus was not as successful as Jesus in his quest. And had not Theseus's youthful descent into the heart of the labyrinth itself been a symbolic, even iconographic, Christlike confrontation with a horned Satan?

But in Rome and its empire he had a unique significance. In a culture in which the cult—the near deification—of the city was as strong, or stronger, than the veneration of any of the gods, Theseus was honored as a legendary founder of cities. And although it was not all his doing, his icon, the labyrinth, became a representation of all cities. Plutarch was one of the earliest to promote Theseus as an urban hero. Indeed that seems to be the implied point of his "Life" of the hero, even if Robert Graves dismisses it as a simple matter of "political propaganda."

Plutarch was born and died in a town near Delphi when Greece was a minor part of the Roman Empire. He was said to have been in Athens when Nero came to visit and later lived for a time in Rome, where he met the emperor Hadrian, who appointed him to a political job back in Greece. He was a prolific writer of philosophy and history. Among his works is a misanthropic three-way debate among Ulysses, the seductress Circe and a pig, in which the pig is clearly the winner, but he is best remembered for his *Parallel Lives*, a collection of forty-six biographies of Greek and Roman heroes. The book is arranged into twenty-three pairs of Greeks and Romans whose lives, in Plutarch's estimation, were similar. Most of the subjects are actual historical figures, with Greeks usually looking a little better than the Romans, but it begins in the realm of legend with Romulus, the mythic founder of Rome, coupled with Theseus, the creator of the Athenian city-state.

After the abandonment of Ariadne, the convenient suicide of his father and his triumphant return to the mainland with the freed hostages from Crete, Theseus began what Plutarch sees as his major achievement. He took over a disorganized place called

Athens and turned it into a great city. He ended the monarchy (while keeping control of the army for himself), unified the various communities that made up Attica, destroyed their town halls and built a city hall on the current site of the Acropolis. The poor, Plutarch writes, were immediately in favor of this; the wealthy took more persuasion. He established a mint that cranked out coins bearing the image of an ox and drew up a constitution that created a democracy ("a commonwealth that embraced all sorts and conditions of men") that was divided among three classes: noblemen, farmers and artisans. It was all so successful that in the *Iliad* Homer refers only to the Athenians as "a sovereign people."

While Theseus and Romulus, unlike other of Plutarch's subjects, such as Solon and Julius Caesar, were legendary rather than historic figures, they could be used as models of the idealized founders of an idealized form of government. It is hardly an accident that Plutarch, writing during an expanding Roman Empire, has Theseus, as his first act after creating the Athenian city-state, go off to the Black Sea to found other cities as Greek colonies. Propaganda, Graves called it, but in Plutarch's hands the conqueror of the labyrinth became the champion of the maze known as the city.

Writing almost a century before Plutarch, Virgil (70–19 B.C.) had already clearly defined, even celebrated, this connection between the labyrinth and the city, and he had added another important element: that mythic prototype of all cities, Troy. Labyrinths and the labyrinth myth play no obvious role in the universally known story of Troy and the Trojan War. Yet the fabled city with its impenetrable walls, its topless towers and its gates too narrow to admit a giant wooden horse would remain associated with the labyrinth down the centuries. When the Greeks sailed to Troy to bring back the abducted Helen and avenge their honor, they encountered—in legend at least—the first major city of the ancient world, the city that all cities that followed, even into the Middle Ages and the Renaissance, would honor as their oldest ancestor.

Many Latin scholars consider Virgil's finest work to be his *Eclogues*, ten long bucolic poems in praise of rural life, the changing seasons and the ripening and harvesting of grapes and olives. These were the poems that won him the attention and the patronage of the man who became the first Roman emperor, Augustus. Virgil is remembered, though, for a city poem, the unfinished epic he wrote for Augustus, *The Aeneid*, a celebration not only of the founding of Rome, the city of cities, but of the destruction of its prototype, Troy. It is filled with images and references to labyrinths and also contains the best description we have of a popular Roman labyrinth game called the Game of Troy.

The Aeneid tells the story of the Trojan hero Aeneas and the circuitous route he takes from the burning city to Italy, where, under the direction of the gods (or at least some of the gods), he will found a city that will become the capital of the world. Virgil writes that Aeneas's task was to "found the Roman people." No less than Jupiter, father of the gods, tells his daughter Venus that Aeneas is "to establish city walls and a way of life." In Book II, having been blown off course to Carthage in North Africa, Aeneas is asked by Queen Dido to tell his story. In a spellbinding monologue he tells of the conclusion of the ten-year siege of his city by the Greeks, of the destruction of the walls to admit the great wooden horse, of the duplicity of the Greeks and the fall of the city. It contains one of the memorable images of classical literature: Aeneas, carrying his aged father on his back and holding his young son by the hand, leads his wife through the chaos of the burning, defeated city. In his confusion, the dying old man thinks he sees the flash of light on the bronze of enemy shields and urges his son to flee. Aeneas says (in Robert Fitzgerald's translation), "I took fright" and

> . . . *turned*
> *Aside from the known way, entering a maze*
> *Of pathless paths, on the run.*

All that follows in the poem is the record of the labyrinthine path through a maze, turning left and right among the islands and mainland ports of the Mediterranean, even, following Theseus, venturing down into the underworld. But the path is always moving toward the inevitable goal, the city to be founded on the banks of the Tiber. Maze images abound, both overtly and inadvertently. At Cumae he and his men visit the votive temple built by Daedalus to commemorate his lost son and their liberation from Minos's prison labyrinth. There, they see on its great doors—anachronistically resembling Lorenzo Ghiberti's doors on the fifteenth-century Florence baptistery—scenes from the life and death of the Minotaur. And on a seacoast in what is now Albania, they find a miniature Troy complete with towers and gated walls. It was built by one of the king of Troy's nostalgic sons and—although Virgil could never have foreseen it—prefigures the many Troy Town labyrinths that would be built in Britain, Scandinavia and northern Europe in the centuries to come. Aeneas's great shield is emblazoned with seven concentric circles, like the seven circles of the path that leads to the center of the classic Cretan labyrinth. And when he fights a climactic duel near the site of the future city of Rome, his movements are described in labyrinthine terms: Aeneus hunts down the "twisted circle" to find his enemy, Turnus. Then, evoking the festive games played earlier in the epic:

> Five times
> They ran the circular track, and five again
> Reran it backward, this way and now that.
> They raced for no light garland of the games
> But strove to win the life and blood of Turnus.

These repeated images are not simply literary devices. They underline the mystical embodiment of Troy in the sacramental founding of Rome. Part of that sacrament was playing a ritual game.

It is the Game of Troy that best establishes the way the labyrinth connects Homer's city with Rome. In Book V, fleeing at last from Carthage and the eager arms of Queen Dido, Aeneas and his little fleet of ships are blown off course—as they so often were— and land near Mount Eryx on the northwest coast of Sicily. Other refugees from Troy have already settled on the mountainside, and there Aeneas commemorates the death of his father with a long day of funeral games that included ship races, footraces, boxing matches, a javelin toss and an archery contest. Aeneas's shipmates, local Trojans and native Sicilians compete for prizes that were both simple and lavish: laurel crowns, garlands, silver cups, battle armor, shields, a bull, even a slave woman nursing twin children.

No prizes are mentioned for the last event of the day, the *Lusus Troiae,* in which the competitors were adolescent sons of Trojan aristocrats, "all shining," Virgil writes, "before their parents' eyes." *Lusus Troiae,* the Game of Troy, combined elements of dressage, war games, polo and mounted acrobatics, all played on a field that was probably marked with the lanes of the seven-circuit classic labyrinth of Crete.

Just as an American novelist writing a chapter set at the World Series would see no reason to stop the action and explain the rules, Virgil assumed everyone knew how the game was played. Unfortunately, modern readers do not and must approach the account as something of a puzzle. There are three teams—that much is clear—each on horseback. Each team consists of a column of six pairs of boys led by a commander and accompanied by an adult "trainer," probably an instructor or coach. They all wear wreathes on their heads, and around their necks are braided bands of twisted gold. Each boy carries two wooden lances tipped with steel, and some also carry quivers on their backs. The three miniature cavalries circle the field until they hear the sound of a whip crack. Then the squadrons break apart in a series of charges and countercharges and mock attack. One translation reads:

"[They] retreat and charge, in figure intricate of circling troop with troop." Fitzgerald's translation of a passage farther along in the maneuvers describes a troop in flight,

> *then whirling round*
> *With leveled points, then patching up a truce*
> *And riding side by side. So intricate*
> *In ancient times on mountainous Crete they say*
> *The Labyrinth between walls in the dark,*
> *Ran criss-cross a bewildering thousand ways*
> *Devised by guile, a maze insoluble;*
> *Breaking down every clue to the way out.*
> *So intricate the drill of Trojan boys*
> *Who wove the patterns of their pacing horses,*
> *Figured in sport, retreats, and skirmishes—*
> *Like dolphins in the drenching sea.*

Hermann Kern, the great German historian of the labyrinth, calls the Game of Troy "a sort of debutante ball for boys on horseback." A coming-of-age ritual (and show of physical competence), it was originally performed on only two occasions: funeral games and the ceremonies accompanying the founding of cities. Although Virgil never actually says the field was laid out as a labyrinth, Pliny the Elder, in his description of the Egyptian labyrinth, mentions such labyrinthine playing fields in Rome.

It also seems likely that the piece of Etruscan pottery mentioned at the end of the last chapter, the Tragliatella jar with its shields and spears and men on the march, depicts the conclusion of a Game of Troy. What we see are two young men on horseback bursting out of a labyrinth marked *Troia*, one clearly getting there before the other. And perhaps the scenes of lovemaking that follow, the ones being pointed out by a long-haired man or woman in a checkered gown, are simply a sign that the boys have reached a new level of maturity.

Virgil ends his account of the Game of Troy with a knowing nod to his contemporaries. He says that Aeneas later staged "this mode of drill, this mimicry of war" when he eventually built the walls of Alba Longa, the precursor of Rome, as part of the ritual of founding a city. Virgil says Aeneas taught the Italians—the ancestors of the Romans—how to play it, and they in turn taught their children and in time "Great Rome" itself took up this "glory of its founders" not as a ceremony reserved for historic occasions but as a sport. Under Virgil's patron Augustus, the Game of Troy became so popular that it was expanded from having two competing troops—as indeed it was originally played—to three. Suetonius, in his biography of the "Deified Augustus," includes the Game of Troy in a section that describes such popular entertainments as chariot races in the Circus and a two-foot-tall dwarf who weighed only seventeen pounds but had an extraordinarily loud voice. The emperor, Suetonius writes, encouraged the game, "thinking it a time-honored and worthy custom for the flower of the nobility to become known in this way." It was a dangerous sport, however. Augustus gave a gold necklace called a torque to a boy named Nonius Asprenas, who had been lamed after a fall from his horse, and allowed him and his descendants to change their name to Torquatus ("wearers of the torque"). The game itself became outlawed after a senator's grandson broke his leg. Whether or not the Campus Martius, the great field dedicated to Mars, the god of war, where they played the Game of Troy, was permanently laid out with a labyrinth design for the riders to follow, its imprint was surely beaten into the ground by the horses' hooves. And there, near the great round mausoleum the emperor was building for himself, it could probably be seen for days after each game was played.

More permanent images can be found on Roman mosaic floors, and they too reveal the Roman custom of equating the labyrinth with the city. Between the second century B.C. and the fifth century A.D. elaborate mosaic floors—and sometimes walls as well—

were constructed in private homes, public buildings, baths, even tombs. It was an expensive art form calculated to showcase the owner's wealth. In its most popular form, thousand of tiny cubes called *tesserae* and made of glazed pottery, glass, stone and terracotta were pieced together to make geometric patterns or pictures. A more economical form used larger, shaped pieces of the material, much as different pieces of colored glass would later be formed into stained-glass windows. Sometimes, especially on the Italian mainland, the pavements are in just two colors, usually black and white, but more often they are indeed great multicolored pictures in stone. A catalog of the hundreds of surviving Roman floors compiled in the 1970s indicates that fifty-four of them—four in Pompeii alone—had a labyrinth design. Interestingly, although the Roman mosaic floor had its origins in Greece and Romans frequently employed Greek artisans to design and build their floors (especially in Roman colonies in North Africa), ancient labyrinth floors are rarely found in Greece. It is a distinctly Roman decoration.

The Greeks, though, did make great use of the meander to decorate their buildings and their pottery. Taking its name from the Meander River, which winds its erratic way through northern Turkey, the meander is a running pattern of sharp right turns that the Romans piled up and bundled together to make a new labyrinth pattern of their own. In the Roman labyrinth, there was still only one way to reach the center, with no choices to make along the way. But the classic Cretan design, with its wide arcs moving from side to side had gone out of fashion. Roman mosaic labyrinths could be round, but most are square, and all of them are divided neatly into four identical quarters, just as Roman cities were divided into quarters. The path to the center fully and doggedly explores each quarter in turn before moving on—never to return—to the next, where it repeats the same pattern. But dividing the design into tidy quarters is not the only way the Romans

urbanized the labyrinth. Surrounding just about every mosaic labyrinth is a mosaic representation of city walls complete with crenellations, watchtowers and fortified city gates. While the labyrinth itself is usually rendered without any attempt to imply depth or a third dimension, the protective walls are often—with dramatic effect—designed with a suggestion of perspective. Forti-
fied walls play no part in the Cretan myth, but they are the defining image in the story of Troy with its "topless towers," and as Virgil explains in *The Aeneid*, plowing a "boundary furrow" to mark the future location of the protective walls is one of the first ceremonial steps in the founding of the city.

This amalgam of Crete, Troy and Rome is the most common aspect of the Roman labyrinths. One of the largest and best-preserved is a late-third-century A.D. tesserae mosaic from the baths of a grand villa near Salzburg, Austria. Counting its elaborate border it is about eighteen feet long and twenty-one feet wide. In the center, Theseus is about to strike what must be the fatal blow to a cringing Minotaur. To the left, beyond the labyrinth itself, is a scene of Ariadne giving a ball of string to Theseus. At the top, the couple can be seen escaping on a ship for Athens. At the right,

Ariadne sits alone, her legs crossed, her chin resting on her right fist. Depending on how you interpret her pose and expression, she has either been abandoned on Naxos or is patiently waiting for her lover to emerge after killing the monster. Surrounding the labyrinth is a design of brick and stone walls topped with battlements. Its only opening is

an archway leading to the beginning of the labyrinth and located next to the pensive Ariadne. Her red string runs all the way along the meandering pathway, making thirteen circuits to the center.

Ariadne's string appears on several of the labyrinth floors. In a fourth-century A.D. pavement now in the Cathedral of Algiers, in North Africa, the string lies slack and abandoned, making it only as far as the second turn. String on the floor, though, may reflect another fashion in Roman interior decoration. A popular mosaic design was called the "unswept room," in which trompe l'oeil bones, half-eaten fruit, hunks of bread and other remains of a dinner party are depicted littering the floor. Perhaps Ariadne's clew was just another visual joke.

There is no gate on the archway leading to the beginning of the labyrinth in the Salzburg mosaic, but the floor of a third-century A.D. underground Roman tomb at Hadrumetum (modern Sousse, Tunisia) shows double doors leading into its pathway. As befitting a burial place, they are closed shut. An inscription reads HICINCLUSUS VITAMPERT (He who is locked in here will die). At the center a presumably dead Minotaur lies on his back, while outside the labyrinth a rather crowded ship sails away. In the lower right-hand corner of the pavement is a circle—two circles actually, one within another—that may represent perfection, eternity or perhaps even Ariadne's clew.

Scenes from the Minotaur legend decorate most Roman labyrinth mosaics, but there are exceptions. The center of a labyrinth in Ostia, the port of Rome, is decorated with a picture of a lighthouse, perhaps the local one. The center of a now lost Pompeii pavement showed a military helmet, and a flower with four petals is the goal on the floor of an early-fourth-century villa uncovered in Yorkshire in Britain.

But no one ever walked a Roman labyrinth. They are purely visual. No pathway on any Roman labyrinth is large enough or wide enough to follow on foot. And Hermann Kern has pointed out that many of the surviving labyrinths are flawed. Mistakes—probably not intentional—keep you from successfully reaching the center even if you follow it by eye. This suggests that the Romans were probably not terribly interested in how a labyrinth actually worked and didn't see great philosophical meaning in following the path. Dr. Bernice Kurchin, an archaeologist who has worked at Pompeii, has suggested that it was not in the Roman nature to be interested in moving inward to the center of things. They were citizens—unless, of course, they were slaves or women—of an ever-expanding empire. Their instinct was to move outward to expand away from the center, which was Rome itself.

The first floor labyrinth that is both Roman and Christian—or, at least, the oldest surviving one—is an eight-foot-wide curiosity in the Algiers cathedral that seems to have remained one of a kind. Originally installed in a fourth-century five-sided basilica in Al-Asnam in Algeria, its neatly quartered labyrinth pathway is just like other Roman mosaics found all over North Africa, although—as mentioned earlier—Ariadne's clew lies abandoned near the entrance. What makes the mosaic unique is its center, its goal, a thirteen-letter by thirteen-letter word square (for want of a better term) that has also been called, incorrectly, a palindrome and an anagram. "Letter labyrinth" may be a better try, but puzzle experts as experienced as Martin Gardner and Will Shortz have been unable to pigeonhole it into any standard category. The message, *Sancta Eclesia* (Holy Church), can be read over and over again by beginning at the S in the center and moving in any direction but diagonally. Will Shortz, the crossword puzzle editor of the *New York Times*, has suggested that the purpose may not have been as a word puzzle at all but as a way to have the phrase repeated as many times as possible in the available space. The same letters get to be used more than once. Indeed, there is a kind of short prayer, two or three words long (for example, "God bless me"), called an ejaculation that is thought to be effective more for its easy repetition than its length. *Sancta Eclesia* may have been a blessing as well as a description. Here it is:

```
A I S E L C E C L E S I A
I S E L C E A E C L E S I
S E L C E A T A E C L E S
E L C E A T C T A E C L E
L C E A T C N C T A E C L
C E A T C N A N C T A E C
E A T C N A S A N C T A E
C E A T C N A N C T A E C
L C E A T C N C T A E C L
E L O E A T C T A E O L E
S E L C E A T A E C L E S
I S E L C E A E C L E S I
A I S E L C E C L E S I A
```

It may be easier to read with a bit of editing:

```
A I S E L C E C L E S I A
I               A               I
S               T               S
E               C               E
L               N               L
C               A               C
E A T C N A S A N C T A E
C               A               C
L               N               L
E               C               E
S               T               S
I               A               I
A I S E L C E C L E S I A
```

This unique floor can be seen as one of the last Roman mosaic pavements, and although it is certainly "Christian" it still reveals

a thoroughly Roman outlook. To reach
the letter labyrinth in the center, the
pathway follows the familiar Roman
route through the quarters. Once in
the center, to decode the message, the
reader—the space is far too small to
walk—must work outward. In all directions, north, east, south and west, the
ever-expanding message is the same. It is
like a fountain spraying from its center or

an empire ever expanding from its capital. Or a new religion spreading across the world from the same capital. It's the Roman way.

Although it may be historically inaccurate to do so, it is
tempting to look at a pavement in Ravenna, Italy, the last capital
of the western Roman Empire, as a symbol of this outlook. On
the floor of the sixth-century church of San Vitale is another
mosaic oddity, a labyrinth in which the triangle paving stones of
the pathway point away from the center and seem to indicate—at
least to modern eyes—that the walker should begin at the center
and move outward to what would traditionally be the entrance.
But the floor, historically, has nothing to do with the Romans,
even the last of the Romans. It is medieval, much newer than
the church, and its design is medieval, not divided into tightly
packed Roman quarters. Some scholars believe the triangles
would not have indicated a way of travel to the builders who had
not seen contemporary traffic signs. Still, it is tempting to think
that the design might indicate some post-twilight flicker of a
Roman outlook in that last outpost of empire.

There is no lack of suggestions as to why Roman labyrinths
appear chiefly in villas and baths. You will look in vain for them
in temples or shrines or on gravestones, which suggests that to
the Romans there was nothing divine in the image. They are
domestic decorations. Labyrinths may have been used as a visual
game, an early form of hopscotch, or as a mnemonic device. It is

popular to think of them as ancient hex signs, their twisting paths used to ward off evil spirits, who—tradition has it—could travel only in straight lines. If so, the Roman labyrinths—which are indeed often found close to the front door—might have been good-luck charms, warding off enemies. Wealthy Romans often decorated their villas with reminders of their occupations. A dealer who imported wild animals to be slaughtered in the Colosseum might decorate his floors with dramatic scenes of wild-animal hunts, as the owner of the villa outside Plaza Armerina, in Sicily, did. Remembering the master innovator Daedalus, Roman architects and builders may have paved their dining rooms with labyrinths as a way of displaying, quite literally, their trade marks. But there is little hard evidence to support any of these notions conclusively. Instead, perhaps these urbanized geometric designs with their quarters of twisted paths, walls and battlements were simply a reminder of Rome. Labyrinth floors are not found in the capital itself but in Africa, Iberia, Gaul, Britain and provincial Italy, where they may well have served as a symbol of "home," the greatest of all cities and the hub of the universe, to the homesick Roman living abroad.

There is one more, highly informal manifestation of the labyrinth in Roman life: graffiti, the folk art of the city. If Pompeii was at all typical, the walls of Roman cities were covered with the scrawls of passersby and loiterers. The excavations of this city near modern Naples that was literally smothered in ash and molten lava on the 24th and 25th of August A.D. 79, have revealed more than six thousand messages written—or more often scratched—on its walls. The most common subjects are gladiators and their exploits both in bed and in the arena. There are lyrical love notes, complaints about fickle women, sexually exaggerated drawings and warnings not to urinate on this wall but to go farther down the street. One writer scrawled, "I wonder, O wall, that you have not yet collapsed under the weight of all the idiocies with which these imbeciles cover you."

And, of course, there were labyrinths. Two were scratched without any additional comments on the walls of a narrow passageway between two theaters, just off Strada Stabia, one of the city's major thoroughfares. Another, not far away, is on the private house of Marcus Lucretius, who has otherwise been identified as a priest of Mars. It shows a squared-off labyrinth and the words LABYRINTHUS HIC HABITAT MINOTAURUS (Labyrinth. The Minotaur lives here). Some have interpreted this as a comment by a disgruntled neighbor or "idler" on the personality of Marcus Lucretius or someone else in the house. Others have seen it as a warning similar to the "Beware of the dog" (CAVE CANUM) notice that appears on another Pompeii house. But by all accounts the graffiti has been scratched onto a red-painted column of the peristyle, a roofless interior courtyard, which must mean that it was made by someone with access to the house. An unsatisfied dinner guest? A rebellious—if unusually literate—servant? A grumpy child in the family? Or maybe it was a young student inspired by his (perhaps even her) lessons in ancient history concerning old King Minos? (Or could it even be a forgery, added long after Marcus Lucretius's house became a ruin?)

The design of the graffiti labyrinths is worth noting. It is not the complexly quartered image of the mosaic floors. No graffiti scrawler would have the time, patience or—probably—artistic skill for that. It is the classic Cretan labyrinth, just like ones on the old Knossos coins and the Stone Age caves of Sardinia. The Roman labyrinth divided into its geometric quarters is far too difficult and time-consuming for any fast-moving graffiti artist. But the markings on Pompeii's walls show that an ancient, unfashionable image continued to be remembered.

It will surface again.

Four

THE CHURCH

LOOKING DOWN IN THE CATHEDRAL at Chartres seems almost unnatural. Everything about the building—the soaring arches, the glowing stained-glass windows—is contrived to draw the eyes upward. But on the floor, stretching across the entire width of the widest Gothic nave in France, is one of the wonders of medieval architectural design. And if architecture is too limiting a category, the Chartres labyrinth can just as well be called one of the defining artifacts of medieval thought. In a sanctuary almost devoid of sculpture, the labyrinth is the largest single stone image in sight. At a little more than forty-two feet across,* it is almost—

---

*Measuring the Chartres labyrinth seems a bit tricky since—according to the German labyrinth cataloger Hermann Kern—the image is not as round as it seems, being slightly taller than it is wide. Also, the 112 teeth that form the uniquely scalloped outer edge of the image give rise to slightly different measurements. Kern cites sources for several different measurements—12.3, 12.5 and 13 meters—and says that one measurer found it to be 12.6 meters east-west (that is, top to bottom) and 12.3 north-south. Kern accepts 13 meters (42.65 feet). Robert Ferré, an American labyrinth designer and builder, believes Kern's elliptical reading came about because he did not measure the floor itself but used possibly distorted photographs to make his calculations. Ferré cites his own measurements in situ and the calculations of Australian architect and Chartres scholar John James to give the diameter as 42 feet, 3⅜ inches, with a 1 percent margin of error.

but not exactly, as some believe—identical in size to the massive rose window that looms nearby over the great west door, the principal entrance of the early-thirteenth-century sanctuary. Today, tourists peering through binoculars often pause to look up at the astonishing details in the window, one of the oldest and grandest in the church, never noticing that they are standing on something equally venerable, the oldest and largest Christian labyrinth in Europe. Indeed, having probably been finished around 1202, it is older than most of the building that rises above it.

If shadows, chairs and the inclination to look upward obscure the labyrinth from modern tourists, medieval pilgrims who came to Chartres to venerate the veil of the Virgin Mary, the cathedral's most prized relic, could not have overlooked it. The huge round design of volcanic black set into the almost beige limestone pavement dominates the open expanse of the nave. With the great doors open, late-afternoon sunlight would have fallen across it. And chairs—those relics of the French Revolution's spirit of egalitarianism (a seat for everyone, not just the clergy and the aristocracy)—would not yet have made their appearance. The nave was the people's portion of French cathedrals, open to all, day and night. Business was transacted there. Pilgrims often slept there, sometimes with their animals. The walls beneath the windows may have been hung with instructive tapestries portraying Bible stories, but unlike most European cathedrals, Chartres's nave has always been free of side altars and chapels. There are no tombs or gravestones. To reach the glitter of the candles and the gold of the high altar rising like a sacred hill far off in the eastern end of the building, the worshippers had to walk the length of the relatively austere nave. To reach the sacred area of the priests and the sacraments—the choir and the apse—they had to confront the labyrinth.

There were three choices. They could detour down the side aisles; they could walk over it, which may in itself have had a spiritual meaning; or they could accept the invitation of the labyrinth's opening—which faced the western doorway—and follow the path to the center and its scene of pagan combat, a large metal disk showing Theseus battling the Minotaur as Ariadne looks on. The center, or goal, of the Chartres labyrinth is wide, nearly a quarter of the circle's diameter, but the disk is long gone, having been melted down as scrap in the aftermath of the French Revolution. Only the scar of a few twisted bolts remain today. But here in the people's nave, the scene on the disk was not pagan mythology but another teaching parable: the Christ-hero, guided by a virgin, defeats evil incarnate, the horned devil. Surrounding the place where the disk was once bolted down are six large circular shapes some see as flower petals—rose petals, the symbolic flower of the Virgin Mary. Others see it as a familiar stained-glass design for round—or rose—windows. Or is the rose a compass rose, the design on maps (and mariners' compasses) that indicates the principal directions? Or does the cluster of six symbolize the six days of creation?

Robert Ferré has pointed out that in the now empty center there is just enough room for a seventh circle the same size as the outer six. In medieval numerology seven is an unusually sacred number (many people, especially gamblers, still think it lucky), while eleven—as in the eleven circuits of the pathway leading to the Chartres labyrinth's center—was considered emblematic of sinfulness, of—paradoxically—both excessiveness and deficiency. One ninth-century French archbishop had even divided the world into eleven zones of evil. Wasn't eleven one more than ten, the sign of completeness and the number of commandments God gave Moses? Wasn't it one less than twelve, the figure Jesus himself chose as the number of disciples?

The most obvious sign of the Christianization of the labyrinth is that it now literally bears the sign of the cross. Back to back 180-degree turns in the pathway (four above and four below the center, three to the left, three to the right of it) leave a clearly defined cruciform imprint. Another numerical curiosity arises from the 112 "teeth" that surround the outer ring of the Chartres design and are found on no other labyrinth. If the number is divided into the quarters indicated by the cross, you get 28, the number of days in a lunar month, and the lunar calendar is the one used to establish the date of Easter, the first Sunday after the first full moon after the vernal equinox. Could the Chartres labyrinth have been a lunar calculator, if only a symbolic one?

The classic Cretan labyrinth had been thoroughly redrawn and converted to Christianity. For the first time, at Chartres and in other new cathedrals in northern France, labyrinths were formally—and expensively—installed as holy paths to be walked and perhaps even danced upon. No longer were they simply sacred icons, artful decorations or clever tricks. In the years, then centuries, following the disintegration of Rome, the labyrinth image—like many artifacts of Western knowledge—disappeared into exile in monastery libraries. Perhaps it was more like a Babylonian captivity. In any case, for about five hundred years labyrinths were ignored.

Then, something stirred and labyrinths—new labyrinths different from the Cretan and Roman models—began turning up on medieval manuscripts, sometimes simply as doodles in the margins. Often the manuscripts had to do with astronomical or mathematical calculations. Hermann Kern, who has made probably the most extensive listing of early manuscript labyrinths, believes the oldest surviving eleven-circuit Chartres-style labyrinth was discovered in the monastic library at St.-Germain-des-Prés in Paris. It was sketched onto a tenth-century flyleaf added to a ninth-century essay on how to calculate the annual and ever-changing date of Easter. In the center of the labyrinth, labeled "prince of the world," is a triumphant-looking devil-Minotaur, enthroned with his feet resting comfortably on a footstool. Clearly, here was a self-satisfied ruler of a world of sin. Among other early examples is an amendment to a ninth-century manuscript from Auxerre, whose cathedral would later have a labyrinth in its nave, warning against tampering with the word of God by adding a *"labyrinthus texatur eerroris,"* a labyrinth of textual error, to the Holy Scriptures. A century or so later the phrase caught the eye of a—perhaps—bored monk who wanted to try out his new compass. For whatever reason, a different hand added a geometrically exact labyrinth to the parchment page. And most intriguing is a badly damaged fifteenth-century Icelandic sketch, clearly a copy of a much older drawing, that shows one of the Three Wise Men who followed the star to Bethlehem kneeling before not a baby in a manger but a labyrinth. None of these drawings was much larger than the palm of a hand.

Not all the manuscript labyrinths are overtly Christian. A thirteenth-century plan of Constantinople by an Arabian geographer, Al-Qazvīnī, looks very much like a labyrinth, but its curious layout, which is neither Cretan nor Chartres-like, leads some to think it represents not Constantinople itself but the course of the Game of Troy played on horseback there during the emperor Constantine's ceremonies celebrating the christening of the city in May 330. Several other drawings, including a fourteenth-century addition of a modified Chartres design to a ninth-century Greek manuscript, claim that the inventor of the labyrinth was not the pagan Daedalus but King Solomon, who in the Judeo-Christian tradition is renowned not only for his wisdom but also as a great builder. The first temple in Jerusalem was his work, and in the Middle Ages, the symbolic roots of Freemasonry were linked to the builders of his temple. Indeed, to this day, there are those who argue with an almost cultish intensity that the geometry of Gothic architecture and the design of the Chartres labyrinth were among the "secrets" of Solomon's Temple brought to France in—they can give the exact date—1128 by a tiny band of

Crusaders called the Knights Templar. Some even believe the lost Ark of the Covenant containing the stone slabs of the Ten Commandments is hidden beneath Chartres's nave.

A whole subcategory of manuscript labyrinths—Kern found fourteen examples—depicts the ancient city of Jericho as a labyrinth; the oldest of these was drawn sometime between 806 and 822 in an Italian monastery in Abruzzi. Jericho, like Troy, was known for its impenetrable walls. In both cities, the fortifications were destroyed not by force but by trickery and—perhaps—the intervention of one or more gods. The Greeks had their treacherous wooden horse. The Israelites had their blaring rams' horn trumpets. And just as Daedalus's labyrinth had Ariadne and her red thread, Jericho had Rahab and her scarlet rope. Both women helped foreign invaders escape a maze. Rahab, however, was no virgin.

As the story is told in the biblical Book of Joshua, Joshua—Moses's general and political successor—was unifying Cannan as a homeland for the Israelites. The walled city of Jericho, which commanded the Jordan River, was a major strategic target, although it was "bolted and barred." Joshua first sent in two spies, who quickly made an alliance with Rahab, a prostitute who lived in a house that conveniently backed up against the city wall. When word circulated in Jericho that spies were within the city, she hid her guests, then lied to authorities about knowing their whereabouts, then helped them escape by providing them with a scarlet-colored rope with which to climb out her back window and over the wall. The spies promised that if she hung a piece of the rope in front of her house, she and her family would be spared when the city fell to the invaders. This could be the scriptural origin of the *red* in *red-light district.*

Following the instructions of the Lord, Joshua had his men march once around the walls of Jericho every day for six days, following in silence behind men bearing the sacred Ark of the Covenant, the Israelites' holiest relic, and seven priests blaring away on seven trumpets made of rams' horns. On the seventh day the entire group was to march not once but seven times around the walls and on a signal from the rams' horns, they were all to shout "a mighty shout." The men followed orders, and after the mighty shout, the walls fell and the invaders slaughtered everyone in sight except for those in Rahab's house of ill repute.

In Hermann Kern's catalog of Jericho labyrinths, some are Jewish, some Christian (both Eastern and Western churches). And just about all of them use the classic Cretan design with its seven circuits. It is difficult not to think of each circuit as a cycle of silent Israelites marching around the ancient city. Most of these labyrinth drawings emphasize the heavily fortified walls, and some show the pathway itself as lined with battlements. And is there anything to be made of the fact that all the Jericho labyrinths in Hebrew-language books and manuscripts are round, while many with Christian origins are square or rectangular?

The parallels among the stories from Troy, Crete and Jericho are probably not coincidental. But perhaps more important is the continued link between the labyrinth and the city. Great cities appear in just about all these manuscript labyrinths, ancient cities with fabled walls: Constantinople, Jerusalem, Jericho. When the first medieval labyrinths were built in the thirteenth century, it was not by chance that they were in cathedrals. In the traditional ecclesiastical definitions of communities, a hamlet is a settlement too small for a church. A village has a church. A town has more than one. And a city is defined by its cathedral, literally—in Latin—the place of the bishop's throne. The city was a labyrinth's natural home.

When the new labyrinths emerged from the monastery libraries at the end of the twelfth century, they settled—with a few notable exceptions—in two distinct areas: across northern Italy from the Po River and Ravenna in the east toward the Mediterranean in the west and in France in a circle around (but oddly not including) Paris.

All of the half dozen or so surviving early Italian church labyrinths are round. Most, like Roman labyrinths, are small when compared to those in France. Many of the designs are also direct descendants of Roman mosaic floors. Signs of the zodiac were included in a now lost—it was last described by someone who saw it in the seventeenth century—labyrinth at Piacenza, along the Po River. The Minotaur legend is retold in many labyrinths, but now—both at Pavia and Cremona—the pictured beast looks much like a classical centaur, a horse or, in this case, a bull with a man's arms, trunk and head.

Pavia, also near the Po, still has at least part of a twelfth-century mosaic labyrinth that was thought to have been lost. Located in the chancel of the basilica of San Michele Maggiore, the labyrinth was once known only by drawings made of a portion of the floor in the seventeenth century. Then, in 1972, the altar was moved, uncovering the floor beneath, and most of what was missing in the early drawings was revealed. The labyrinth itself is in the Chartres style, but otherwise what was discovered when both the lost and found portions were put together is a mosaic that would not have been all that out of place in a Roman villa. Theseus and the centaur-Minotaur in the center are surrounded with a litter of half-eaten body parts that could have been a macabre "unswept room" pavement. The round labyrinth itself is squared with vignettes in each corner showing other uneven battles. A naked man fights a dragon with a spear, a goat battles a wolf, a man wrestles with a goose, and if the boy facing off with a giant turns out to be David, that simply tells us that someone was familiar with the Old Testament.

A key distinction—besides the design of the labyrinth pathway—between the Roman and medieval Italian labyrinths is their location: none of the Roman ones was placed in a temple or a sacred site. All of the medieval ones are in or on a place of worship.

Two small, nearly identical labyrinths located not far from each other in western Tuscany demonstrate the easy cohabitation of pagan and Christian elements. One is in Lucca, the other Pontremoli. Both are stone carvings of Chartres-style labyrinths about eight and a half or nine inches in diameter with entrances on the right-hand side. The pathway in the Lucca stone, however, is hollowed out as a groove while the Pontremoli pathway is cut in relief so that it is raised up. In effect, they are positive and negative representations of the same image.

Lucca is a walled city with its ramparts still intact and walkable. Sometime in the late twelfth or early thirteenth century a labyrinth was carved into a column in the narthex of the Cathedral of San Martino. It is along a wall on the north side of the bell tower, at shoulder height, just next to the cathedral's principal doorway. In the labyrinth's center was once the familiar battle scene between Theseus and the Minotaur, but that was rubbed away long ago by fingers that traced along the pathway and still to this day leave it shiny with frequent use. Next to the entrance to the labyrinth, on the right, is carved a Latin text that reads: "Here is the labyrinth that Daedalus from Crete built, and which no one can exit once inside. Only Theseus was able to do so, thanks to Ariadne's thread." There is no overt religious message, but no one needed a sermon to understand Theseus's role as a surrogate for Jesus. The smoothly worn pathway is evidence that centuries of worshippers—and perhaps passersby as well—have run their fingers over it just as they might have dipped them into a holy-water font as they entered the cathedral.

The history of the Pontremoli stone is so dramatic there is no telling where—exactly—it was originally placed, but there is a good chance it was used much as its neighbor in Lucca was. To begin with, it was part of a twelfth-century church attached to Pontremoli's Convent of San Pietro de Conflentu, a popular stopping place for Italian pilgrims headed for the shrine of Santiago de

Compostela, in northern Spain. In 1567, the church suffered the fate of many medieval buildings: it simply collapsed. In 1750, San Pietro was rebuilt and the labyrinth stone reused, probably on the façade near the doorway. The fact that the stone was carefully preserved for 183 years indicates that it must have been given special meaning. All went well until 1945, when the church was hit by a bomb during the Allied campaign in Italy and again destroyed. The labyrinth once more survived and is now preserved in a local institution.

At first glance, the Pontremoli stone seems to have far more Christian content than its counterpart in Lucca. No pagan scene appears in the center. Instead there is the traditional abbreviation of Jesus the Savior's name in Greek, the letters IHS. And below the image is a quotation in Latin from one of Saint Paul's letters to the Christians in Corinth. Yet a second glance reveals some signs of paganism. That quotation is curious: "So run, that ye may obtain." The complete verse (it's 1 Corinthians 9:24) reads: "Know ye not that they which run in a race run all, but one receiveth the prize? So run, that ye may obtain." That, coupled with the carving that appears above the labyrinth of two men on horseback greeting each other with upraised right arms, makes it impossible not to think—once again—of the ancient Game of Troy and the wild race around its labyrinthine course.

The labyrinth wall plaques at the church doorways in Lucca and Pontremoli, whether their designs are engraved or raised, create a pattern or template to guide the hand in making a "sign" of the labyrinth. It's similar to the gesture of worshippers at the holy-water font when they bless themselves by making the far less complex sign of the cross. There is no evidence that this was the stones' purpose, and there seems to be no record that the sign of the labyrinth drawn in the air was ever used as a blessing. But it is a possibility worth considering, if only to dismiss it.

Vertical labyrinths, rather than ones on the pavement, are

unusual in the post-Roman world. These two rare Tuscan examples show that the new Christianized labyrinth still carries with it memories of its past. Signs of modernity—late-medieval, early-Renaissance modernity—began to appear in twelfth-century Italian pavements as multicolored near-patchwork quilt combinations of marble chips, mosaic fragments and porphyry. These floors can be seen in many of Rome's oldest churches, including the Basilica of San Clemente and Santa Maria, in Trastevere, where there is what may or may not be a labyrinth. The ten-circuit Trastevere image—that number in itself is highly unusual—certainly begins as a labyrinth, but its inner circles are just that, concentric circles with no openings. Some believe that it was a true labyrinth that has been ineptly repaired over the years. Others think that however beautiful it may be, it was never a labyrinth in the first place. Another eye-catching Roman Chartres-style labyrinth, now destroyed, was five feet wide and made of bands of yellow, green and red. It was in the twelfth-century church of Santa Maria Acquino. Already mentioned in chapter 3 was the dazzling but curious labyrinth on the floor of the octagonal sanctuary of San Vitale, in Ravenna, the city that was the last capital of the western Roman Empire and the burial place of Theodoric, one of the first post-Roman, so-called barbarian kings. Again, the design (possibly from as late as the sixteenth century) is startling, with a parade of arrowlike triangles—some decorated with floral patterns—leading out from the center, a sight seen in no other early church labyrinth.

It makes sense that a discussion of the early Italian labyrinths ends with such words as *color, design* and *originality*. Although these images carried their theological and metaphysical weight, there is rarely a sense that the medieval Italians took the labyrinth symbol as seriously as the French did in that circle of cathedrals around Paris. For the Italians, the labyrinth was an aid to devotion. Following the winding path—even with a finger—might help save one's soul, but labyrinths were also wonderful visual ornaments to be enjoyed for their sheer beauty. They remained small, and like the paths on the mosaic Roman floors, were too small to walk. Even San Vitale's labyrinth, the largest, is only about eleven and a half feet wide. Some are vertical, like pictures or Roman mosaic murals. In Italy, the labyrinth remained something to look at or maybe, however briefly, to touch. It was primarily a visual experience. In France, it became a pathway to walk, a sacred pathway.

The names of the French cathedral cities, the labyrinth cities, peal like a great church bell: Amiens, Arras, Auxerre, Bayeux, Chartres, Reims, St.-Omer, Sens and—although it is a collegiate church and not a cathedral—St.-Quentin. When they were built, mostly in the thirteenth and fourteenth centuries, all but one of the labyrinths were round or octagonal, usually with an eleven-circuit design that became known in the twentieth century as Chartres-style after the largest and best known of the survivors. Survivors? Of the original church labyrinths, only Amiens, Bayeux, Chartres and St.-Quentin remain as they were built, and Amiens is a late-nineteenth-century replica, an exact reconstruction of a labyrinth that had been ripped out of the cathedral nave earlier in the century.

The cathedral in Bayeux once housed the late-eleventh-century embroidered tapestry that tells, in a rollicking, almost cartoonish fashion, the raucous story of the Norman conquest of Britain. It is also the home of the most Italianate French labyrinth. It is not in the nave. Locked away, as it has been for the past seven hundred years, in the center of the floor of the cathedral's high Gothic chapter house is a little tile labyrinth. Now so badly worn that the designs on the individual tiles are known (perhaps incorrectly) only from an early colored illustration, it is still obvious that this church labyrinth is unlike any other in France. None other is too small—only about twelve feet across— for an adult to walk. None other is located in a part of a church restricted only to clergy. And although at first it looks like a standard Chartres design, it isn't. There are only ten rings.

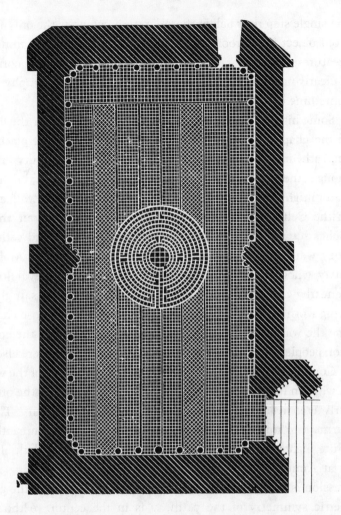

The floor of the roughly twenty-four-by-forty-five-foot room, dominated at one end by a huge painting of the Adoration of the Virgin, seems to have been rubbed clean of any decoration. But as the eye adjusts, like mushrooms becoming visible amidst the leaves in a forest, tile designs spring into view: many variations of the fleur de lys, fanciful castles, lion's heads, a triangle formed by three left hands, oak leaves, a griffin, a wild boar, a man blowing a horn. An entire, well-preserved hunting tableau runs along the single step riser below the Adoration, which is the only religious object in the room. Even a fish, that most symbol-prone of creatures, that appears on one tile protected by being in a corner, is clearly not from the zodiac or early Christian iconography. It's something to be cleaned, fried and eaten.

Some highly colored illustrations now mounted near the door of the chapter house, which was the formal meeting place of the cathedral's clergy, suggest what a nineteenth-century artist thought the tiles looked like, and some look as through the illustrator might have been influenced by William Morris's wallpaper or the Celtic revival. The actual surviving tiles, about three inches square, are predominately brown, red, green and yellow. They were likely made in a local village now called Le Molay-Littry, whose pottery also produced tiles found in medieval floors in nearby Caen. It is tempting to imagine their shiny salt glaze being worn away by the dancing feet of the canons whose chairs line the walls of the room, dancing free of the gaze of the common people whose property the labyrinth was everywhere else.

Compared to Bayeux—which is, after all, rather out of the way in western Normandy, almost as far away as Brittany—the other early French labyrinths have an almost Shaker austerity. They are made of stone, not decorated tile, and the pathways are either white, light gray or beige, as at Chartres, or black or dark blue, as at Amiens and St.-Quentin. Either way, the prevailing impression is black and white. The only decoration beside the geometric symmetry of the pathway is in the center. (Although the octagonal center of the late-fifteenth-century labyrinth at St.-Quentin is blank, a seven-pointed star lies between the labyrinth and the basilica's west door. Such a star is not only a symbol of the Virgin Mary but also of the Egyptian goddess of measure and geometry, Seshat [her name means "seven"], who is usually depicted in tomb art in scenes showing the building of temples.) Traditionally, some reference to the Theseus-and-Minotaur story appeared there, and most historians have assumed—working from seventeenth-century illustrations—that the missing metal disk at Chartres showed such a scene. A few, Hermann Kern among them, disagree. They point out that the Knossos trio appears in not a single cathedral labyrinth in France. Instead, in both Amiens and Reims the labyrinths honor Daedalus and his heirs, the architects and master builders who created the great cathedrals whose walls surround them. And at Chartres, they argue, the missing disk might even have revealed the name of the cathedral's unknown designer.

Names are—or were—recorded within the labyrinths at both Amiens and Reims, and portraits as well. The late-thirteenth-century Reims labyrinth was destroyed in 1779, but elaborate sixteenth-century sketches and descriptions reveal its details. It was octagonal, with eleven circuits, like so many others, but at each corner were small octagonal additions usually called "towers." The entire image was about thirty-four feet square and, with its watchtowers, resembled the floor plan of a medieval fortress or walled city.

A single male figure stood in the center and in each of the four towers. Except for the central, almost phantasmagoric figure, whose face had been completely obliterated by 1587, when a local architect named Jacques Cellier made his sketches, each of them has been identified. In the margin, Cellier called the labyrinth *un dédale*, a daedalus, and identified the men simply as architects who "directed the work of the construction" of the cathedral. Fifty years later, a canon, Pierre Cocquault, recorded the pavement's badly worn inscriptions and made more specific identifications. The figure holding a carpenter's square is Jean le Loup, who was master of works for sixteen years and began work on the portals. Jean d'Orbais (holding a compass) began the upper stories of the chevet. Bernard de Soissons (drawing a circle with a compass) was master of works for thirty-five years and designed

the vaults and great rose window, and Gaucher de Reims (pointing with his hand) was master for eight years and worked on arches and portals. And that mysterious faceless figure in the labyrinth's center, which was often called *le ciel,* heaven? That shrouded figure who neither holds nor points? He may have been the archbishop who ordered the cathedral built. Or perhaps he was the architect of architects, the master of the masters of works, who created the overall plan for the cathedral. That the concentration of wear and tear centers on his face and head may be significant. They may have been worn away by the faithful who believed the only true architect of architects was God in heaven, who, Saint Augustine wrote, "made the world in measure, number and weight." Was rubbing his face a sign of devotion, even veneration, akin to the urge to trace the labyrinth's path in Lucca?

But the medieval architects and their masters of works were indeed little gods creating small, if complex worlds. There was no single, accepted unit of measure. Although the Romans had established a standard foot (295 millimeters, or 11.614 modern inches), it was now often forgotten or ignored. Not only was a yard in Siena often a different length than it was just a few miles away in Florence, it varied from construction boss to construction boss within a single cathedral. John James, who has studied Chartres literally stone by stone, claims to be able identify different construction crews not just by the quality of their work and their individually unique designs of small details but by their different units of measure. Each crew's foot was a different length—however minor the differences—and each master, James writes, carried a metal rule that indicated its length. It was his hallmark. Some believed it was a contemporary equivalent of the rod carried by Aaron, Moses's brother.

The three architects pictured in the Amiens cathedral *ciel* also carry tools of their trade, a ruler, a square and a compass. Amiens has one of the tallest Gothic naves in France and the second-largest—about two feet smaller than Chartres's—labyrinth, locally called the House of Daedalus. It's also the most informative labyrinth, being—as labyrinths go—downright chatty. We believe construction to have begun in 1220 because the lengthy inscription in its *ciel* says so, or at least it did until it was vandalized during the French Revolution. The complete inscription read, in Latin: "In the year 1220 when work on this cathedral was begun, Blessed Evrard was bishop and Louis the King of France, who was the son of Philip Augustus. He who directed the work was called Robert, surnamed Lazurches. Master Thomas de Cormont came after him, and after him his son, Master Renaud, who had this inscription placed here in the year of the incarnation, 1288." That is the sort of wealth of information investigators were hoping to find in Chartres when, in the nineteenth century, they dug under their labyrinth, searching in vain for the rumored grave of their still nameless architect.

The original, if damaged, Amiens *ciel* now displayed in the local Museum of Picardie shows four human figures, three builders and Bishop Evrard, who carries the tool of his trade, a bishop's crook. Each man appears between the equal-length arms of a Greek cross. They are all the same size, unlike in Reims, where the tower figures were smaller than the one in the center. The attending angels are considerably smaller than the men. There are four of them, each hovering over the end of one of the cross's arms. Surprisingly, the cross does not line up with the top or bottom of the labyrinth and looks like a slightly off-kilter X. It may indeed, as some believe, even align with the angels' gaze on the spot where the sun rises on August 15, the Feast of the Assumption, the cathedral's principal feast day.

Although the pathway of the Amiens labyrinth follows the classic Chartres pattern, the labyrinth itself is a simple octagon, with no added Reims-style watchtowers. Most of the labyrinths in northern France are octagons, including the smaller, plainer survivor in nearby St.-Quentin. Throughout Christendom, the octagon and the number eight are associated with baptism and rebirth. Baptisteries are almost always eight-sided. Baptismal fonts to this day in most Christian churches, both Catholic and Protestant, are octagonal. It can be argued—indeed well argued—

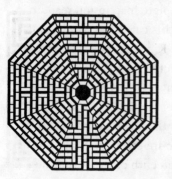

that walking the labyrinth's path is an act of spiritual rebirth, that the person reaching the center is no longer the person who entered its western gate. But in this part of France, there may also be a political meaning to the symbol of baptism.

In 496, Clovis, king of the Franks and vanquisher of the Romans, was baptized by the bishop of Reims and became a Christian. In effect, all of what was then France was baptized with him. According to legend, four thousand of his troops also converted. As the sixth-century historian Gregory of Tours described it, the entire city became a baptistery: "The public squares were draped with colored cloth, the churches were adorned with white hangings, sticks of incense gave off clouds of perfume, sweet-smelling candles gleamed bright, the holy place of baptism was filled with divine fragrance. God filled the hearts of all present." Gregory compared Clovis with Constantine, whose conversation to Christianity in 313 changed the face of the Roman Empire. What better way to commemorate and celebrate the rebirth of a nation than to bend the labyrinth into an octagon, the very symbol of baptism? It was an act of both piety and patriotic nationalism. In centuries to come, French kings on their way to their coronations at the high altar of the Reims cathedral walked across the octagonal labyrinth just inside the western portal. Whether or not they realized it, they were crossing a monument to the baptism of their earliest predecessor.

The pathway of the eleven-circuit octagonal labyrinth is identical to the round Chartres original, but the straight sides force the pattern into sharp turns—rather than swooping curves—that produce a walk that is jerkier and more angular. The most angular—and the most original—of all the French church labyrinths was the late-fifteenth-century square that was once in the south transept (not the nave) of the Benedictine Abbey of Saint Bertin in St.-Omer, near the English Channel. It was all straight lines and right angles and owed more to the quarters of Roman mosaic floors than to either the Crete or Chartres prototypes. The effect is al-

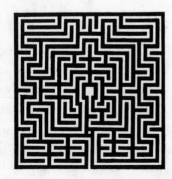

most reminiscent of Piet Mondrian's jittery Jazz Age painting *Broadway Boogie-Woogie,* except for the dominating image of the cross that rises out of the Golgotha-like center. It was destroyed centuries ago, and one would be tempted to say it was like no other, except for the fact that it was copied on the floor of the Ghent city hall in Belgium in 1533 and more recently in the cathedral in St.-Omer.

There is no record of early French kings actually following the labyrinth's pathway as they made their way through Reims's nave. They probably did not. Indeed, the earliest historical commentaries on cathedral labyrinths say nothing at all about walking. What they do mention, however, are dancing, singing and a liturgical ball game.

Links between dance and worship, as well as dancing and the labyrinth, are as old as religion itself. Ariadne danced. Theseus and the survivors of the Minotaur danced. The Bible tells how King David the Goliath slayer—who, as the partially destroyed labyrinth at Pavia shows, was seen in medieval times as a Theseus figure—danced before the Lord and the Ark of the Covenant. Early Christian fathers began banning dancing in churches as early as the fifth century, which means there must have been something to ban. Early records include passing references to ceremonial dancing on the labyrinths at Sens, Amiens, Reims and Chartres, but little is known of the details. The best account of dancing on a cathedral labyrinth dates from Auxerre in 1396.

The lost labyrinth at Auxerre, a city south of Paris, is thought to have been circular and all together similar to Chartres's, though smaller. No one knows for sure what it looked like. It was destroyed before 1690 and there are no known sketches of it. A description of its Easter dance in its chapter records, however, makes Auxerre's live on as one of the best remembered cathedral labyrinths.

The dance begins early on Easter afternoon with a leather ball, a *pilota,* provided by the most recently ordained priest, who was probably one of the youngest of the church's clergy. The *pilota's* size is unclear: so large that it must be held with two hands but small enough to throw with one. Judging from complaints made over the years by newly ordained priests, it was also expensive. The young canon gives the *pilota* to the dean, probably one of the older men in the cathedral, who takes his place in the labyrinth, probably at its entrance, in front of the great western door. The rest of the cathedral clergy hold hands and dance around the labyrinth, while the dean, performing a distinctive three-step movement (which may have involved a bit of foot stamping), throws the ball, using his left hand only, one by one to each of the other dancers, who, in turn, return it. The organ—which then, like at Chartres, was located near the labyrinth—plays and they all sing, presumably over and over again, a brief Latin hymn that begins, "Christians, sing forth praises to the Easter victim, / The lamb redeems the sheep."

There are several obvious questions. First, about the chorus of hand-holding dancers. According to the account, they dance "around," *citra.* Does that mean around the outside or around—along—the pathway through the labyrinth? Many modern commentators, thinking of labyrinths in terms of walking them, have the clergy in something of a crack-the-whip formation speeding—in time to the music—along the path. But then from where does the dean throw the *pilota*? Is he dancing in place in the *ciel*? The labyrinth would be extremely crowded with the chorus of clergy and the dean all maneuvering on the same narrow path. It makes more sense to have the dean dancing the pathway to the center while the rest of the clergy circle the perimeter.

And if they are holding hands, how do they catch the ball? Perhaps it was a variation on dodgeball, although that seems unlikely. The receiver probably simply dropped hands, caught it and threw it back. Craig Wright, a historian of music at Yale University, has shown that the construction of some medieval musical works—with their repeats and reversals of notes—follow the form and structure of the labyrinth. He suggests that the dancers might have had to kick the ball back or butt it with their heads. He doesn't make the claim, but this sounds suspiciously like the divine origin of soccer.

The ball and the dean's three-step dance are the key elements here. The ball could refer to Ariadne's clew, but it also symbolizes both the Easter sun—a new, living sun rising in glory after the darkness and death on Good Friday—and a world born anew after the Resurrection of Jesus. The three steps of the dance celebrate the Father, Son and Holy Ghost of the Trinity.

But all this talk of death and resurrection should not obscure the fact that the dancing and the ball playing were fun. Here was a group of men, many of them young, singing, dancing and throwing a ball around. Things were bound to get out of hand. Surely that hymn about Easter's victim was interrupted with a good deal of laughter. The privations of Lent were over. Christ had not only risen from the dead but had also returned victorious from his descent into hell. It was a time for celebration, even for some approved mischief. In Chartres, each canon was given five sous on Easter afternoon to gamble with. The Auxerre account says that after the dancing was done, the clergy went to the chapter house, where they sat in a circle on benches and were served "sweet meats, fruit tarts and game of all sorts: boar, venison, and rabbit, and white and red wine was offered in moderation, each cup being refilled no more than one or two times." It was all so much fun that the canons at Sens, about forty miles away, petitioned in 1413 that "according to custom" they, too, be permitted to "play freely the game on the labyrinth"—they had one of their own—the following Easter.

As early as the 1280s bishops were denouncing the Easter dance as a pagan throwback, and it was formally condemned in

Auxerre in 1531, although the minor clergy protested not for religious reasons but for the loss of entertainment the dance provided the townspeople, who apparently came to watch. Although there were attempts to "reform" the game (which usually meant removing the ball from the ceremony), it was officially ended in 1538 by a ruling of the parliamentary court in Paris.

In spite of all the mysticism and mystery, there is something about a labyrinth that is playful. It's a game. Children sense this immediately. The thread of playfulness inherent in the labyrinths' pathways was one of the major reasons they were eventually removed from most French cathedrals. Children, like the priests freed from their Lenten vows, found the large labyrinths filling the width of the naves of dark, possibly frightening cathedrals irresistible playgrounds. They were places to run and invent games and dances of their own. Many suspect it's where hopscotch was born. The children's laughter interrupted services and disturbed prayers, or so it was claimed. What happened in Reims was typical. In 1778, one of the priests, Jean Jacquemart, offered to pay a thousand francs—presumably his own money—for the cathedral's pavement to be torn up and the ancient octagonal labyrinth destroyed. A year later, it was gone.

Liturgical dances performed only on Easter are well represented in collections of surviving medieval music. Craig Wright has found more than thirty-five different tunes. But the raucous canons danced upon the labyrinths only one afternoon a year, and although we have those reports of noisy children, there is amazingly little said about how the pavements were used on all the other days. The activities must have been so ordinary, so much a part of everyday life, that it was hardly worth mentioning. The lack of solid factual information has produced a bonanza of speculation and anachronistic second-guessing.

The contemporary British designer Adrian Fisher, who may well have created and actually built more mazes than anyone else in history, has suggested a highly detailed analysis of the meaning of the Chartres design. Among his interpretations is that the three rather cramped counterclockwise arcs encountered fairly early on in the pathway represent the time between Jesus's crucifixion and resurrection, while later, larger, more sweeping arcs—over which the walker can move more quickly—stand for the hope of eternal life. Such speculation is more the result of self-confidence, and perhaps personal experience walking a labyrinth, than historic documentation.

A favorite gambit employed by writers on the history of labyrinths—one that will be repeated here—is to set up the straw man of indulgences, the grant of absolution from sin. It was a popular belief in the nineteenth century, when guidebook writers rediscovered the cathedral labyrinths, that medieval pilgrims walked them—or perhaps made their way around them on their knees in prayer—to win the indulgences awarded to those who had visited the holy shrines in Jerusalem, a trip the Crusades had made even more difficult than usual. Many labyrinths were indeed, as the guidebooks pointed out, called the *chemin de Jerusalem*, the path to Jerusalem. But that term came later, well into the eighteenth century, and although over the centuries some of the faithful may have seen and used the labyrinth as a way to absolution and the gateway to heaven, there is no evidence that thirteenth-century Christians—be they clerics, pilgrims or architects—saw it that way.

Walking the Stations of the Cross, also called the Way of the Cross, was another substitute for visiting Jerusalem that began to become popular at the end of the twelfth century, especially among Franciscans. In it, worshippers followed a trail of "stations" that traced Jesus's procession from his trial to his execution on the Hill of Golgotha, just as pilgrims in Jerusalem followed the path of what was said to be the actual sites, the Via Dolorosa. The practice continues today in most Catholic churches, with fourteen stations situated around the nave observing such moments as "Jesus Falls for the First Time," "Simon of Cyrene Helps Jesus Carry the Cross" and "Veronica Wipes the Face of Jesus."

The image of the cross is imposed on the Chartres labyrinth by the pattern created when two 180-degree reversals of direction in the pathway meet back to back on the vertical and horizontal axes. The back-to-back image reminds some twentieth-century observers of the double-headed axes Sir Arthur Evans reported finding at Knossos. As a result, these points are sometimes called the labryses. Four labryses are aligned above the center, and there are three on either side. The four turnings below the center do not form perfect labryses, but all together the U-turns create the cruciform image.

That the total of these turns on the Chartres-style labyrinth is fourteen has made some believe they were somehow used as a site for the Stations of the Cross. Indeed, a nineteenth-century guidebook discussing the destroyed labyrinth at Reims claimed pilgrims often read from a locally published prayer book entitled *Stations on the Path to Jerusalem Found in the Cathedral of Our Lady in Reims* as they made their way to the center. No publication date was given for the book (which very likely resembled the "Way of the Cross" section of prayers and devotions in the contemporary *Roman Missal*), but it was certainly centuries after the labyrinth was built. And however popular "doing the stations" later became, it is unlikely that the labyrinths were built for that purpose. As for the stations themselves, the actual number of them varied from place to place and time to time, the number fourteen not being officially enshrined until as late as 1731.

There is little doubt that worshippers have always walked the labyrinth. What they were walking toward is the mystery. Saint Jerome, the mystic and scholar often remembered today because so many early Renaissance painters depicted his friendship with a lion, wrote lovingly of "the labyrinth of the mysteries of God." But to others the labyrinth had a decidedly grim aspect. Its eleven circuits proclaim its symbolic sinfulness. Boethius, the most read philosopher of the Middle Ages, contrasted the "inextricable labyrinth" with the "wonderful circle of the simplicity of God." Erasmus, the most enlightened man of his age, wrote of the "labyrinthine errors of this world," while in "The Knight's Tale" of *The Canterbury Tales,* Chaucer, that otherwise most amiable and amused of authors, also described the world in grim but downright labyrinthine terms: it is "but a thoroughfare full of woe" and we, its inhabitants, are "pilgrims passing to and fro." One person has counted the turns on the pathway to the center and back of the Chartres labyrinth and come up with the number seventy (most count only sixty-eight), the biblical "three score years and ten" of a human lifespan.

But the church labyrinth can be many things at once. On Easter afternoon it is a commemoration of Jesus's triumphant return from hell, where he successfully confronted the devil, just as Theseus defeated the Minotaur. Another time, when the cathedral clergy walked in procession across it singing the psalm "When Israel Came out from Egypt" it could represent Moses's wandering through the desert. It could celebrate the work of the architect who, using—in the words of both Augustine and the Apocrypha's "Wisdom of Solomon"—"measure, number and weight," created however imperfectly on earth what the Great Architect had done with perfection before man's first sin. It could record everyman's progress through life to death and the hope— and promise—of eternal life thereafter. Its coiled and entwined serpentine design could be emblematic in God's house, a cathedral dedicated to Notre Dame, the Virgin Mary, of the snake in the Garden of Eden, the deceitful creature that introduced sin into paradise. Prophecy said it would be crushed beneath the heel of the Virgin herself. And it could be a game for bored children on a rainy afternoon.

Most of all, it could be the path to Jerusalem, not that fortified hill town in the Judean desert but the New Jerusalem, the City of God described in the next-to-last chapter of the last book of the Bible as descending from heaven "prepared as a bride adorned for her husband." It is the place that Saint Paul, in a phrase that would later be borrowed by Gertrude Stein, called "the mother of us all" (Galatians 4.26). Buried deep in the phantasmagoric, near hallucinogenic stanzas of William Blake's epic 1804 poem *Jerusalem* are four simple lines that connect the labyrinth to the New Jerusalem with Ariadne's clew. It is addressed "To the Christians":

> *I give you the end of a golden string*
> *Only wind it into a ball:*
> *It will lead you in at Heavens gate,*
> *Built in Jerusalems wall.*

Let us look again at the *Mappa Mundi,* Hereford Cathedral's giant thirteenth-century map of the world. As mentioned in the first chapter, it is round, and as with most medieval maps, east is at the top, west on the bottom, north to the left, south to the right. If you had the map before you as you entered the west portal of Chartres or Amiens or any of the labyrinth cathedrals, it would be correctly oriented. You would be facing the east both in the cathedral and on the map. The entrance to the labyrinth is directly in front of you. If the labyrinth were the round map itself, you'd be standing at the western edge of the world, beyond the Pillars of Hercules, the Strait of Gibraltar. In the middle distance is the center of the labyrinth, the *ciel,* just as Jerusalem is at the center of the map. Straight ahead in the east, far off in the distance, is the high altar, and on the top of the map, at the edge of the known world, you find the Garden of Eden.

In medieval geography, the west is the place of the dead, Indeed, "going west" survived as a synonym for dying well into the twentieth century. The western interior walls of churches and cathedrals traditionally bear scenes of the Last Judgment, with Jesus sitting as judge dispatching the saved to his right, the damned to his left. The ferocity of the punishment varies from place to place. The twelfth- and thirteenth-century mosaics on the back wall of the Torcello basilica in the Venetian lagoon show severed heads, brutally ripped body parts burning in eternal fire as snakes slither through empty eye sockets, while not so many miles away in Padua, Giotto's more humanist fresco on the rear wall of the Arena Chapel includes a timid sinner hiding behind a tree. In Chartres, the judgment, which is neither particularly grotesque nor gentle, is filtered through the dark stained glass of a great rose window.

The walker entering the Chartres labyrinth moves first toward the *ciel*, then must turn left, the direction of the damned, then right, toward the saved, then left again, passing next to the great rounded petals that ring the inside of the center. Then, just as quickly, the walker is thrust away from the goal and because of the labyrinth's design seems to be headed farther and farther away from the center. High above in the west, the land of the dead, the walker sees centered in the rose window the figure of Jesus, not on the cross (there are very few crucifixion scenes in Chartres) but displaying the wounds inflicted on Him by men during His time on earth, the bloody nail holes through His hands and feet, the jagged spear slash on His side. From time to time when the walker moves toward the east, there are glimpses of the altar, the place of the priests and the holy sacraments, but more time is spent moving westward, through the sinful world of ordinary people. To the left and right, on windows donated by the medieval guilds, are scenes of everyday life, shoes being sold, horses being shod. From the high, round window, angels and apostles watch the judgment as the Archangel Michael—who was also said to have visited the souls in hell—assists Jesus the judge. Demons herd the damned away with tools American farmers would call pitchforks. Hell itself yawns as an open, fanged mouth. If the labyrinth were indeed a medieval map of the world, the walker would visit and pass by every land, continent or island. Finally, from the outermost ring, the path takes a sharp, right-angle turn directly toward the east, and after a few more quick turns the walker, facing away from death and judgment and toward the altar and eternal life, moves into the circle—just as Jerusalem is a circle on the *Mappa Mundi*—of the Holy City, the *ciel*, the New Jerusalem, Saint Paul's "mother of us all."

Through much of its long history the labyrinth was associated with cities. In naves of the great cathedrals of France, the city became the City of God.

Five

THE FIELD

THE GREAT FRENCH CATHEDRAL LABYRINTHS may well have been showpieces for medieval architects and builders. But at the same time they were being laid out under the high, vaulting arches of the long naves, cruder labyrinths made of earth and local stone were being constructed outdoors—not in France but all across northern Europe, from Iceland to the British Isles to arctic Russia. And they were not the work of professionals. Whether built by villagers, farmers, shepherds, fishermen or monks and whether inspired by Christianity, Viking paganism or local folk-lore, the labyrinths were created by amateurs. They were such common sights on England's village greens and near the shores of Swedish and Norse fishing towns that—for an American—it is tempting to think of them much as one would neighborhood baseball diamonds. Back, that is, before the local ball field be-came the responsibility of parks departments or Little League franchises, back when it was made and maintained by the people who played on it.

Except for the basic design (usually variations on either the traditional Cretan or Chartres images), the English and Scandina-vian labyrinths are very different. The English turf labyrinth was made by cutting away and removing the top layer of soil, the turf,

Stone Age cup-and-rings rock carvings, Achnabreck, Scotland.

Traditional Scandinavian stone labyrinth,
Valbypark, Copenhagen, Denmark, 1996.

Roman mosaic floor, late third century A.D., uncovered near Salzburg, Austria.

Medieval labyrinth, early thirteenth century, located near the west door of Chartres Cathedral, Chartres, France.

Turf labyrinth known as Julian's Bower, Alkborough, England.

Island of Crete, detail
from the *Mappa Mundi*,
thirteenth century,
Hereford Cathedral,
Hereford, England.

Petroglyph on the surface
of the canyon rim in
Arroyo Hondo, near Taos,
New Mexico.

The 2002 Amazing Maize Maze, created by Don Frantz,
at Cherry-Crest Farm, Lancaster County, Pennsylvania.

to create a pattern; the Scandinavian, by placing rocks—large and small—in a geometric design on top of the ground. Compared to the carefully cut and fit stone of the cathedral floors, they are surprisingly fragile. Without constant care, turf paths become overgrown, while the Scandinavian stones sink deeper into the earth with each spring thaw. And the very act of maintaining these labyrinths can easily change their size and shape. The image in the nave at Chartres looks, after more than eight hundred years of wear and tear, almost exactly as it did in 1202. No surviving outdoor medieval labyrinth looks as it did when it was created. To survive, each had to be continuously remade.

Shakespeare, who grew up in a relatively small town, must have been familiar with turf labyrinths. Several passages from his plays have labyrinthine allusions, but only one is a specific, unquestionable reference to a British turf labyrinth, and it deals with how easily the path can disappear. It's in the first scene of act 2 of *A Midsummer Night's Dream*. Although Theseus, ruler of Athens, is one of the characters, nothing is made of his adventures in Minos's labyrinth on Crete. Instead, the reference is thoroughly British. In the course of complaining about the unusually foul weather, another British tradition, Titania, queen of the fairies, talks of a labyrinth that would have been familiar to the sixteenth-century audience. She mentions the weeks of terrible rain and high winds. The fields are too muddy for either spring plowing or outdoor round dancing ("ringlets"). She adds, "And the quaint mazes in the wanton green, for lack of tread, are indistinguishable." That is, the old turf labyrinth on the unusually lush village green is overgrown through lack of use. Her audience would have understood. Who, after all, wants to walk or run a muddy labyrinth in a drenching downpour?

A Midsummer Night's Dream was probably first performed in 1595. The Shakespeare scholar G. B. Harrison has pointed out that the year before saw a summer in which it rained almost steadily, sometimes inches a day, from May to September. What crops there were rotted in the fields. Annals written at the time comment on how odd this was and on the terrible fogs as well. The first audience that heard Titania's speech probably nodded their heads in recognition of that dismal summer, but they would also have been familiar with the ease with which turf labyrinths could become lost in the weeds from disuse. And they were far more at ease with both those quaint mazes and the wanton greens than would have been the ancient Greeks Titania was supposedly addressing.

What's revealed by cutting away the ground cover and topsoil in many parts of Britain is dazzling white chalk. Exposing these chalk lines is an ancient folk art in England. Centuries before crop circles began appearing in local wheat fields, gigantic chalk line drawings made by cutting away the topsoil were appearing on British hillsides. The oldest is a 360-foot-long elegantly abstract horse (some prefer to see it as a dragon) that stretches along a hillside at Uffington, near Oxford. It was first written about in the twelfth century and is probably considerably older than that. The most notorious chalk figure is a heroically proportioned naked man wielding a club—very much like Hercules—on a hillside at Cerne Abbas, in Dorset. Although you can buy postcards claiming the "Giant" is fifteen hundred years old, it probably dates to the seventeenth century. There are dozens of others, including a map of Australia near Bath, all crafted with the same technique that was used to make the turf labyrinths, and all needing to be recut about every three to five years.

Perhaps it is this almost intimate sense of turf labyrinths as living things that accounts for the wealth of folklore that has accumulated around them. And although it was popular in the nineteenth century to find Christian origins for the mazes (most of these labyrinths are usually called mazes), almost none of the stories have anything to do with Christ or his church. A common claim was that all the labyrinths were built near abbeys, monasteries or other Christian institutions. True enough. They are, but just about anything built in medieval and Renaissance Britain was probably located equally close to some sort of house of worship. But the surviving turf labyrinths seem to lie just as close to Roman ruins—the walls of lost forts and camps—as to any church. A much-reproduced drawing shows two pious monks on their knees, heads bowed, hands folded in prayer, making their way along a turf pathway. Its distinctive design, based on the cathedral labyrinth at Reims, makes the maze easily identifiable as a much-described but now destroyed outdoor labyrinth in Nottinghamshire in the Midlands. Located near a holy well and a chapel dating to 1409, both dedicated to Saint Anne, it was plowed over and destroyed in 1797. The illustration looks suitably antique, but it was in fact drawn during the reign of Queen Victoria, and the notion that monks "walked" it on their knees is simply that, a conjecture.

Over the centuries, the labyrinth's neighbors in Nottinghamshire sometimes called it Shepherd's Maze, sometimes—to further celebrate a well-known local hero—Robin Hood's Race, but never Saint Anne's anything. But just as designs evolve over the years through use and recutting, their very names show how secular they became: Julian's Bower, Mizmaze, Troy, Walls of Troy, Troy Town, Maiden's Bower and, very often, simply the Village Maze. Only the maze on St. Catherine's Hill has kept a suggestion of a religious source in its name.

Julian's Bower, one of the best preserved and most beautifully situated of the surviving turf labyrinths, has all the ambiguities necessary for a good archaeological mystery. It is located in the village of Alkborough, high on a bluff overlooking the wide valley where the Trent and the Ouse rivers flow together to form the Humber. Although tamer, the spot is reminiscent of Achnabreck, the rocky ridge in Scotland covered with the ancient cup-and-rings carvings. In the distance lies Yorkshire, and in the late spring and early summer the far hills are bright yellow with rapeseed plant. The labyrinth is cut deeply into a terrace on the edge of the ridge. It has eleven circuits, in the Chartres style, but is slightly larger than the one in the cathedral.

Let's start with the name, Julian's Bower. Or, in some very old accounts, Julian's Bore. Julian is a form of Julius, and in medieval Britain almost anything Roman was attributed to Julius Caesar. Nearby, hidden in the trees, are traces of Roman walls that may be the remains of a camp the Romans called Aquis. Julian is also a variation of Gillian or Jill, a familiar word for "girl," like Sheila in Australia or Colleen in Ireland. One of the most common stories about turf labyrinths concerns footraces in which a girl stands alone in the center and boys run down the pathway toward her to see who gets there first and claims the prize.

In the middle of the nineteenth century, an old man in Alkborough recorded his memories of racing along pathways, "running it in and out," and of the games played there on the eve of May Day. He remembered feeling "the indefinite persuasion of something unseen and unknown co-operating with them." May Day? Any reader of James Frazer's *The Golden Bough* or Joseph Campbell's *The Hero with a Thousand Faces* would know those games were remnants of spring fertility rites.

The oldest surviving mention of Julian's Bower dates from a century earlier, the turn of the eighteenth century. Abraham de la Pryme, who seemed to be called "the Yorkshire Antiquary," wrote sometime between 1671 and 1704 that besides Julian's Bower there was another labyrinth six miles away in Appleby called Troy's Walls. Both, he wrote, were Roman games "cut into the ground with a hill cast up around them for spectators to sit round about on to behold the sport." He does not mention what the sport was, but it was probably a race. One more classical allusion: another Julius (or Iulius) was Aeneas's son, the boy who rode in the Game of Troy described by Virgil in Book V of *The Aeneid*. Which, frankly, sounds a bit too literary an explanation of how the labyrinth got its name.

A Benedictine monastic house was located near the labyrinth site between 1080 and 1220, and perhaps the monks made the labyrinth. Another explanation of its origin is that a knight involved in the murder of Thomas à Becket, archbishop of Canterbury, in his cathedral in 1170 made it, or had it made. His penance for the crime was to undertake a pilgrimage to Jerusalem, and finding that impossible—or perhaps too dangerous, given the Crusades— he built a labyrinth instead. The fact that the Chartres labyrinth dates to about 1220 (and probably as early as 1202) may render this explanation improbable.

The nearby rivers also contribute to the legend. There was indeed a medieval saint named Julian, a nobleman and an avid hunter, who built a famous bower. Legend has it that, by accident, he murdered his parents, perhaps an honest mistake. He had, it seems, returned from the hunt unexpectedly and found a couple in his bed. Thinking that his wife was up to no good, he killed them without looking to see who they were. Unfortunately, his parents had come on an unannounced visit and his hospitable wife had given them the best bed. In penance, he built a bower, a refuge, next to the ford on a river as a resting place for travelers. (One of them turned out to be a leper, but that is another story.) The upshot was that a forgiven Julian became the patron saint of innkeepers. It seems all but impossible to make the labyrinth and the rest stop the same place, and anyway sites of fords on the rivers are much too far away.

An equally doubtful river story smacks strongly of nineteenth-century faux mythology and imaginative guidebook writing. According to this legend, a river god or spirit—he even has a name, Gur—so hated the Christian labyrinth (perhaps he believed the tale about the guilt-ridden knight) and the throngs of pilgrims that visited it that he sent a combined flood and tidal wave to wash it away. The bower on its high ridge was untouched, but to this day, every spring a rush of high water called the Trent Bore roars up the river valley and annually fails to sweep away its intended goal.

Themes from these stories that have attached themselves to Julian's Bower are also associated with other turf labyrinths: a site with ancient associations, running, games, penance and an available maiden. There is another theme that should not be ignored: the labyrinth's recurring urban connection. Just as Julian may be a linguistic variation of Gillian, *bower* may well be a corruption of *burgh* or *borough*, words meaning "town" or "protected place" that live on in such place-names as Pittsburgh, Edinburgh and the borough of Brooklyn. And, for that matter, Alkborough. By the late seventeenth century, John Aubrey, an antiquarian fascinated with what he called curiosities, both human and otherwise, was using *borough* as a synonym for "labyrinth."

Toward the end of the nineteenth century, the justice of the peace in Alkborough, who had the bower trimmed and recut several times and knew its fragility, saw to it that the design was preserved in something more permanent than turf. When the local St. John the Baptist Anglican Church was renovated in 1887, James Goulton Constable of Walcot Hall—the local J.P., also described as "lord of the manor"—had a smaller version of the labyrinth replicated in stone on the new floor of the church porch. It also appears—even smaller but high up—in the stained-glass window over the altar, and in later years women of the congregation made needlepoint reproductions of the bower on some of the church kneelers. Just down the road in the cemetery, the Chartres design also appears on a metal disk at the center of the stone cross that marks Goulton Constable's grave. All of which makes little Alkborough one of the most thoroughly "labyrinthed" villages in England.

Other eleven-circuit Chartres-style turf labyrinths in England share some of the qualities of Julian's Bower. At Wing, in Rutland, a seventeenth-century labyrinth fifty feet in diameter was once adjoined by an ancient tumulus, or mound, that a 1901 guidebook described as "flat-topped, bowl-shaped." The tumulus was said to have been seventy feet in diameter and four feet high, and spectators used it as bleachers to watch the footraces in the maze. A monastic link with Alkborough can be found at the Mizmaze at Breamore, near Salisbury. It is beautifully situated in the woods on a high hill. Monks from the local priory—St. Michael's, founded in the twelfth century and dissolved in the seventeenth—were said to have made it, but, then, another story says it was the work of a bored shepherd who dug it with his crook.

There are the usual tales of penitent monks doing the Mizmaze on their knees, but the quantity of thirteenth- and fourteenth-century pottery shards that can still be found near the labyrinth's edge suggests that it might have also been put to more festive use. The most repeated story about it, obviously dating from a much later period, is that you can run the maze in the same time it takes to run from it to Gallows Hill, three-quarters of a mile away. And that sounds suspiciously like the basis of many a wager made in the local pub at closing time. An intriguing near-contemporary possibility exists about the Breamore maze. In the weeks before D-day, General George S. Patton, then in disgrace for slapping wounded G.I.s in Sicily, was stationed briefly at Breamore Manor House, the estate on which the maze is located. (Indeed, the Mizmaze's present look dates to the recutting Sir Edward Hulse, lord of the manor, ordered in 1783.) Could the general have taken the old farm road to the hill a mile or so behind the house and walked the Mizmaze and stood on the raised mound at its center? He was a notably impatient man, but he was also fascinated by such ancient sites as Carthage. It might even have been an act of penance. Or maybe he ran it all the way.

The credit—at least in one story—for cutting another Mizmaze, this one on St. Catherine's Hill just outside Winchester, is given to a seventeenth-century schoolboy, a busy, possibly tragic schoolboy. Mizmaze is a common name for turf labyrinths in southern England, and according to the story, the student at Winchester College, Britain's oldest public school, committed some offense that put him on detention for Whitsuntide, or Pentecost (the seventh week after Easter, a popular time for baptisms). That is, when his schoolmates went home for spring break, he was required to remain on campus. Either simply to fill his time or as an act of penance, he crossed the Itchin River behind the school, climbed a hill that can be seen from town and cut what is now England's only square turf labyrinth. Close by, in a grove of beech trees, was the now-destroyed eleventh-century chapel dedicated to Catherine of Alexandria, patron saint of wheelwrights and spinners. Then, apparently with more time to fritter away, he composed the school song *"Dolce Domum"* ("Sweet Home") before—in some but not all versions of the tale—he drowned himself in the Itchin.

There are familiar elements here: penance, of course, and the adjacent church, to begin with. Also, the church is built within the ditch of an Iron Age fort, much like the Roman camp near Julian's Bower. Then there is a tradition of running. A guide published in 1794 describes the Mizmaze as "a very perplexed and winding path, running in a very small space over a great deal of ground." The maze was, it adds, "the usual play-place of the school." Part of the play was a game called "tolling the labyrinth," in which the boys started in the center and raced outward along the pathway. There are no maidens mentioned here, but the turf was supposedly cut in the spring, on the week of the Sunday—Whitsunday—named for the virginal white robes worn by the newly baptized.

The schoolboy story is a good example of how the labyrinth can absorb other local legends. In an early history of Winchester

College by the Reverend H. C. Adams, vicar of Dry Sandford, we learn that the unnamed boy was indeed put on detention, and then, in a version the vicar clearly doubts, was chained to either a tree or a pillar, where he wrote the Latin lyrics to "*Dulce Domum*" before pining away and dying of heartbreak on the last day of the vacation. The vicar prefers to think he was simply seen sitting under the tree on the banks of the Itchin writing his poem. In any case, the lyrics were written to a popular tune, a rather merry one, it seems, composed by John Reading, who had nothing to do with Winchester but who was "at the height of his reputation during the reign of William III" (1689–1702). Since there is no mention of drowning or St. Catherine's Hill, those touches must have been nineteenth-century flourishes. Young dead poets, like suicide maidens, were popular fascinations of the time.

Even without the macabre appeal, it is easy to see how the Mizmaze could be attributed to a boy. Although its present version comes from an 1833 recutting that made it larger and perhaps more rectangular than the original (it now measures about eighty-six by ninety feet), its pathway moves along irregular, imprecise lines. They could be thought to resemble a rather untidy sketch in a schoolboy's copybook.

Another, nearly unique, feature of the Mizmaze path is that it is a ditch. In just about all the other turf labyrinths, the path is on the turf that was not cut away. On St. Catherine's Hill, the walker moves along the cut-away trail with the raised, uncut turf on either side. When W. H. Matthews published his pioneering study of labyrinths in 1922, he assumed this was a mistake on the part of the warden of Winchester, who supervised the 1833 cutting. But a more recently discovered plan from 1710 shows that the path was always a shallow trench. In this, it resembles the small labyrinth on the wall of the cathedral porch in Lucca, on which worshippers' fingers can trace Theseus's route along a groove carved into the stone.

The pathway of one other turf labyrinth is lowered, and since the last century paved in brick, and it is just about a mile long, making it England's largest. It's the Town Maze in a corner of Saffron Walden's village common, just northeast of London in Essex. The design resembles the one on the floor of the Reims cathedral and Robin Hood's Race in Nottinghamshire, both long gone. Like them, it is a circle with a horseshoelike bulge (called variously a bastion, tower, ear or bellows) at its northeast, southeast, southwest and northwest edges. Compared to other turf labyrinths, it's huge. There are seventeen circuits, six more than Chartres and Reims, with a diameter across the center of about 90 feet, and about 138 feet from corner to corner. Deep, sculptured banks spill off the bastions, and a small mound in the center (called "Waterloo" in the post-Napoleon nineteenth century) once sported a giant ash tree. The first mention of the maze was in 1699, when village records show that the Guild of the Holy Trinity paid fifteen shillings to have it recut, which means it must have been old enough to become overgrown. Legend has it, and aerial photographs suggest that this may be true, that an even older labyrinth was once located more toward the middle of the common.

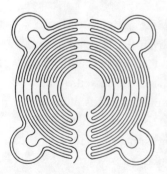

The Guild of the Holy Trinity was a tradesmen's organization with religious aspirations that dated back to the fifteenth century, and its members may well have used the maze for devotional purposes, but what has been remembered is decidedly secular. A late-eighteenth-century manuscript book has been quoted as saying, "The Maze at Saffron Walden is the gathering place of the young men of the district. Who have a system of rules connected with walking the maze, and wagers in gallons of beer are frequently won or lost. For a time it was used by the beaux and belles of the town, a young maiden standing in the centre, known as *Home,* while the boy tried to get to her in record time without stumbling." No mention of whether gallons of beer were also involved in this sport.

Even though the design of the maze obviously had Christian roots, there is no persistent claim that monks or any other religious group had anything to do with its founding. Indeed, unlike Robin Hood's Race, which it otherwise resembles, no images of the cross are cut into the turf. In the race, which was placed next to a holy well, each bastion bore a rather daggerlike cross cut, like the path, from the turf and pointed toward the center. According to the story, the maze was dug by itinerant shoemakers or disbanded soldiers, which—as Nigel Pennick has pointed out—are not mutually exclusive categories. Shoemakers were associated with several now-lost turf labyrinths, the best documented being the Shoemakers' Race built in Shrewsbury on land owned by the Patriotic Company of Shoemakers. It probably dated to 1598. And it may well have been built as an attraction to draw customers, since it was located next to an "arbour" where shoes were sold and guild members "made merry." No drawing of the race has survived, but it may have been octagonal since its enclosure had eight sides. Nigel Pennick quotes a source as saying that in the center was an image of a "giant's head" (the Minotaur perhaps?), and runners—it was a runners' game—on reaching the center would leap and try to land with their feet on each of the giant's eyes. He adds that an almost identical maze seems also to have been built by shoemakers in Pomerania in either Germany or Poland, depending on the date of the map you look at. The Shoemakers' Race was destroyed in 1796 so that its land could be used as the site for a windmill.

Two coincidences—if that's what they are—are worth mentioning. One is that in the cathedral at Chartres, the stained-glass window donated by the shoemakers' guild, depicting the story of the Good Samaritan, is located next to the labyrinth, on its south side. The other? The shoemakers' feast day is the Tuesday after Whitsunday, when the Winchester schoolboy was supposedly building his labyrinth.

Shepherds are another group historically associated with turf labyrinths. A Welsh book (*Drych y Prif Oesgoedd*) published in 1740 claimed that the local shepherds cut curious designs in the turf that they called *caerdroias*, which has variously been translated as City of Troy or City of Turnings. An Englishman wrote in 1858 that they were still doing it. And a legend in eastern Germany, which has—or had—a few turf labyrinths of its own, tells of shepherds digging mazes with their crooks. (In Scotland, on the other hand, bored shepherds were said to have used their crooks as clubs and invented the game of golf.) Given the romantic view of shepherds that dates back to the ancient Greeks, some people thought that creating and running mazes was just what they *should* be doing. W. H. Matthews quotes a seventeenth-century poem by Thomas Randolph that berates a tired—or perhaps lazy—shepherd for sleeping under a bush rather than doing what shepherds were supposed to. Instead, he ought "to tune his Reed and chant his layes / Or nimbly run the windings of the Maze."

Robin Hood's Race was originally called the Shepherd's Maze for a more prosaic reason: the shepherd who tended the flock on the common also tended the labyrinth. As for the name change, it came about when, in the eighteenth century, "relics" of Robin Hood—such as his chair—were displayed on the maze as a tourist attraction.

With the coming of the Christian Middle Ages, the classic Cretan labyrinth fell out of fashion, but two of the surviving British turf mazes are both Cretan and named after Troy. They could not be more unlike each other.

Troy Town, at Somerton in Oxfordshire, is huge. It is about sixty by fifty-one feet, with an astonishing fifteen circuits, and it is on private property. It has always been private. Visitors without permission cannot see it, and the only hint of what is hidden beyond the trees is a small sign saying TROY on a farm building across the road. Troy is the name of the farm, which like Troy Town itself, probably dates to the sixteenth century. The maze was likely to have been just one feature of a much larger garden containing, perhaps, several different botanical designs, or knots, as they were called, and formal orchards of fruit trees. Troy Town was clearly designed for a grander scale than the tight, well-maintained clearing it now fills. Besides the unusual number of circuits and the fact that it was never public, it is right-handed. That is, rather than turning left as you do in most labyrinths, you make your first turn to the right.

The "City of Troy," outside Dalby in the open hills of North Yorkshire, is small and round (about twenty-six feet in diameter), a near dollhouse of a labyrinth built on the edge of the road. It is traditionally left-handed and seven-circuited. Far off to the south, when the weather cooperates, can be seen the spire of the cathedral at York. If the Somerton maze is a model of stability and tradition, the Dalby City of Troy is almost antic and modern. Cut around 1900 to replace an 1860s labyrinth believed to have been destroyed by traffic driving over it to avoid mud puddles in the road, its design is said to have been copied from the same image drawn on a now-lost barn door that had inspired the first. Another version of the story, however, says that the door had been lost much earlier, and the replacement was based on an illustration in a newspaper.

In any case, whoever dug it must have been a runner. The pathway is skillfully banked inward for easier fast turns. It may not now be a local legend, but the fact that at least one book warns that running it nine times in succession brings bad luck may make it one.

An ash tree was once at the center of the Saffron Walden Town Maze, just as trees stood in some of the German mazes. But other British turf labyrinths have empty centers, all except the one in a corner of the village green at Hilton in Cambridgeshire. The maze—it is also one of the few English labyrinths without a name of its own—was once a variation of eleven-circuit Chartres design, but sometime since the beginning of the twentieth century, several of the innermost rings were cut away. Maybe their sharp turns were too hard to cut, but now it has only nine circuits. At its center is a square column topped with a stone ball—the whole thing is about a dozen feet tall—erected in memory of one William Sparrow. On the north side of the column was once a sundial, now gone, and on another we learn, in English, that Sparrow died in 1729 at age eighty-eight. And in badly weathered Latin you can read the real reason for the memorial: in 1660, at age nineteen, he cut the circuits (*gyros*) of the labyrinth. What isn't said is a matter of politics.

Any villager in Hilton would know the meaning of 1660, the year the monarchy returned and Oliver Cromwell's puritanical Commonwealth came to an end. Among the acts banned by the Puritans—along with dancing around maypoles, going to the theater and confessing to a Catholic priest—were walking, running or praying on a labyrinth. It was all deemed to be either too frivolous or too idolatrous (i.e., suspiciously Catholic). Either way, the devil was at work.

Young William Sparrow may not have actually created a turf labyrinth on the Hilton green but simply restored one that had been allowed to grow wild. Maybe it was his way of welcoming back the Stuart dynasty and Charles II, or maybe it was just his way of celebrating the return of fun.

A recent sunny spring afternoon at the labyrinth at Hilton provides a vignette of a turf labyrinth in England today. Two young mothers, one pushing an empty stroller, stop on their way across the village green to watch four—or maybe it was five—children who had run ahead of them race along the freshly clipped path of the labyrinth. The air still smells of newly cut grass. The mothers sit on the embankment carved by centuries of cutting and recutting the turf and talk. The children make up their game as they play, and it involves a lot of running and tagging and falling on top of one another.

But they are not alone on the pathway. The mothers seem to know the two men, one of whom could be the father of the other, working away with a power mower, clippers and a wheelbarrow. The men aren't happy, and the older one, speaking in a voice intended to be overheard, complains to no one in particular about whoever it was who "dreamt up mazes." To foreign ears it sounds as though he is saying "mizes."

And foreigners are indeed also on the labyrinth, a vanload of them, mostly Americans. They solemnly and a bit self-consciously make their way along the pathway toward the battered column with a pristine stone ball (a "reconstruction," says the guidebook) on its top. They skirt around the laughing children and the grumbling workers. The first to get to the center pauses, bows slightly as though in prayer and pulls out a camera to photograph the crowded labyrinth and the "wanton" green beyond.

But earth labyrinths are not limited to England's green and pleasant land. In far-off India, several Cretan-style outdoor labyrinths may be far older than any surviving site in Britain. Those who like to believe that just about any cultural artifact actually came from somewhere else like to suggest that the labyrinths there are a result of Alexander the Great's invasion of India in 327 B.C. It's a curious notion, picturing Alexander spreading Mediterranean artifacts the way nineteenth-century British missionaries once scattered wildflower seeds from "home" in the exotic lands they hoped to convert. But that's unlikely. In any case, Alexander spent his time in the north, and the principal concentration of labyrinths is in the Tamil south. Oddly enough, the Tamil labyrinths most resemble the stone mazes of Scandinavia. Near a small village in the state of Tamil Nadu is what has been described as a Cretan "Troy Town," about eighteen feet in diameter, placed next to what is thought to be an ancient standing stone. One scholar has dated it to 1000 B.C., but its age is actually anyone's guess. A slightly larger Troy Town, with the same seven-circuit design (and with an added spiral in its center) can be found in the same state. Another, about fifty feet in diameter and located near Orissa in the south, is said to date from the eighth century and was reputedly made by yogis.

Scandinavia, though, may have the corner on the labyrinth market. Even with the most generous count, there are fewer than ten pre-nineteenth-century turf mazes remaining in the British Isles. Extending out from the Baltic Sea, along largely uninhabited coastlines and islands in Sweden, Finland, Russia and Denmark, are five hundred or more stone labyrinths, the largest concentration of labyrinths in the world. Most are between twenty and sixty feet across. And almost all of them have exactly the same design, the seven- or eleven-circuit pattern, much like the ones on the ancient coins from Knossos.

John Kraft, a Swede who has spent decades studying, cataloging and collecting stories about these labyrinths, estimates that there are more than 300 of them in Sweden, 150 in regions of Finland settled by Swedish-language speakers, and at least 60 in Russia, chiefly near the White Sea. Perhaps as many as 20 percent of the Swedish labyrinths can be traced to the late nineteenth century. Then a Norse revival (much like the Celtic revival experienced in Ireland at the same time) inspired schoolteachers to take their classes along the coasts and into the fields to make labyrinths, just as their ancestors had.

Making them the Scandinavian way is not difficult. The classic Cretan design is simple to lay out, and then it is just a matter of finding stones and dragging them into place, where they sit on top of the ground. No digging is involved. The stones—which seem to be placed in no particular size order—range from cobbles to small boulders. As to situating the stone labyrinths, there seems to be no rule concerning which direction they face. Unlike in French cathedrals, where most labyrinth entrances are in the west, nothing is uniform about the way stone labyrinths line up with compass readings. In this they resemble turf mazes. One thing, though, can be counted on: just about every single one faces inland, with their entrances toward the sea.

Assigning dates, however, is a problem. The usual carbon tests do not work on stone, and attempts to date labyrinths by analyzing lichen growing on the stones has proved to be erratic and unsatisfactory. So have attempts to estimate the age of a labyrinth by the age of nearby buildings. Some of the inland labyrinths, rare as they may be, now stand close to ruins of chapels that date to the fourteenth or fifteenth centuries. Were the churches built near the labyrinths to "Christianize" pagan sites? Or were the labyrinths the work of the church builders? And what about the inland labyrinths that stand next to Bronze Age, or older, burial mounds? Which came first? Eggs? Chickens? As a result, some have been dated as early as 500 B.C. (which seems doubtful), some to the medieval period, and most to the sixteenth to eighteenth centuries. And they all look almost exactly alike. Several impressive-looking monuments in former Soviet territory along the White Sea were taken seriously by some archaeologists, only to turn out to have been the work of bored soldiers (or perhaps, in some cases, prisoners) in the 1950s.

Two parchment manuscripts from Iceland (where Kraft counted the sites of four stone labyrinths) dating from the fourteenth and fifteenth centuries show modified Cretan labyrinths labeled *volundarhus*, or Volund's House, just as in medieval France a cathedral labyrinth was sometime called *la maison de Dédale*, the house of Daedalus. Volund could be called the Nordic Daedalus, an ingenious wonder-worker. According to legend, he escaped an evil king, who had crippled him to keep him from running off, by constructing wings and flying away, much as Daedalus fled Crete. In Britain, where Volund was also a legendary figure mentioned in several Anglo-Saxon and early English works, including *Beowulf*, he is called Wayland the blacksmith.

At the center of the seven-circuit labyrinth in the fifteenth-century Icelandic manuscript is a rather plump leonine creature, and around the edges is an explanation of the name Volund's House. This brief caption—written in Icelandic—may confuse the name of Theseus with that of his father, Aegeus. It tells a tale of Egeas, "a very able bodied and agile" prince of Syria, who goes off to a neighboring kingdom to win the hand of the king's beautiful daughter. But to wed her, he must pass a test. He must—alone—capture the terrible half-man, half-beast Homocentaurus, which "no one with mortal powers could ever defeat." The princess, who seems to have taken a shine to Egeas, tells him how to conquer the Minotaurish monster. First, he must kill all the animals in the forest that the beast usually feeds upon. Then he should take the meat of a wild boar, smear it with honey and place it at the center of the twists and turns of an ingenious trap, the *volundarhus*, the design of which she draws for him. The prince builds the *volandarhus* out of bricks and stones and follows her instructions. The hungry Homocentaurus smells the delicious bait and follows Egeas into the labyrinthine trap. (The story doesn't say so, but he must have either carried the boar-and-honey treat or smeared it on his body.) The prince, who had climbed to the top of the wall in the center, jumps down and seizes "the creature with all his strength" before bounding over the wall and getting away. The beast, which presumably can't find its way out, "bellowed terribly and was found dead in this same trap seven days later." And the prince won his princess, or perhaps it was the other way around.

The labyrinth as a trap for catching animals: it is a notion heard earlier, when Robert Graves suggested the Greek partridge trap as a possible prototype of the Cretan labyrinth. And here, a trap with a similar design appears in far-off Iceland and is linked to the name of a northern master artificer.

Just because the Chartres—or Christian—labyrinth is almost unknown in Scandinavia does not mean the labyrinths were pagan there. The other Icelandic manuscript showing a Cretan-style House of Volund—this one from the fourteenth century—has a handwritten caption saying that a particular Icelandic unit of measure was one-sixteenth the length of Christ's body. The immediate connection between the labyrinth and this bit of information is not immediately obvious, but the writer was clearly thinking of the design in both religious and geometric terms. More important, Cretan labyrinths appear painted on the walls of a few fourteenth- and fifteenth-century churches in Sweden and Finland. Often they seem randomly placed and crudely drawn, almost like graffiti resembling those wall scratchings in Pompeii, but they are in fact proper church murals that must have conveyed a Christian message. Their eccentric placement in rather austere sanctuaries that could hardly be considered ornate suggests, in itself, that their purpose was not simply decorative.

Usually, these small seven-circuit figures appear in the murals as geometric shapes without embellishment and unaccompanied by humans or mythological beasts. An exception is in the Old Church in Sibbo, not far from Helsinki. Its eleven-circuit labyrinth is a little more than three feet wide, and was probably

painted in the fifteenth century, although it doesn't seem to have been commented upon until 1935. High up on the wall and faded, a mysterious, almost ghostly figure stands in the center, a woman wearing a long skirt and facing the incoming path. Her arms are upraised, perhaps in welcome or maybe in supplication. John Kraft cites it as a near-iconic prototype of the *jungfrudans,* the maiden's dance, one of the common names for stone labyrinths in Sweden and Finland.

In collecting folklore about the stone labyrinths, Kraft heard variations on the same story over and over again. A maiden stands in the center of the stones as young—or maybe not so young—men run along the winding path to reach her—much as the Homocentaurus rushed through the *volandarhus* toward the boar-and-honey bait—and "win" her. In some labyrinths the men win a dance, in others a wife. In some a man wins through speed, by getting there first, and in others by not making a mistake, such as stepping off the pathway or stumbling. But the girl is always the prize, just as she was in the story told about those footraces for the girls in the town maze at Saffron Walden, in England.

Some stone labyrinths are associated with particular stories. In Köpmanholmen, in northern Sweden, the tale told about a site called Jungfruringen (Maiden's Ring) is that a troll had kidnapped a young girl and kept her hidden in his mountain (the center of the labyrinth) and to free her the men of the village had to circle it seven times (walk the seven circuits), much as Joshua's army circled Jericho seven times, until the troll fell asleep and the girl could be seized and saved. Kraft reports an account from the 1930s from Västergötland, again in Sweden, in which a winter labyrinth was made of ice and snow to reenact the legend of Grimborg's bride. A young girl, representing the beautiful daughter of a king, stands in a "castle" at the center, watched over by a guard on ice skates. A young man, Grimborg, then skates his way along the frozen pathway and defeats or outwits the guard and saves (or captures) the girl, who becomes his bride. That is, she will after—according to the legend—he kills at least forty-eight thousand of the king's men. While all this is going on, the participants and a chorus of onlookers (this sounds as though it were a rather grand annual festival) sing the "Song of Grimborg," a well-known folk song. In it, the hero is described, to quote a line cited by Kraft, fighting his way "through fences of iron and steel."

The Virgin's Ring, the Virgin's Dance, the rescued maiden, the stalwart hero, the perilous journey, the May games at Julian's Bower, the Easter afternoon ritual ball games on the cathedral labyrinths, Whitsun races at the various mizmazes: it is difficult not to believe that these are remnants of some basic, universal spring ritual of rebirth. Stripped of place-names and local gods' personal quirks and identities, the story is the same from India to Egypt to the Arctic Circle. Every year the sun goddess is captured and imprisoned underground, and every spring she must be saved by a hero, a god or a son of a god, and be brought through the winding path back to earth. Otherwise there would be no springtime rebirth. In the arctic and near-arctic north, the return of the sun after the long, dark winter must have seemed dramatic indeed.

Even if stone labyrinths had first been built thousands of years ago to commemorate or perpetuate such a cycle of vernal rebirth, the image has been used for many other purposes since then. Here are some suggestions about the origins and purposes of those stone designs in Scandinavia, Finland and Russia:

- They were placed outside harbor villages where they could be seen from the sea to announce—or advertise—a local pilot who could be hired to steer visiting boats safely into the unfamiliar port.

- They were built by fishermen—and visited before setting sail—to ensure favorable winds and weather, and perhaps a good catch as well.

- They were troll traps fishermen ran through just before setting sail to ensnare slow-footed trolls, evil beings who would bring chaos and trouble if they followed the seafarers on board their boats. (This may be the product of nineteenth-century folklorist romanticism, but it is also another suggestion of the *volandarhus* trap.)

- They marked the sites of fresh water. (This is based on the debatable theory that it was a common pre-medieval practice to mark springs and locations of underground water with rocks carved with a spiral design.)

- They were built as diversions by bored lighthouse keepers or their wives and children. (This indeed seems to have been the case for the only stone labyrinth in Britain, a much-rebuilt eighteenth-century Scandinavian-style labyrinth on St. Agnes in the Scilly Islands, off the Cornwall coast.)

- They were playgrounds to keep children amused while their fathers mended their nets.

As mentioned earlier, many of the northern stone labyrinths are named after ancient walled cities such as Jericho, Constantinople, Jerusalem and Nineveh, but the most common city name—as usual—is Troy, including such variations as Trojenborg, Troyeborg, and Troyborg. Besides the sites named for maidens, there are also Steintanz (stone dance), Trellborg (troll's castle), Rundborg (round castle) and Jatulintarha (giant's fence). And some patriotic Finns have argued that not all the labyrinths in their land have Swedish—that is, Scandinavian—origins. Finns are not Scandinavian and call some of their labyrinths in the far north Jatulintarha, "Jatuli gardens," for the Jatulis, an ancient, if mythic, Finnish people.

The most visited of them all is probably Trojaborg, on Gotland, which, located not far from Stockholm, sometimes calls itself "Sweden's major holiday island." The Troy Castle there is the standard design, about sixty feet across and with eleven circuits. Located next to the sea and at the foot of a small mountain, its combination of shining white stones and well-maintained green grass, backed by the bright blue of the water, makes it a natural picture-postcard subject. And there are even park benches to rest on. Trojaborg comes with its own legend, a variation on the captured-maiden motif. Only this time it also contains a faint echo of Scheherazade and the 1,001 tales she told to stay alive during her captivity. In this case, the princess is captured and kept in a cave on Gallows Hill, next to the labyrinth's present location. (For the second time in this chapter, that macabre place-name turns up in conjunction with a nearby labyrinth.) She keeps herself alive by placing one stone each day on what will become the Trojaborg, until she is finished, and then, just when you expect the hero-prince to storm down the stone-lined pathway to save her, she is freed: a rare folktale without a male hero.

Farther inland and not nearly so picturesque are several smaller, less frequented labyrinths that are noteworthy for being associated with graves. One is next to a church cemetery, and others seem to be part of Iron or Bronze Age burial grounds. This is highly unusual. Graves are almost never found under labyrinths. Even Chartres Cathedral is free of tombs. Only two gravestones in England are known to bear labyrinth or maze carvings, both twentieth century and both for men associated with either labyrinth preservation or maze making. Mary Watt's labyrinth-decorated cemetery chapel in Compton, England, is unique. Members of the American Association for Gravestone Studies have not identified a single example in the United States. Strange as it seems for an image as ancient and mysterious as the labyrinth, it has rarely been associated with death, only with renewal and rebirth.

Although they are rich in folklore, the hundreds of labyrinths scattered outward from the Baltic Sea remain, for the most part, empty and unvisited. They are not—and probably never were— found in populated areas or along the tourist or trade routes. Many lie overgrown and hidden on tiny islands and seem to mark abandoned fishing camps that are—or were—used only seasonally. In spite of the rousing stories of "winning" the maiden, the real point of these stone-lined paths seems to have been the building of them, not how they were used. And they were easy to make, like graffiti, a simple, uncomplicated, yet still mysterious curving line created just by placing rocks in a field or along a beach. Stone labyrinths move across the landscape with the ease of handwriting on a page. Their paths are rarely worn with use. Making them was the important thing. Like calligraphy, they remain more a message than a game.

Six

THE GARDEN

A FEW MONTHS AFTER THE TURN of the twenty-first century, the London entertainment magazine *TimeOut* listed under "Bars and Clubs" a place called Sleaze and promised "sordid goings-on." Its attractions, the magazine said, included not only a host named Spike and "music pumping all night long" but also "a backroom maze." As for what to wear: "Dress code: dirty, horny or just plain cheap."

By the end of the sixteenth century, people—both men and women—walking the new and tricky hedge mazes in private gardens throughout England and Europe were taking the first steps toward Sleaze's back room. No one ran in these mazes. No demure maidens waited passively at the center. Prayers were probably rarely uttered, and there were no quests for a holy city. Labyrinths, as they evolved—or mutated—into mazes, became both social events and elaborate garden ornaments, definitely something to dress for, and sometimes there was music. Just like Sleaze. As a sixteenth-century landscape architect who called himself Didymus Mountaine—formerly Thomas Hill— recommended in *The Profitable Art of Gardening* (1568), empty or "voide" spaces in gardens should be set aside as mazes "for the onlye purpose, to sporte in them at times."

With the addition of high hedges and dead-end passageways, the labyrinth as a maze was changing into a rich man's expensive plaything as fashionable as the latest clothing style. For the first time, the labyrinth had actual walls more tangible than myth, and its walkers had the opportunity of become truly—if just momentarily—lost. If the classic Cretan and medieval Chartres labyrinths had been journeys with the goal always in clear sight, the new mazes, with their dead ends and wrong turns, were puzzles, mysteries with hidden solutions to be enjoyed simply— "onlye"—for the sport of it. And in the right company there was also, to use the words of novelist Terry Southern, "a chance for vice." Or, at the very least, an opportunity for flirtation.

By the early seventeenth century, no respectable—or at least fashionable—garden was without a maze, often with more than one. At the Villa d'Este, on one side of Rome, identical mazes are displayed among the fountains in pairs, like sets of matching luggage. At the Villa Lante, on the other side of Rome, a single maze is coyly tucked away out of sight in the woods. In the pattern books of Dutch architect Jan Vredeman de Vries the ideal gardens are filled with mazes like tidy patches on a neatly ordered quilt. At Versailles, near Paris, a convoluted path wanders like a giant outdoor Way of the Cross but at each stop or station, instead of representations of Christ's last passion, there are sculptures depicting Aesop's fables. At Hampton Court Palace, outside London, a maze that will become the most famous and long lasting of them all is fit into an odd-shaped corner of a side garden called the Wilderness. Close to it is a tight little spiral planting named the "Plan-de-Troy."

Mazes, mazes everywhere.

But the high-walled puzzle maze with its nonflowering hedges of yew, boxwood and privet did not spring into the world like Eden. With a certain amount of ingenuity its roots can be traced back to winding pathways lined with low hedges in ancient

Roman gardens, but for all practical purposes the hedge maze grew out of the so-called knot gardens of the late Middle Ages.

These small gardens—usually about twenty feet square—with their intricate designs of low, flowering plants were well named. They look like giant well-tied seamen's knots, the sort of thing displayed far less elegantly on the walls of Boy Scout meeting rooms. There was nothing new or rare in using knots as decoration. Single "knots" that play with the illusion of perspective and three dimensions appear in Roman mosaics. Visitors to the ruins of the ancient city of Ephesus, in modern Turkey, can see one on the floor of a second-century A.D. hillside villa. Its seemingly endless cord, like a knotted Möbius strip, may symbolize eternity. In the sixteenth century an architect from Padua, Francesco Segala, included a slightly more complex version of the same image in a book of suggested labyrinth designs. Some see the knot as a basic motif of Celtic art, as it is revealed in the intertwined lines in illuminated manuscripts such as *The Book of Kells* and in sculpted decoration on ancient high crosses. In France knot designs were called *entrelacs*, interlacings, and may symbolize not just eternity but—more immediately—endless love. Cupid, after all, tied a knot to bind Venus and Mars together when the goddess of love met the god of war, and "tying the knot" remains a slang term for wedding.

The knot designs can also be seen as outdoor floral versions of the finely knotted Middle Eastern carpets that began to be imported into Europe in the fifteenth century and soon became all the rage. (Curiously, the carpets themselves may have been inspired by Persian gardens.) Another possible Islamic source may just as easily have been geometric ceramic tiles remembered from the mosques and palaces of the Holy Land, or possibly brought back as souvenirs of the Crusades. Indeed, some believe the Chartres labyrinth design itself was brought to Europe by returning Crusaders.

Didymus Mountaine/Thomas Hill (whose name is sometimes spelled Hyll) published knot garden designs in his *The Gardener's Labyrinth* (1577) and suggested they be planted in thyme and hyssop, a bushy perennial. Some were composed solely in lavender and herbs. By 1620, when John Parkinson recommended that knots were "more proper . . . for outlandish flowers" such as daffodils, saffron flowers, lilies, tulips and anemones, the gardens had become more colorful, if not downright outlandish. Some knots were large and quite complex. Henry VIII had his initials and those of his second wife, Anne Boleyn, intertwined in plants in the Hampton Court knot gardens. (One can only imagine the feverish replanting when she was beheaded. And did the busy gardeners devise new knotted monograms for each of her replacements?) Individual knots became linked together by grass or graveled ornamental pathways and with elaborately trimmed hedges until entire gardens became a vast panorama of individual or matching knots. But none of them was allowed to grow much taller than knee high.

The very complexity of the knot pattern attracted some artists as a challenge. Leonardo da Vinci, who tried everything, tried his hand at them, and Albrecht Dürer followed suit, producing six virtuoso "knot" woodcuts in Venice between 1506 and 1507. The results were endless weaves of lines moving above and beneath one another with no beginnings or ends. They are dazzling feats of draftsmanship, but even with all their bravado, they are not labyrinths.

Ben Jonson, Shakespeare's younger, rowdier and possibly more popular contemporary, coupled knots and labyrinths in some lines from a masque titled "Pleasure Reconciled to Virtue" (1618). Masques were usually elaborate spectacles with music, dancing and astonishing theatrical effects performed outdoors in a garden. By their very nature they became temporary garden ornaments in themselves. Daedalus is one of Jonson's characters and, sounding very much like a dancing master, says:

> *Come on, come on, and where you go*
> *So interweave the curious Knot,*
> *So ev'n the Observer scarce may know*
> *Which Lines are Pleasures and Which not. . . .*
> *Then as all actions of Mankind*
> *Are but a Labyrinth or Maze*
> *So let your dances be entwin'd.*

Francis Bacon, another of Shakespeare's contemporaries, hated knot gardens and, unlike Jonson's Daedalus, saw no great metaphysical truths hidden there. Part of Bacon's genius was that he could—and did—write about anything, even how to design a four-acre garden. In his essay on just that ("On Gardens") he observed, "As for making knots or figures . . . that they may lie under the windowes of the house . . . they be but toyes: you may see as good sights, many times, as tarts." Toys, designs on pastry (or is he punning with "tarts"?): Bacon makes his point on the triviality of knots, but the key distinction is that bit about looking out at them from a window. Knots are not labyrinths, which are designed for one to walk through and interact with. Their designs are to be looked at from a distance, from a terrace, a nearby house, a window of a drawing room or—given their amorous connotations—a bedchamber. Their ornamental networks of paths do not lead anywhere. They were never intended to be walked upon. Indeed, knots can be seen to their full advantage only at a distance and from above. Only the gardeners get close to them. Even today, tourists who have bought their tickets to see the great houses more often than not stand, after a quick glance around them, with their backs to the magnificently crowded rooms to look out the windows at the empty gardens below. By its very nature the knot garden is an empty garden.

The homely herb knot near the kitchen had its practical uses; it was the great house's spice shelf. But herb knots were few. The great ornamental displays were less emblematic of the intertwining of Virtue and Pleasure than of the emptiness of the garden itself. People were rarely in them. Over the course of the seventeenth and eighteenth centuries, as the knot was transformed first into a unicursal labyrinth and then into a multipathed puzzle maze, the garden became urbanized, with its high, green walls, dead ends and wandering pedestrians. The garden became more than a passive spectacle as people found their way back in by way of the maze's path.

The puzzle maze, in fact, was the first physical manifestation of the mythic labyrinth, with its confused and confusing path to the center. As mentioned earlier, the simple, elegant Cretan labyrinth never reflected the chaos of the story it told. In the puzzle maze, the panic can become both real and actual. Yet the Minotaur story plays almost no role in garden-maze mythology. At Versailles's now-destroyed labyrinth, a statue of Cupid, not Ariadne, stood at its entrance holding a ball of string.

In English folklore, the best remembered "historical" maze is not the one in ancient Knossos, but Rosamond's Bower in twelfth-century Woodstock. Its ambience was not slaughter, but romance, befitting the spot where Henry II, father of Richard the Lionheart and the reviled King John, was said to have hidden his mistress, "the fair Rosamond," as she always seems to be called. The supposedly deceived party was Henry's wife, the politically powerful but perhaps not-so-fair Eleanor of Aquitaine. (The fractious royal household is probably best known to modern audiences from James Goldman's play and film *The Lion in Winter*.) The maze or bower—once again those two words are linked—was said to be located near the spot where centuries later the duke of Marlborough's Blenheim Palace, birthplace of Winston Churchill, was built. The bower/maze was impenetrable to the uninitiated. But no one has ever been able to find a trace of it. If the bower actually existed, it was probably not a maze at all but a house hidden in a forest. Perhaps a secret tunnel led to it. Whether real or legend, the important thing is that the story became folklore and the maze is remembered as part of a secretive love story, an illicit trysting spot hidden away from prying eyes. For the same mildly erotic reason Cupid, the goddess of love's little helper, stood guard at Versailles and statues of Venus decorated the centers of many a maze, including one built in the garden of Elizabeth I's adviser William Cecil. It was atop a mound called, with a nice continental flair, "Venusberg."

In May 1591 when the queen visited Cecil's garden at Theobalds in Hertfordshire, she was welcomed by a gardener, or an actor playing a gardener, who explained a maze to her with a little speech written for the occasion by the poet George Peele. As cited by historian Nigel Pennick, it begins:

The moles destroyed and the plot levelled, I cast it [the garden] into four quarters. In the first I formed a maze, not of hyssop and thyme, but that which maketh itself wither with wondering, all the Virtue, all the Graces, all the Muses, winding and wreathing about your majesty, each contending to be chief, all contented to be cherished, all this not of potherbs, but of flowers and flowers fairest and sweetest, for in so heavenly a maze, which astonished all earthly thought's promise, the Virtues were done in roses, flowers fit for the twelve Virtues, who have in themselves, as we gardeners have observed,

above an hundred; the Graces of pansies, partly-colours, but in one
stalk, never asunder, yet diversely beautiful, the muses of nine several flowers, being of sundry natures, yet all sweet, all sovereign.

All this, in the spring of 1591, may not yet have been considered old-fashioned, with its hundred roses and multicolored pansies and no ordinary potted herbs. But those flowers with their
allegorical meanings were about to become passé. Fifty years earlier, Elizabeth's father, Henry VIII, had already installed a much
more modern puzzle maze at his new, and now destroyed, Nonsuch Palace. A visitor described it: "You will enter a tortuous
path and fall into the hazardous wiles of the labyrinth" with
shrubbery walls so high you could not see over them. This was
the maze of the future, and Henry, as usual, was ahead of his
time.

The Theobalds "gardener" seems not to have mentioned
Venus in his talk of Virtues and Graces, perhaps in deference to
the Virgin Queen. (A half century later, the statue and the maze
were not overlooked by Oliver Cromwell's army of militant Puritans, which destroyed the garden—as well as the house—on
April 15, 1643.) More likely, however, the flowering maze shown
to the queen was not Venusberg but a traditional knot garden also
on the estate. The welcoming speech began by saying once the
moles were driven out and the land prepared, the plot was divided
into quarters, as was typical of gardens of the time. A traditional,
flowering knot maze could take up one quarter, a seductive
puzzle maze another, perhaps an ornamental orchard a third, and
so on. But the maze or the labyrinth was almost never the garden's centerpiece. There were fountains for that, statuary, reflecting pools, obelisks and other curiosities. The labyrinths and
mazes were there as supporting diversions, for pleasure or—if one
took that business about Pleasure and Virtue seriously—moral
instruction.

By the beginning of the seventeenth century, the walls of some labyrinths were allowed to grow taller and thicker, flowering plants were replaced with shrubbery, and the element of choice was added to the now-branching pathways. In parts of Germany, the name given the new puzzle maze was *irrgarten,* error garden. (In one of his short stories the twentieth-century Argentine writer Jorge Luis Borges calls it "the Garden of Forking Paths.") But the maze never completely replaced the knot. The puzzle maze simply went its separate way. Knots continue to this day as the basic elegant, if antique, building blocks of traditional, formal gardens throughout the world, sometimes even being called labyrinths. And in recent years there have been some surprising variations. In the garden behind Dublin Castle, for example, is a giant knot made of stone, designed by Ana Dolan to represent intertwined eels, in memory of the dark pool that once stood on that spot and gave Dublin its name. Only when the switch is thrown and the eels' red eyes light up does it become clear that the knot is actually a helicopter landing pad.

The popularity of the new garden labyrinth spread quickly. Some of its success was a matter of fashion and envy. Henry VIII was said to have built Nonsuch and its gardens to outdo his French rival François I's château at Fontainebleau. Cardinal Wolsey is thought to have been inspired to build the original section of Hampton Court after he saw the archbishop of Rouen's maze garden at Gaillon. The most powerful men in Europe built mazes. Emperor Carlos V of Spain had a labyrinth with tiled walks installed at the Alcázar in Seville, and next to it he put a hedge maze. Even a pope—in this case Clement X—gave his unofficial blessing. The pontiff was rumored to enjoy sitting on the balcony of his estate at Altieri and watching the servants at play in the maze. After the beheading of England's Charles I, a Puritan inventory of property seized from the crown included a labyrinth of "very young trees" in Wimbledon, on property the king purchased from the

Cecils, the labyrinth enthusiasts who had owned Theobalds. In earlier years, according to garden historian Robin Whalley, no less an artist than Leonardo da Vinci had mazes to deal with. Twice in his notebooks from the 1490s does this otherwise unexplained item appear on his things-to-do lists: "Repair the labyrinth."

But the spreading popularity of garden mazes and labyrinths was not limited to princes of the church and the state. The merely wealthy began building them. Their interest was spurred not only by stories of what their "betters" might have been up to in their gardens, but also by books. Publishing was new, and books on architecture and design found an eager audience. Andrea Palladio might have remained an innovative architect with a strong following in the Veneto, but he published the plans and drawings of his great country houses and became not only the most influential architect of his day but also one of the most copied architects in Western history. The first examples of the new garden labyrinths appeared just as printed books were becoming truly accessible. In Venice, Holland and other printing centers, lavishly illustrated books and elaborate folios were appearing that showed gardens—new gardens—and told how to build them and what plants would do well. Through their books, innovators and popularizers such as Thomas Hill, André Mollet (son of a famous French family of gardeners) and Jan (or Hans) Vredeman de Vries were finding audiences of garden builders throughout Europe. De Vries's designs appeared not only in his native Holland but in Prague, Hamburg, Heidelberg, even Versailles. The style was truly international. Mollet, who designed labyrinths for England's Charles I, became Sweden's royal gardener under Queen Christina and published a number of both fanciful and more traditional designs that were widely copied.

Not much is known about why the sixteenth- or seventeenth-century owners of Troy Farm in Oxfordshire decided to include a labyrinth, albeit a turf labyrinth, in their garden, or why—later—

a wealthy Quaker family in Saffron Walden chose to cultivate a puzzle hedge maze in their Bridge End Garden, within easy walking distance of the town's famous turf labyrinth, or why El Laberinto, a late-eighteenth-century cypress labyrinth, grows in Barcelona. But there is a good chance that the designs for all of them came from books and not from folk memory or tradition.

Perhaps because the very existence of hedge mazes rested on the whims of fashion, perhaps because their function seems so trivial, perhaps because of intervening revolution and war, or perhaps it is simply a matter of the fragility of plants and the availability of experienced gardeners, but very few of the original mazes have survived. At the Villa Pisani, along the Brenta Canal near Venice, is probably the best-preserved and most-visited hedge maze in Italy. Built for a doge of Venice in the 1720s—and based on plans published nearly seventy years earlier—it contains nearly four miles of tortuous pathways with a round stone tower at its center. Topped with a statue of Minerva, usually called the goddess of wisdom, the tower has an exterior staircase so that upon reaching the goal successful walkers can climb up and watch others struggle frantically along the difficult course. With its statue, the tower may represent the triumph of wisdom over folly (all those wrong turns), although wisdom has little to do with mastering a maze—unless wisdom is simply a matter of learning from past mistakes. Minerva was also the goddess of inventiveness—yet another echo of Daedalus—and perhaps that is what is being celebrated.

The Pisani maze is only a small part of a huge garden that features an ornamental canal. Perhaps the tower's solidity kept the maze from being destroyed during numerous garden renovations and reconstructions, including one by Napoleon's Italian viceroy, who lived at the villa after the French emperor conquered Venice. However it came to be preserved, few structures built on mazes have survived. It's been suggested that some mazes contained

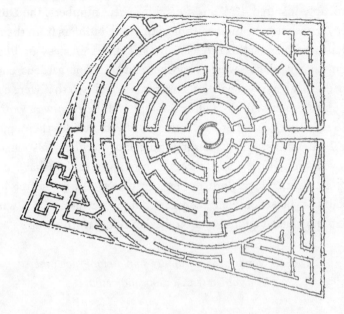

highly decorated wooden Houses of Daedalus, little fun houses whose interiors may have resembled topsy-turvy M. C. Escher architectural sketches or miniature versions of the library-maze in the film version of Umberto Eco's *The Name of the Rose*. The Daedalus houses may have also served as romantic hideaways or trysting spots, but this is all speculation since—if they existed at all—no one ever described them in detail or made a sketch that has come down to us. As it now stands, the Villa Pisani's stubby little labyrinth tower (eighteenth-century sketches make it look taller than it actually is) remains a true rarity.

Near Hannover, Germany, a seventeenth-century octagonal puzzle maze still exists in remarkably good condition in the Herrenhausen Gardens. Nearly seventy-five feet across, it was built soon after 1666 and rebuilt in 1937 and again in the 1970s. Originally designed by an associate of Versailles's Le Nôtre, it has somehow managed to survive better than the French designs that probably inspired it. When it came to sheer numbers, the Dutch may have been the most enthusiastic maze builders from the sixteenth to the eighteenth centuries. Garden mazes—*doolhofs*, confusion gardens—were everywhere, in bourgeois gardens, country estates and royal palaces. Amsterdam had two that were even open to the public, the *Oude Doolhof* and the *Nieuwe Doolhof*. None, either private or public, has survived. Besides their appeal to Holland's strong gardening tradition, *doolhofs* also had a bawdy reputation. One in Middachten was said to have been closed by the local lord for being "the venue for secret love affairs." The seventeenth-century Dutch poet Jacob Cats wrote (in a translation quoted by a Netherlands labyrinth group):

> *The way young people stupidly spin around each other*
> *Resembles a garden with a thousand detours*
> . . . .
> *A garden, an entangled web, and still*
> *one considers wandering a pleasant game.*
> *The garden, a special place, where everyone with desire*
> *fulfils his lust with a thousand turn-arounds.*

In Dutch, *dool*, used in *doolhof*, is also incorporated into the word for a teacher who instructs incorrectly, misleadingly or heretically.

Nothing remains of the most complex—or at least the most expensive—maze of all, the labyrinth at Versailles. The massive royal gardens created for the intentionally intimidating palace of the Sun King, Louis XIV, were laid out in 1662 by André Le Nôtre, that most spectacular of landscape artists. Space was allotted for a maze, about two acres in a rather out-of-the-way spot called the Petit Parc, a short walk southwest of the palace. Designed by Jules Hardouin-Mansart, it was finished in 1674 and—fittingly for a Sun King—was unlike any labyrinth ever made. The principal entrance was placed on a corner and guarded by statues of a large-winged Cupid (looking more adolescent than childlike) and a rather disheveled Aesop holding a scroll that presumably contained his fables. But there were two other ways to get in, or out, and its "walls" were made not so much of hedges but of closely planted trees and thick undergrowth with no center goal. Instead, thirty-nine bronze sculptures depicting the fables could be visited in any order. And to keep the maze suitably entertaining, the sculpture groups were actually fountains, a small part of Versailles's vast water garden, an engineering marvel driven by ingenious hydraulic pumps and fourteen giant waterwheels far off in the Seine River.

According to Charles Perrault, it was called a labyrinth because it had an "infinity of little *allées*" in which to become lost. Perrault is remembered today as the seventeenth-century collector and author of fairy tales who preserved and no doubt elaborated upon such classic stories as those about Cinderella, Little Red Riding Hood, Bluebeard and Sleeping Beauty. He also had close ties to the court of the Sun King, designing a grotto for Versailles based on Ovid's *Metamorphoses*. In 1679 he published a little book of Aesop's fables, illustrated with drawings by Sebastien Leclerc of all the sculptures as well as a map of the entire maze. Titled *Labyrinthe de Versailles* and published in both Paris and Amsterdam, it is the best record we have of the unique little garden.

Beginning with the massive *Owl and the Birds* just inside the entrance, there was considerable variety in the bronze sculpture groups. Some were painted and some left natural. Some, like *The Hen and Her Chicks*, were freestanding and meant to be walked around, while others were placed in apselike trellised niches. Some were huge and complex, such as *The Battle of the Animals*. Some, like *The Fox and the Crane*, were simple. *The Eagle, the Rabbit and the Snail* may have been just that, an unimaginative

little water-drenched totem pole of the three characters. But the whimsical *Council of Rats* consisted of a dozen or so rodents sitting in a circle facing one another, each spitting out a great, well-aimed *jet d'eau* so that they all splashed together at the center. In Aesop's fables the animals speak and—except for a few cascades—most of the water in the fountains come from the animals' mouths and represent speech. The streams of water, some directed upward, some down, some thin and needle-sharp, some gushing, all added to the splashy "conversational" din.

The labyrinth, as depicted in the first edition of the book, is empty of people. But in the 1693 Dutch version, it is teeming with visitors. And workers, too. Judging from their dress, most of the walkers are courtiers. There is a good deal of flirting going on among the couples, with some lounging about on the ground and sipping from wineglasses. Men together are almost always deep in conversation, while groups of women seem more interested in the stories the statues are portraying. There are a few children, daughters mostly, and many, many dogs, who seem to be thoroughly enjoying themselves. The number of workers—some with wheelbarrows, sharp-pointed shovels and pruning hooks—suggests that the maze must have required almost constant attention. Even the king makes an appearance, passing between the statues of Cupid and Aesop as onlookers bow and doff their floppy hats.

As for the maze itself, the walls are represented as being unreasonably tall, as much as three or four times taller than the people. The paths, the *allées*, are narrow but widen to form rooms for the fountains, some of which are in sight of one another. Most curious of all are the walls themselves. Perhaps it is artistic license, like their exaggerated height, but some are clipped as smooth as a well-trimmed hedge. Others are as wild and shaggy as a dense forest, which, of course, is what the walls actually were. None of the editions of Perrault's book show the gilded plaques that accompanied each sculptural group and identified the fables.

The entire area was cleared in 1774, the paths put in concentric order and Aesop's birds and beasts hauled away to be replaced with a single representation of a very ordinary Venus.

The maze that has survived the best both in memory and in fact is the one at Hampton Court Palace. From the United States to Australia, it is the most-copied maze ever built and so famous that even some mazes not based on it—such as the one at Bridge End Garden in Saffron Walden—are *thought* to be either a replica or a modification. Mazes built for laboratory mice by the first British behavioral scientists were based, it's been said, on Hampton Court's. A January 25, 2001, page one story in the *New York Times* reported that tests on muscle and brain activity in sleeping laboratory mice suggest that they dream at night about the mazes they run all day. If so, the Hampton Court design may live on in a dream world its first builders never imagined.

The palace's maze history is tidy enough. Early in the reign of Henry VIII, while the king was still Catholic, Thomas Wolsey, archbishop of York, became a cardinal, lord chancellor of England and probably the richest man in the kingdom. He bought property along the Thames and in 1514 built the original section of Hampton Court as a country retreat, one that—if necessary—could accommodate four hundred overnight guests. He was said to have been much taken with mazes he had seen in France and may have built one at his new estate. In 1529, he "gave" Hampton Court to Henry, went into hiding briefly and somehow managed to die while en route to London from York to stand trial for treason. Henry, most of his wives and all his children lived there at one time or another, and there are unverified reports that a turf labyrinth was on the property during the Tudor years.

The present maze, which may well have replaced an earlier one, is usually said to have been built in 1690, during the dual reign of William and Mary. They came from Holland, where William was the prince of Orange, and were probably well aware of the many *doolhofs* designed by the busy Jan de Vries. On the other hand, some—including the British government's Ministry of Public Buildings and Works—claim the maze was built under their successor, Mary's sister, Queen Anne, who came to the throne in 1702 and had twin "his-and-her"—as Nigel Pennick called them—spiral labyrinths on the grounds of her Kensington Palace in London. The only known illustration of them (each had a tall cypress in its center) shows two dogs playing on the pathway, just as the dogs were doing in the Versailles picture book.

The hedge in Hampton Court's maze, which now grows to about eight feet tall, seems first to have been hornbeam, later patched, fortified and replanted with specimens of privet, yew, holly and sycamore. As mentioned earlier, the maze fits into an odd corner of a more raffish garden on the opposite side of the palace from the river and the more elegant knot gardens. Because of its lack of formality, it was called the Wilderness, although nothing about the place seems particularly wild. As a result of being fit among existing paths, the maze is a trapezoid, a shape mirrored in almost none of its usually rectangular copies. The longest side, the side opposite the entrance, is about 222 feet long.

Serious labyrinth enthusiasts often seem almost embarrassed by Hampton Court, the old maze having perhaps been too popular for its own good. The tone adopted in 1922 by the pioneering labyrinth historian W. H. Matthews is typical and not a little pained. He wrote:

> It is of no great complexity, but . . . is of a neat, symmetrical pattern, with sufficient of the puzzle about it to sustain interest and to cause amusement but without a needless and tedious excess of intricacy. The area occupied by it is more than a quarter of an acre—not a great amount of space, but enough to accommodate about half a mile of total pathway.

One reason the maze has survived so long is that since 1760, when George II—the palace's last royal resident—died, the grounds have combined aspects of a public park and a museum. Daniel Defoe, in his *Tour Through Great Britain* (1726), mentioned it in

passing as one of the sights, but the big explosion of interest came at the end of the nineteenth century. Queen Victoria opened part of the palace itself as a museum and in the 1880s the railroads began promoting the new notion of Sunday outings to Hampton Court, Windsor and other Thames Valley sites, with cheap excursion fares from Waterloo Station. And then, in 1889, came the astonishing success of Jerome K. Jerome's *Three Men in a Boat,* a little book that combines comedy with sentimentality as three friends with little better to do travel up the Thames in a small boat. A scene set in the Hampton Court maze; less than two pages long, became what amounted to the comic turn of the year, something read aloud at parties. A year later, when the book was published in the United States, its success was repeated, with sales totaling more than a million copies. It would be hard to underestimate the importance of *Three Men in a Boat* in establishing the maze's new popularity. The little adventure begins:

> Harris asked me if I had ever been in the maze at Hampton Court. He said he had been in once to show somebody else the way. He had studied it up in a map, and it was so simple that it seemed foolish—hardly worth the twopence charged for admission. . . . It was a country cousin that Harris took in. He said:
>
> "We'll just go in here, so that you can say you've been, but it's very simple. It's absurd to call it a maze. You keep on taking the first turning to the right. We'll walk around for ten minutes, and then go and get some lunch."

They met some people soon after they got inside, who said they had been there for three-quarters of an hour, and had had about enough of it. Harris told them they could follow him if they liked; he was just going in and should turn around and come out again. They said it was very kind of him, and fell behind, and followed.

They picked up various other people who wanted to get it over, as they went along, until they had absorbed all the persons in the maze. People who had given up all hopes of getting either in or out, or of ever seeing their home or friends again, plucked up courage at the sight of Harris and his party, and joined the procession, blessing him. Harris said he should judge there must have been twenty people following him, in all; and one woman with a baby, who had been there all the morning, insisted on taking his arm, for fear of losing him.

Harris kept on turning to the right, but it seemed a long way, and his cousin said he supposed it was a very big maze.

"Oh, one of the largest in Europe," said Harris.

"Yes, it must be," replied the cousin, "because we've walked a good two miles, already."

Harris began to think it rather strange himself, but he held on until, at last, they passed the half of a penny bun on the ground that Harris's cousin swore he had noticed there seven minutes ago. Harris said, "Oh, impossible!" But the woman with the baby said, "Not at all," as she herself had taken it from the child, and thrown it down there, just before she met Harris. She also said she wished she had never met Harris and expressed an opinion that he was an imposter. That made Harris mad, and he produced his map, and explained his theory.

"The map may be all right enough," said one of the party, "if you know where abouts in it we are now."

Harris didn't know, and suggested the best thing to do would be to go back to the entrance, and begin again. For the beginning again part of it there wasn't much enthusiasm, but with regard to the advisability of going back to the entrance, there was complete unanimity, and so they turned, and trailed after Harris again, in the opposite direction. About ten minutes more passed, and then they found themselves in the centre.

Harris thought at first of pretending that that was what he had been aiming at, but the crowd looked dangerous, and he decided to treat it as an accident.

Anyhow, they had got something to start from then. They did know where they were, and the map was once more consulted, and the thing seemed simpler than ever, and off they started for the third time.

And three minutes later they were back in the centre again.

After that, they simply couldn't get anywhere else. Whatever way they turned brought them back to the middle. It became so regular at length, that some of the people stopped there, and waited for the others to take a walk round, and come back to them. Harris drew out his map again, after a while. But the sight of it only infuriated the mob, and they told him to go and curl his hair with it. Harris said that he couldn't help feeling that, to a certain extent, he had become unpopular.

They all got crazy at last, and sang out for the keeper, and the man came and climbed up the ladder outside, and shouted out directions to them. But all their heads, by this time, were in such a confused whirl that they were incapable of grasping anything, so the man told them to stop where they were, and he would come to them. They huddled together, and waited, and he climbed down, and came in.

He was a young keeper, as luck would have it, and new to the business, and when he got in, he couldn't find them, and he wandered about, trying to get to them, and then *he* got lost. They caught sight of him, every now and then, rushing about the other side of the hedge, and he would see them, and rush to get to them, and they would wait there for about five minutes, and then he would reappear again in exactly the same spot, and ask them where they had been.

They had to wait until one of the old keepers came back from his dinner before they got out.

Harris said he thought it was a very fine maze, so far as he was a judge, and we all agreed to let [someone else] go into it.

About a century later, another fictional hero had a very different reaction to his first visit to the Hampton Court maze. In Carol Shields's novel *Larry's Party*, Larry Weller, a young Canadian on his honeymoon, enters the maze alone (which raises immediate questions about the success of this marriage) and becomes—of course—lost. Larry thinks, "And now, in this garden maze, getting lost, and then found, seemed the whole point, that and the moment of walled abandonment, the unexpected rapture of being blindly led." Larry thinks he hears a cheery American voice calling, "This way" and ignores it. Shields continues, "He shrank from the sound, its pulsating jollity, wanting to push deeper and deeper into the thicket and surrender himself to the maze's cunning, this closed, expansive contrivance." He doesn't know it yet, but he will spend much of the rest of his life designing mazes.

More in the spirit of Jerome K. Jerome is a London Transport poster that appeared all over the city in 1956. Beneath a cartoonish faux-Victorian drawing of a maze full of crying children (not, in fact, the one at Hampton Court) are these words:

> *A harassed school teacher from Hayes*
> *Took her students to Hampton Court Maze.*
> *They got thoroughly lost*
> *At a moderate cost*
> *And then had a wonderful time admiring*
> *The Great Vine and imagining Henry VIII*
> *Serving double faults on the Tennis Court.*
> *It was easy to get there, too—Green Line*
> *Coaches 716, 716A, 718 and 725 run to the gates.*

And once again, the great old maze comes to the aid of public transportation and Thames Valley tourism.

When it comes to mazes, the recurring question, one as old as Theseus, is: how do you get out? It is often even more pressing than: how do you find the center? Harris thought there was a trick to it. (Always take the right turn.) Whoever put the statue of Minerva on the tower at Villa Pisani seemed to think it was a matter of wisdom or inventiveness. They were both wrong. There is no surefire trick. It's all a matter of the maze makers' whims. Of course, if the walker has a great deal of time to spare (and little sense of adventure) there is the time-honored hand-on-the-wall technique, which actually works on relatively simple mazes. With it, the walker places a hand—either one will do—on the wall of the maze and follows along as though walking in the dark, always keeping in contact with the wall, even, indeed especially, going around corners. It will be a dogged trip down one side of numerous dead-end passages and back again on the other. Eventually the hand dragger reaches the center, perhaps with scuffed knuckles. Equally unsatisfying is the business of memorizing the turns in advance. Many know that the "secret" of Hampton Court is that you turn left as soon as you enter, take the next two right turns, and then it is left turns all the way to the two white oak trees planted at the center. (Walkers who forget to count how many turns will find their adventure on the way out.) But early on, puzzle-maze designers found a way to confound the drones. The fourth earl Stanhope is usually given credit for adding "islands" to further confuse the puzzle. Islands are minimazes within the larger maze that are not connected to the perimeter wall and send the hand-on-wall devotees walking first in a circle and then back to the entrance. The islands can be as simple as a single, isolated meander. In the 1820s, the earl, a prominent amateur mathematician, built at least three mazes on his estate at Chevining, in Kent. At first glance they look very much like the familiar—indeed overfamiliar—Roman floor labyrinths, but in fact islands isolate the centers to make them trickier than they seem. Only one of them has survived.

But no one wants a simple maze. As Larry Weller realized on his honeymoon, the whole point is to become lost, safely lost, and then find yourself again. It is the same emotional mix of danger followed by relief that sends travelers off on mapless walks in labyrinthine cities such as Venice or Fez.

The puzzle-maze boom, or at least the first bout of it, did not survive the eighteenth century. Although eccentrics, antiquarians and enthusiasts such as the earl Stanhope continued to build new puzzles, popular garden fashions changed dramatically, first in England and then across Europe. Perhaps it was the influence of the newly discovered—or at least newly noticed—gardens of China, with their brilliantly contrived "wild" look. Perhaps it was the influence of philosophers such as Rousseau and talk of freedom and the natural world. Perhaps the right person simply looked out across the trees and lakes of the countryside and saw not a frightening wilderness but a beautiful landscape. In any case, by the middle of the century, English landscape architects such as William Kent and Lancelot ("Capability") Brown were ripping out such "unnatural" contrivances as fences, walls and mazes and replacing them with lakes, waterfalls, hills and blooming groves more artfully artless than anything the Creator had imagined on His own. As Royal Gardener, Capability Brown lived from 1764 to 1783 at Hampton Court, and tradition has it that the maze there survived only because he was ordered, perhaps royally, to keep his hands—and his axes—off it.

William Kent proclaimed: "all nature was a garden," while Isaac Ware ("Of His Majesty's Board of Works," so said the title page of his book *A Complete Body of Architecture*) bemoaned what he called "serpentines" with their "curled and twisted" narrow paths and closely packed shrubbery. All of which was "disagreeable, damp and dark." Or, to use another of his phrases, it was a place of "savage darkness or dreary wet." Not a proper garden at all.

Labyrinths, as mentioned earlier, by their very nature are not natural. They are one of the earliest signs of man's intellect upon "natural" forms. If hedge mazes were an indication of the urbanization of the garden as pedestrians walked and played in their narrow streets and alleys, their destruction was a logical result of this new celebration of nature and the natural, however romantically conceived.

Bernard Rudofsky, an architectural historian and critic, has written of England's traditional distrust, even hatred, of cities and its romanticized notions of country living. He believed this urban aversion at least partially explains why he found English cities so inhospitable and uncomfortable (not to mention ugly), while in Italy—where he felt people loved cities and pedestrian life—they were so livable and inviting. Rudofsky had a knack for brilliantly overstating his case, and it is an opinion that takes little notice of the differences in weather between northern and Mediterranean Europe, but this aversion may partially explain the rejection of the urbanized garden. The English taste for a natural, uncontrived look—even if achieved by totally rebuilding the countryside—spread abroad as puzzle mazes disappeared all over Europe in favor of the "natural" *jardin anglais.*

Mazes will return in the twentieth century. Novelist Julian Barnes, after all, has written that their enduring popularity is rooted in two basic British passions, horticulture and crossword puzzles. And when they return it will be as the more "spiritual" labyrinths' rich, worldly, moneymaking, perhaps even vulgar cousins.

Seven

THE NINETEENTH CENTURY

IN 1879, THE EDITOR OF A Christian socialist newspaper in Brooklyn published an account of his visits to a number of America's backwoods utopias, a tour that took him from the Amana settlement in Iowa to a Shaker village in New England. William Alfred Hinds's opinions of these *American Communities*, as his book was called, are generally favorable, and he himself had long been associated with the highly successful Oneida Community in upstate New York. But there was something about the Harmony Society in western Pennsylvania that he found—to use his word—"un-American." The people were pleasant enough and obviously industrious. The village, named Economy and located just down the Ohio River from Pittsburgh, was neat and tidy. It had a strong economic tradition, over the years owning a railroad (the Pittsburgh and Lake Erie); at least six working oil wells; cotton, wool and silk mills; a whiskey business (the Golden Rule Distillery) and a profitable mail-order seed catalog. Yet to walk down its streets, he said, "is to imagine yourself in some old town in Germany." And it was not simply because the villagers were speaking German.

Among the more exotic foreign elements mentioned by Hinds is a labyrinth. Economy was past its peak in 1879 and the labyrinth itself was gone, but outside the village was something called the Round House that had once stood at its center. When the labyrinth was intact, he was told, the

> house was so carefully concealed by hedges and vines, and there were so many paths crossing and recrossing one another, that the visitor might lose his way many times, and waste hours even, before finding its entrance.

The "Labyrinth" (he capitalized it) and the garden in town with its mysterious "Grotto" were "great objects of pleasure and interest in the days of Economy's greatness."

The Round House now, too, is gone, and the site of the labyrinth is the Ambridge High School's football field. But the Grotto remains, with its rough stone exterior, bark-covered door and thatched roof, preserved and restored as part of Old Economy Village, a state historical site and museum. Many visitors—and a number of writers—have assumed incorrectly that it was the Round House at the center of the village labyrinth. A similar Grotto built by Harmonists along the Wabash River in Indiana was indeed the center of a maze, and to add to the confusion, the labyrinth now on display in New Harmony has a reconstructed copy of the Economy Grotto as its centerpiece. But at Economy, the Grotto was in the Garden of Eden. The Labyrinth, with the Round House, was outside of town.

The Harmonists built at least three labyrinths, one in each of their three successive settlements. George Rapp, their theocratic leader, came to Pennsylvania from Württemberg, in southwest Germany, with a small band of followers in 1805, and they built their first community north of Pittsburgh in Butler Country. It was called Harmony and a few of its buildings remain, although not the labyrinth. They were escaping Lutheranism, the state religion, although they continued to use Martin Lu-

ther's German translation of the Bible, which they believed
literally as God's Word, especially focusing on the Book of Revelation and its details about the end of the world and the Second
Coming of Christ. They believed they were building the garden
Christ was returning to, going so far as to adopt celibacy in
preparation. But unlike the celibate Shakers, who maintained
sexually segregated sleeping quarters, the Harmonists lived together chastely—or so they claimed—simply as "brothers and
sisters."

In 1815, finding Harmony too isolated for their growing commercial activities, Father Rapp led his flock to the banks of the
Wabash, where they built another town, New Harmony, and
another labyrinth. In 1825, they sold the entire Indiana operation
to Robert Owen, the Welsh utopian millionaire who had already
built what he considered an ideal industrial community in Scotland and wanted to experiment further in the New World. The
Owenites expanded New Harmony but kept the labyrinth (and
possibly built a new one of their own), while Father Rapp and his
people began anew in Economy to create even greater prosperity.
And they continued to await the return of the Lord. Although the
populations of Rapp's three villages varied over time, each aver-
aged about six hundred inhabitants.

In 1809, John Melish, a Philadelphia cartographer, visited the
original Harmony, in Pennsylvania, and later described the labyrinth, which had been shown to him by Father Rapp himself. Perhaps playfully or perhaps teaching a lesson on the difficult path
to spiritual harmony, Rapp dashed ahead of his visitor and waited
at the center while Melish became thoroughly lost. "[It] is a most
elegant flower-garden," he wrote, "with various hedge-rows, dis-
posed in such a manner as to puzzle people to get into the little
temple, emblematic of Harmony, in the middle." He went on to
contrast the little building's ugly exterior with its beautiful interior. In his autobiography, Robert Dale Owen, Robert Owen's

son, described the almost identical labyrinth in New Harmony. When his father bought the village it was "without a touch of fancy or ornament" except for a few flowers in the gardens and the Labyrinth, which was

> a pleasure-garden laid out near the village with some taste and intended—so my father was told—as an emblematic representation of the life these colonists had chosen. It contained small groves and gardens, with numerous circuitous walls enclosed by high beech hedges and bordered with flowering shrubbery, but arranged with such intricacy that, without some Daedalus to furnish a clue, one might wander for hours and fail to reach a building erected in the centre. This was a temple of rude material, but covered with vines of the grape . . . and its interior neatly fitted up and prettily furnished. Thus George Rapp had sought to shadow forth to his followers the difficulties of attaining a state of peace and social harmony.

Melish described the interior of the rough-hewn temple only as being "smooth and beautiful." *Angel in the Forest*, Marguerite Young's 1945 account of New Harmony, is an often eccentric mixture of fact and fancy. In it she re-creates the temple's interior, presumably working from her own historical research:

> It is a house of a wished-for death, really. The interior was furnished pleasantly. Blue silk curtains stitched by Rosina [George Rapp's daughter] adorned the walls. The cupboards were well stocked with cheese and wine. There was a bench to rest on. There was a golden book on a higher shelf, but written in a fine, spidery print, which no one had the eyesight or patience enough to read. It was said to contain directions for the building of a city foursquare, the length, breadth and height of which should be equal.

The city foursquare, just as prophesized in Luther's translation of Revelation. The labyrinth was the "mother" of another City of God.

But we do know what the interior of the Economy Grotto looked like. Even if it were not in the center of a labyrinth, it is likely that the Round House or Temple in all three labyrinths were similar. Inside the rough exterior, through the bark-covered door, was someone's notion of a miniature Roman temple, with a coffered domed ceiling and a life-sized—or larger—wooden statue by Philadelphia sculptor William Rush of a classical-looking woman holding a lyre. On the walls were painted important dates in the history of the society.

As their devotion to the images and numbers in the Book of Revelation suggests, the Harmonists loved symbols and symbolism. The garden in Economy was the Garden of Eden. But—says Raymond V. Shepherd, Old Economy Village's historian—this Eden was also one of the best specimen gardens in the state, with three kinds of goldenrod, specially bred black roses, twenty varieties of dahlias and even a few orange and lemon trees. The labyrinths stood for more than just a difficult way to reach the symbolic houses at their centers. Although it is unclear what. Father Rapp heard his followers' confessions, but no evidence exists that the labyrinth was used for penance. The society employed a number of symbols associated with Freemasonry. Could the labyrinths have been used as part of a Masonic ritual? Researcher Lilan Laishley has discovered that the society owned a hundred copies of *The Pilgrim's Progress* and raises the possibility that John Bunyan's 1678 allegorical account of Christian's circuitous journey to salvation (the complete title: *The Pilgrim's Progress from This World to That Which Is to Come*) may well have been a spiritual guidebook to the Harmonists' labyrinth.

Unidentified and undated watercolor drawings of at least three

labyrinth designs dating probably from the 1840s are in the Economy archives, and although serious attempts have been made by Laishley and others to assign them to the different Rappite communities, no one knows what the actual labyrinths looked like. Raymond Shepherd says efforts to identify possible prototypes in Württemberg have also been unsuccessful. The archive drawings seem very much like the decorative images Thomas Hill and other early garden designers published in their pattern books. The Pennsylvania and Indiana labyrinths may have had their source there. The society had a few copies in its library. Ornamental garden structures closely resembling the rustic exterior of Economy's Grotto appear both in an album of garden designs published by Charles Over in 1758 (identified as a Gothic "Banqueting Room") and in *Grotesque Architecture, or Rural Amusements* (published by William Wrighte in 1767), where it is called a "Hermitage." Frederick Reichert Rapp, George's adopted son and chief deputy (critics might say henchman), served as the society's architect and builder and probably adapted the designs of all the Harmonist grottoes and labyrinths.

Education—usually adult education—was a major interest of the Harmonists. They prided themselves on the fact that everyone in their community was literate. They maintained a five-thousand-volume library and an art and natural history museum— displaying paintings, rocks and fossils—open to the public for a small fee. And as their name might suggest, music—both instrumental and choral—was ingrained in everyday life; a small brass band even played from the church tower.

One of the books in Economy's library was a first edition of *The American Gardener's Calendar* by Bernard McMahon, an Irish horticulturist living in Philadelphia. Published in 1806 and reissued in new editions throughout the century, it was the first how-to book devoted to gardening in an American climate. With 648 tightly packed pages (and no illustrations), it was as thorough as its subtitle suggests: *A Complete Account of All the Work Necessary to Be Done in the Kitchen-Garden, Fruit-Garden, Orchard, Vineyard, Nursery, Pleasure-Ground, Flower-Garden, Green-House, Hot-House and Forcing Frames for Every Month of the Year; with Ample Practical Directions. . . .* It keeps on going. A description of a labyrinth appearing under "Pleasure-Grounds," one of the shortest sections of the book, gives an idea

of how they were considered in America at the beginning of the
nineteenth century.

> A Labyrinth is a maze or sort of intricate wilderness-plantation,
> abounding in hedges and walks, formed into many windings and
> turnings leading to one common centre, extremely difficult to find
> out; designed in large pleasure grounds by way of amusement.
>
> It is generally formed with hedges, commonly in double rows,
> leading in various intricate turnings backward and forward, with
> intervening plantations, and gravel-walks alternately between
> hedge and hedge; the great aim is to have the walk contrived in so
> many mazy, intricate windings, to and fro, that a person may have
> much difficulty in finding out the centre, by meeting with as many
> stops and disappointments as possible; for he must not cross, or
> break through the hedge; so that in a well-contrived labyrinth, a
> stranger will often entirely loose himself, so as to not find his way to
> the centre, or out again.
>
> As to plans of them, it is impossible to describe such, by words
> any more than the above hints. And their contrivance must princi-
> pally depend on the ingenuity of the designer.
>
> But as to the hedges, walks and trees: the hedges are usually
> made of hornbeam, beech, elm, or any other kind that can be kept
> neat by clipping. The walks should be five feet wide at least, laid
> with gravel, neatly rolled, and kept clean; the trees and shrubs to
> form a thicket of wood between the hedges, may be of any hardy
> kinds of the deciduous tribe, interspersed with some ever-greens;
> and in the middle of the labyrinth should be a spacious open, orna-
> mented with some rural seats and shady bowers, etc.

The labyrinth McMahon describes, with its "thicket of wood"
between the hedges, is more like the densely planted Versailles
maze than the standard country estate puzzle maze, and he goes
on to describe adjoining hedges cut into "trained figures" of
columns, obelisks and pyramids and long, straight avenues of

trees. This was no labyrinth for run-of-the-mill gentlemen farmers or even a wealthy utopian community. Perhaps the pre-Revolution colonial governor in Williamsburg, Virginia, had something like it. When the old capital was re-created and rebuilt by the Rockefeller family in the 1930s, its designers gave the Governor's Palace a garden maze, a squared-off, truncated version of Hampton Court's. Completed in 1935, it is now probably the oldest surviving hedge maze in the country. But the Harmonists had something less substantial. That there was no trace of it in Economy in 1879, except for the ruins of the Round House, suggests as much. But still, for fifty years or so, an American community—one that had existed in three different settings—had lived intimately with a labyrinth.

The mysteries of the Harmonist labyrinths seem almost trivial when compared to the questions raised by labyrinths that were being discovered in the American Southwest by the end of the nineteenth century. They come primarily in three forms: petroglyphs carved in stone, graffiti scratched onto adobe walls and designs woven into baskets. They are found in rather limited areas of Arizona and New Mexico, the homelands—at least for a while—of the Hopi and the closely related Akimel O'odham, or People of the River (formerly called the Pima), and Tohono O'odham, or People of the Desert (formerly the Papago). All the labyrinths—and they are true labyrinths, not mazes—have nearly identical designs, which follow the seven-circuit pathway of the classic Cretan labyrinth.

The mystery is how the designs got there. How did a symbol on a silver coin minted thousands of years ago on a Mediterranean island turn up on an ancient adobe tower near the Gila River in the Arizona desert?

Casa Grande would have to be on anyone's list of the oldest buildings in the United States, even as a ruin. It was probably built out of adobe in the twelfth or thirteenth century and inhabited until the fifteenth by the Hohokam, ancestors of the People of the Desert and the People of the River. On an inside wall close to where the floor once was on the second story is inscribed a Cretan-style labyrinth nearly two feet wide. Once the four-story-tall center of a complex of smaller structures, Casa Grande is now reduced to a central tower with walls two to five feet thick. The labyrinth was first recorded in 1889, when a photographer climbed up on the rubble from the collapsed upper stories that filled the ground floor to take a picture of it. Those who believe the symbol was introduced into the local culture by Spanish explorers or missionaries point out that mass was said in the already abandoned Casa by an itinerant Jesuit in 1694 and that the design could date from then. Hermann Kern, however, believes it unlikely that a missionary would introduce something as complex as a labyrinth and if he did, it would be of the medieval Christian style and not a pagan one. He also points out that there are no other designs of any kind on the building's walls and that to inscribe it while the building was still intact, the drawer would have had to sit on the floor. Instead, he suggests, whomever the graffiti artist was had probably climbed up on the same pile of rubble as the nineteenth-century photographer.

This does not mean that the drawing must date from the 1800s. The building has been a ruin for centuries and tribes of the People of the Desert and the People of the River, both of which use Cretan labyrinth images in their basketry, have lived in the region since the seventeenth century. The people white men once called

Pima and Papago have long woven what is now called the Man in the Maze motif. It is an angular, somewhat spider-like version of a Cretan labyrinth with a figure of a man standing enigmatically at its entrance—which is at the top—much as the silhouette of a woman appears near the center of the labyrinth in the Sibbo church mural in Finland.

The People of the Desert call the design the House of Iitoi, or Elder Brother, who combines qualities of Noah, Lot, Moses and Jesus, not to mention some aspects of Br'er Rabbit in the Briar Patch. According to legend, as summarized by Terry DeWald, Iitoi was the one good man in an evil civilization. In the beginning, the Creator brought forth a Desert People, but over the generations they had gone bad, all except Elder Brother, whom the Creator placed upon the sacred mountain, Baboquivari, and let him watch as he destroyed the sinful tribe with a great flood. Afterward, Iitoi descended from the mountain and helped found the Hohokam people and taught them the rules of how to live. All went well for a time, but then the people turned against Iitoi and killed him. His spirit escaped to the peak of the sacred mountain, and from time to time he would return disguised as a very small man to take things from the villagers. Sometimes he was seen and chased, but all his cunning twists and turns as he made his way back to Baboquivari confused his pursuers, who could never capture him.

The design on the baskets, then, is not the flat surface of the traditional European labyrinth but a topographical rendering of a mountain. And, as Helen Raphael Sands has pointed out, it is a totally masculine labyrinth, one without an Ariadne to guide the hero through a world of confusion. Terry DeWald believes that the labyrinth has an additional allegorical meaning, one reflected by elderly members of the tribe today, who refer to changes in their lives in terms of the reversals in the design. It is, DeWald says, a depiction of a lifetime that gains wisdom as it moves on. The figure in the maze, as it nears the end, comes to a final U-turn in the path, just before reaching the center, and there the figure pauses and reflects with all his gained wisdom before making the final turn onto the mountaintop and death.

The People of the River refer to the design as the House of Tcuhu, the legendary founder of their tribe, and the labyrinth was

said to be the walls he built to protect himself. The earliest out-
sider's depiction of one of these labyrinths was drawn in 1761 or
1762 by Father Juan Nentvig, a priest who had traveled in the
Gila River region. It was his version of a drawing he had seen
made in the sand by a local Indian who said it was a map of a
great palace that had once been there. Casa Grande (like Minos's
Knossos) was not a labyrinth, but perhaps the symbol stood for
any large building, just as in Europe, where the labyrinth design
became associated with cities. One of the other tribal names for
Casa Grande was the House of Motechuhzoma, an Aztec chief
who could only have been known as a mythic king. Whoever
drew the labyrinth on the wall of Casa Grande might have been
saying that even in ruins it was indeed still a Great House.

Since 1900 Man in the Maze baskets, trays, even cigarette-
pack holders have become popular as items turned out for the
tourist trade, and other tribes, including the Navajo, have copied
the design in their commercial jewelry. But Jeff Saward has written of evidence that the labyrinth was not always simply a matter
of iconography. In the published archives of anthropologist Carl
Schuster, he has seen photographs taken in 1906 (on the Yaqui
Reservation) and in 1929 (in the Salt River Valley) showing Pima
Indians walking small—less than twenty feet wide—temporary
labyrinths. The designs were either scratched in sand or marked
with stones, as they are in Scandinavia. It is unclear how common this was. It was certainly not a tradition that survived, but
however briefly, people did walk labyrinths in the American
Southwest early in the twentieth century.

The other southwestern tribe with a labyrinth tradition is the
Hopi. If Oraibi, a Hopi pueblo in Arizona, was indeed settled in
1100 or 1200, as many believe, it is one of the longest continuously inhabited spots in North America. On rocks just south of
the pueblo are six labyrinth carvings that keep their secrets well.
One is circular, five are square, and they are all small, only five to

seven inches in diameter. It is impossible to date them. It is impossible to know when the Hopi cut them deep into the stone. Or why they did it. But thanks to an oral history project in the 1960s that resulted in Frank Waters's *The Book of the Hopi*, we know what a number of tribal elders believed about the origins of their tribe and what the labyrinth designs—there are two— signify.

The common name for both the round and square labyrinths, Waters writes, is *tapu'at*, "mother and child." The theme of emergence plays a major role in Hopi mythology, both the tribe's emergence from Mother Earth into the world at the beginning of time and the everyday emergence of a child from a mother's womb. They are clearly related, and both can be seen in the *tapu'at*. The square labyrinth is the more literal, being in fact two separate labyrinths, one within the other, and can be seen as both the child within the womb and a child held—and protected—in a mother's arms. The straight line, unattached to either labyrinth, denotes the passage out, maybe even the umbilical cord. Waters does not suggest it, but in some southwestern tribes a sand painting was made while a woman labored to give birth, and the newborn baby was placed upon it almost immediately. Perhaps the stone carving was a more lasting version of a design made in the sand to receive the new baby. Or perhaps the making of the square labyrinth was a ritual to ease or advance the emergence of birth.

The rounded labyrinth, as explained by Waters, is more cosmic than the square. That center line at the entrance is connected on both ends to the overall design and forms a cross that, he writes, symbolizes the Sun Father, "the giver of life." The labyrinth reveals the Creator's universal plan, and the four places where the lines come to an end to form a turning point stand for the four cardinal point on the compass. In this case, the *tapu'at* serves as a divine map. There seems to be no tradition of walking the labyrinth, but every year at Wuwuchim, the first in the annual cycle of ceremonies, Hopi priests walk around the pueblo four times to reclaim the earth according to the universal plan revealed in the labyrinth.

Hermann Kern does not see the roots of these labyrinths in Europe but in Asia, particularly in India, where he believes the labyrinth tradition has many similarities with the traditions of the Hopi and the Peoples of the Desert and of the River. As descendents of the oldest tribes in the Southwest, they have perhaps best preserved some ancient traditions brought to America from across the Bering Strait.

There is a Hindu tradition of linking the labyrinth with birth. As mentioned earlier, pregnant women in India rehearsed giving birth by tracing a labyrinth design with their fingers and, according to some reports, making a design in saffron on a metal plate, then sweeping the powder off and drinking it. Painted in red on a rock overhang on a path to a temple dedicated to the goddess Kali at Tikla, in central India, is a labyrinth similar to the carved petroglyphs of the Southwest, and on a dolmenlike shrine in Tamil Nadu are carved several seven-circuit labyrinths that may date to the first millennium B.C. The women in the Tamil (southeastern) section of India, to this day, continue to decorate their doorsteps with protective, if temporary, labyrinthine designs called *kota*s.

According to Kern, during the month of Margali (mid-December to mid-January on the Western calendar), which is thought to be a time of particular bad luck, women mark their families' doorsteps with a white powder. The images are not always true labyrinths, but pattern books are sold with suggested designs, and most of them seem  to be based on variations of the classic seven-circuit labyrinth. Since the powder is soon obliterated by people coming and going or by the weather, the power of the labyrinth does not seem to reside in the design itself, but in the act of making it. A historic— or mythic—example of the defensive power of the labyrinth is found in the epic *Mahabharata*, in which an army arrayed as a *chakra vyuha* is invincible. In Sanskrit, *chakra* means circle, *vyuha*, battle formation.

As the story of the Battle of Kurukshetra goes, Drona, a wise man with magical powers, was called upon to lead the Kaurava army against the Pandavas and swore to create a military formation that would outwit even the gods. As illustrated by carvings in three twelfth- and thirteenth-century temples in Mysore, he then arranged his troops in the shape of a classic Cretan labyrinth. The *chakra*'s power did not come from enemy soldiers entering the "pathway" and being destroyed (although that did happen once, when a single brave young soldier was told the secret of how to get in but not how to get out) but from the very image embedded in the formation, which re-  pelled the Pandavas. The magic was in the image itself. The *Mahabharata* as it now appears probably evolved between 4 B.C. and A.D. 4 and the *chakra vyuha* may originally have been simply a formation of concentric circles, but by the time the temple carvings were made labyrinths had made their mark in India, especially in the south. This was centuries before Casa Grande and the Oraibi pueblo were built.

There is something patronizing (not to mention improbable) about the notion that the labyrinth had to be introduced into the American Southwest from an outside source. Perhaps the Spaniards did bring it. Perhaps there was some deep racial memory of Asia. But let's not forget the anthropological principle mentioned earlier that given the same raw materials, people the world over come up with almost identical solutions to the same problems. This can be as true for concepts as it is for corbel arches. And it is worth noting that the same people who argue that the Hopi or the People of the Desert got the idea of a labyrinth from European Christians or Asian Hindus probably suspect the labyrinth was brought to India in the first place by Alexander the Great.

At the same time as an ancient labyrinth tradition was being discovered in the American Southwest, the second half of the nineteenth century saw a modest revival of what might be called officially blessed labyrinths, blessed by either church or state. One was even ordered by Prince Albert himself. His pet project, London's Great Exhibition of 1851, housed in Joseph Paxton's architecturally innovative Crystal Palace, was such a success that it made a profit. The excess money, in turn, was used to buy land near the present location of Albert Hall for the Royal Horticultural Society to create a garden showcase.

And Albert, Queen Victoria's consort, is supposed to have "recommended" that part of the twenty-five-acre botanical garden be set aside for a hedge maze or labyrinth. William Andrews Nesfield, a retired naval officer who had become a popular society garden designer, was hired for the job. Perhaps best known for his landscaping in the royal gardens at Kew, Nesfield was partic-

ularly admired—and hired by estate owners—for his faux-Tudor knot gardens. He
had also designed labyrinths before. The
original Bridge End hedge maze in Saffron
Walden was his, and an eccentric one fea-
turing three large circles with a somewhat
bug-eyed appearance can still be seen at
Somerleyton Hall, near Great Yarmouth in
Sussex. The Royal Horticultural Society
hedge maze, which opened in 1861, was
more conventional, containing only one

circle. It was intended to hold a fountain but a statue of Galatea
was put there instead. Nesfield's critics complained—as they
usually did—of his "excessive" use of gravel throughout the
entire garden. Unfortunately, over the years the site became overgrown and in 1913, when it was replaced with the South Kensington Science Museum, Central London lost its only hedge
maze.

In addition to his perhaps liberal use of graveled walks, what
set Nesfield apart from most other labyrinth and maze designers
of his time was his originality. In most cases, tradition prevailed.
Australia got its first hedge maze in 1862, in the botanical garden
of the rich gold rush city of Ballarat, and it lasted—with one
replanting—until 1954. It was a copy, more or less, of Hampton
Court, as was New Zealand's first in 1911 in Dunedin. It, too, is
gone. Although similar mazes appeared and soon withered in a
number of colonial outposts in Africa and Asia, the revival was
not limited to the British Empire. The Netherlands, for one, experienced a major labyrinth and maze boom in the 1880s and '90s.
The best-known survivor is on the floor of the Gothic thirteenth-
century addition to the far older Romanesque St. Servaas, in
Maastricht. Designed by architect Petras Cuypers as part of his
1886 renovation of the city's oldest church, the roughly thirty-

foot-square variation on the Roman-style labyrinth shows mosaic silhouettes of six cities: Maastricht at the entrance, Jerusalem in the center and Rome, Constantinople, Aix-la-Chapelle and Cologne at the four corners. A second, less visible Cuypers labyrinth is located in the choir, this one closely resembling the labyrinth with a cross that appears in both St.-Omer in France and in the Ghent city hall. It is about twenty-four feet square. Two churches built late in the century also contain more or less traditional labyrinths at their entrances, St. Nicholaskerk in Nieuwegein (about twelve feet square) and St. Martinuskerk in Oud-Zevenaar (about fifteen feet square). At the center of the St. Nicholaskerk labyrinth are the words *Per Crucem ad Coronam,* By way of the cross to the crowning. About the same time as the church labyrinths were being built, a number of hedge mazes began appearing across the Dutch landscape. Four still exist, all variations of the Hampton Court design, at Rurrolo (the largest), Paterswolde, Weldam and Sypesteyn.

The most startlingly original of the late-nineteenth-century church labyrinths came from an unexpected source. Sir George Gilbert Scott made his name, his fortune and his knighthood building—or more often renovating—structures that could pass for authentic sixteenth- or seventeenth-century architecture of the noblest kind. How many visitors over the last century and a half have praised the magnificent Gothic ceiling of the Abbey Church in Bath knowing it was not Tudor at all but Victorian? Scott could create a medieval railway station (St. Pancras in London), tidy up a national treasure (Westminster Abbey) or save a perhaps dangerously decaying country cathedral, as he did at Ely, near Cambridge.

The angels he had painted high over Ely's transept would never fool anyone into thinking they were anything other than nineteenth-century creations, but the true surprise is the black-and-white stone labyrinth on the floor at the cathedral's entrance. It is

the first and only one in an English
cathedral, and it is located in just about
the place where labyrinths would be in
French cathedrals. But with its sharp
turns and nearly twenty-foot-square
shape (an optical illusion makes it
seem rectangular) Ely's is unlike any
other labyrinth built before it. And
although cathedral guides have a suit-

ably medieval story about it—that the labyrinth was designed to
turn the devil around and send him back out the door he had just
come in—there is no mistaking it as a dramatic, thoroughly modern piece of work.

The end of the century's renewed interest in labyrinths combined with an even stronger fascination with new science and
new building materials is reflected—quite literally—in a new
kind of puzzle maze. On both sides of the Atlantic, some of the
most popular mazes of the late nineteenth and early twentieth
centuries were glass. They owed little in either their design or
how they worked to Crete, Chartres or Hampton Court and a lot
to the science of physics and optics. Mirror mazes were ideal carnival attractions. They were easy to set up, easy to maintain and
did not take up much space. Indeed, they could make the area
they filled look as much as six times larger than it was. The typical carnival wagon was only eight feet wide; most could fold out
to sixteen feet. Robert Goldsack, a historian of carnivals and traveling shows, has pointed out that the secret of success for a "glass
house," as they were called in the trade, was not to be so confusing as to keep the customers inside too long. There simply wasn't
room for them.

The typical glass house consisted of, first, a corridor, which
often doubled back on itself, lined with distorting mirrors having
curved glass that made the walkers look taller or fatter or smaller

than they were. Sometimes the floors were set on springs to throw the customers off balance. Sometimes the corridor also included house-of-horrors touches such as hanging string (to imitate cobwebs), spooky lighting (although if it were too dark the mirrors wouldn't reflect) and prop skeletons and monsters. The corridor led into the mirror maze itself, in which arches, doorways and more corridors seemed to stretch in all directions and walkers could catch glimpses of themselves, sometimes dozens of them, often heading in unexpected directions. The purpose was not to reach a central goal but to navigate an escape route that would lead you back outside without your bumping your nose too often on unexpected panes of glass. Most people soon learned to walk with their hands extended in front of them, like so many road-company Lady Macbeths.

C. W. Parker of Leavenworth, Kansas, a leading manufacturer of carnival rides and sideshows, probably made many of the traveling glass houses, but some were permanent installations at amusement parks. A handbill for Steeplechase Park ("Coney Island's Only Funny Place") listed twenty-five attractions you could see for only twenty-five cents, and number 19—between 18: Moving Pictures and 20: The Roller Coaster—was the Glass Works, located in the Sunken Garden. Since 1906 a mirror maze has been on exhibit at the Musée Grévin, Paris's version of Madame Tussaud's waxworks. It had been built for the 1900 International Exhibition, held in the shadow of the Eiffel Tower, the modern engineering marvel left over from the 1889 world's fair.

Gustav von Ptittwitz Palm, if that indeed was his real name, described himself as "a subject of the Emperor of Austria-Hungary, residing in New York" in the papers he took out on May 30, 1893, for a United States patent on a "Device for Producing Optical Illusions." It was a mirror maze that offered two illusions. The first was an elusive woman (or "any suitable attraction") the "visitor" sees in the distance on entering but when approached turns out to be elsewhere. Palm wrote, "Whichever way he tries to get at the object or person so shown he will be baffled." The second is a crowd scene. As Palm described it, the visitor enters "a maze" (the inventor himself put the word within quotation marks). Then:

> Looking in front of him he perceives a number of visitors but on examination he will find that what may appear to him numerous persons, are only reflections of the same individual. . . . In like manner he is seen by other visitors. In fact, any visitor in any part of the "maze" is seen reflected in every other part of the "maze." Not so the "attraction" [the woman or suitable object glimpsed on entering]. . . .
> Thus two distinct illusions are created, the one that the locality is enormous in extent and filled with visitors, the other . . . that is comparatively speaking near the visitor and easily accessible.

Awarded patent number 498,524, this device owed all its illusions to mirrors, twenty-five of them. Later in 1893, Palm received additional patents on his mirror maze, for "improved" arches and frames and a standardization of sizes that made the attraction more portable.

What's generally considered the best of the surviving nineteenth-century mirror mazes was also constructed as an exhibition attraction, the 1896 Swiss National Exhibition in Geneva. After the fair closed the maze was rebuilt in Glacier Gardens, in Lucerne, where it had the good luck to be renovated and restored in 1991. At first glance the grand hall seems to be a multicolumn Moorish fantasy, probably inspired by the Alhambra in Spain, with corridors and passageways seeming to lead off in six—or is it more?—directions. Walkers trying to find their way are greeted with endless doorways that turn out not to be doorways at all, glimpses of themselves at the far end of corridors they are entering, a roomful of flowers and even a few surprising encounters with a caliph.

Overhead are what seem to be a series of Moorish arches, and the floor, like the floors of most mirror mazes, is decorated with a pattern of equilateral triangles. These are the key to how the maze deceives. Not every triangle is used. Some remain purely decorative. The tall rectangular mirrors (which do not distort the images they reflect) have the same width as one side of the triangles, and are placed along the triangles' edges. Sometimes there is a mirror along only one side. Sometimes there are two mirrors on two sides. Sometimes there is a mirror and a clear pane of glass. Because of the triangles, all of these mirrors are set at an angle of sixty degrees, and those that are aligned on the correct pattern can communicate and reflect one another. It is also possible in more complex mazes, such as Gustav Palm's double illusion, to have smaller mazes within mazes, in which an independent network of mirrors—ignoring the triangles—is set at forty-five-degree angles and reflect one another but not the ones set at sixty degrees. This added complication, though, is rare and may indeed exist today only in literature, such as William Bayer's mystery novel *Mirror Maze*.

In 1986, Jearl Walker, writer of "The Amateur Scientist" column in *Scientific American* magazine, entered the Lucerne maze and found it far more difficult than he expected. So, journalist as he is, he returned with a notebook, had his wife walk in front of him so he would avoid crashing into any unexpected glass walls, and mapped the whole thing. The sketch he published in his June column shows what seems to be a simple route of alternating left and right turns (with one true dead end) that meanders past the walls of angled mirrors. It also reveals that there is no actual maze at all, only an illusion created through optics and geometry for befuddled eyes. The ever-changing maze exists only within the walker's head. As "modern" nineteenth-century science, it is as intricately meshed—and as playfully ingenious—as its contemporary, the Eiffel Tower.

Mirror mazes still can be found in a few carnivals and amusement parks. In some gimcrack versions glass mirrors have been replaced by Mylar. At the Wookey Hole Caves, near Bath, England, there's a new brightly colored maze clearly inspired by Lucerne, if a bit simplified. (There's really no need there for wives to walk ahead of any earnest mapmakers who might wander in.) And unlike Lucerne, it ends with a giant mirrored fountain. The Navy Pier in Chicago holds a maze that reproduces landmarks of the Windy City, and at Longleat House, a stately mansion in southern England, the story of King Arthur is played out in a mirror maze built in a stable. All these new creations are the work of the inventive Adrian Fisher. A curious variation on the mirror maze could once be found in the garden of the Hotel Tjaarda in Holland. Built early in the twentieth century and expanded several times, since the 1980s the site has become a parking lot. It first seemed to be an ordinary hedge maze, but when the walkers reached the center, they were confronted by six distorting mirrors. So, what would normally be a moment of triumph became a moment of mockery. And the Minotaur turned out to be a grotesque version of one's self.

But the glass house to remember is the one in an abandoned San Francisco amusement park that appears at the end of Orson Welles's 1948 movie *The Lady from Shanghai*. Rita Hayworth is the lady, caught up in what seems to be a grim marriage. Welles, in addition to directing, is a not-so-innocent bystander with an Irish accent who gets more than he bargained for. It's a classic American film noir with dialogue to match. "The world is bad," says Rita. "Everybody is somebody's fool," says Orson. The shoot-out between the lady and her husband (a famous criminal lawyer played by an especially evil Everett Sloane) is reflected in the shattering glass of a fun house Hall of Mirrors. The gunfire may last for only about twenty seconds, but it's the reason people still remember the movie's other eighty-seven minutes.

Yet with all this fascination with gadgetry and innovation and the titillation of an unsolved puzzle, the mystical appeal of the labyrinth continued. And nowhere, at the end of the nineteenth century, was this better embodied than in a little red-brick chapel on a hillside in a cemetery in Surrey. The name of the village is Compton, and it was the home of painter and sculptor George Frederic Watts and his young wife, Mary. Watts's huge, heavy paintings, with their muscular heroes and melodramatic settings, have long been out of fashion, but in his lifetime he was hailed as "England's Michelangelo." Mary was his second wife—the first was the then-sixteen-year-old actress Ellen Terry—and although there is no doubting her devotion to the "Signor," as Watts was called around the house (Mary's biography of him runs on for three volumes), her artistic taste was considered more "modern" than his. A Scot, raised in her family's castle, Aldourie, on Loch Ness, Mary found inspiration for her own work in Celtic sources, in the highly ornamented *Book of Kells* and *Book of Durrow* and the intricately carved high crosses of Ireland, Scotland and Wales. She was also devoted to William Morris and the Arts and Crafts movement, with its philosophy of uplifting the masses through art. That included not only art appreciation but also the actual making of beautiful things that could then be put to practical use. For example, distressed by the ugliness of most gravestones, she briefly entertained the notion of teaching people to make their own out of locally available materials.

When the village of Compton bought some land near the Watts house in 1895 for a new cemetery, Mary came up with a more ambitious plan than single gravestones. She would design a chapel for it and train the villagers to prepare the symbolic terra-cotta architectural elements that make the building one of the most remarkable in England—although some have called it grotesque. She set up clay modeling classes at the Watts estate, where the "terra" for the terra-cotta was also dug, and had more volunteers than she could cope with. In *The Word in the Pattern*, her little book on the meaning of the chapel's symbolism (in which she apologizes—not very convincingly—for having so much of it to explain), she lists seventy-three names, including her own, of those who fashioned her designs. The clay was kneaded and molded into hundreds of angels, peacocks, ships, mice, intertwining branches of the Celtic Tree of Life, quasi-Arabic scriptural quotations and dozens and dozens of other details, including more than a few labyrinths. Then they were fired in a kiln William De Morgan, William Morris's brilliant tile designer, helped set up.

The way to the chapel, which was completed in 1898, is up a closely planted yew-lined walk that passes through the cemetery. Emerging from the trees, which is rather like coming out of a hedge maze, the first impression is that the little brick building, even after more than a century of fading, is still very, very red. The second impression is of the massive Romanesque doorway surrounded by intricate stone carving (actually terra-cotta) that could have come from a medieval Irish monastery or—farther across the sea—from many a New England or Chicago building by Henry Hobson Richardson or Louis Sullivan. The floor plan of the chapel is of a Greek cross superimposed on a slightly smaller circle. On the domed roof, where the unusually narrow bricks make the chapel seem taller than it is, there's a small bell tower. And everywhere can be seen swirls of deeply detailed terra-cotta.

On each side but the front is an angel holding a labyrinth, part of a trio of angels representing the Way, the Truth and the Life. The labyrinth is emblematic of the Way and resembles the pavement labyrinth in San Vitale in Ravenna. Nigel Pennick points out that it is actually a copy of the Italian labyrinth as it appears in an inaccurate drawing published in *Architecture, Mysticism and Myth* by William Lethaby, one of the principal philosophers of the Arts and Crafts movement. Inside, in the chapel's only room, a swirling mixture of Celtic, Art Nouveau and Arts and Crafts elements that Mary Watts herself called—perhaps half jokingly—"glorified wallpaper," another, larger labyrinth, this one with eleven circuits, appears on the altar.

The building's most unusual labyrinths probably go unnoticed as figures on the bases of columns around the windows. Mary Watts writes that she saw the design on a Celtic cross in Carew, Wales. It combines a version of the swastika (which she believed may have represented the path of the sun in the pre-Christian world) and the T, or tau, mark, anticipating the cross of Jesus, that the Israelites in Egypt put over their doors on the night of the first Passover. It was a sign to the Angel of Death to pass over and spare the lives of the firstborn sons, but tau was also, she writes, "a symbol that had been used for thousands of years before Moses by the Egyptians as a sign of immortality."

Mary claimed that the Carew labyrinth was used as an identification sign by early Christians in Britain, and sometimes written around the labyrinth itself were the words "God Leadeth." She found strength in this. Although the chapel was not built as a memorial to G. F. Watts, as many believe, his ashes are there, next to the altar, in a small box Mary had designed years before for another purpose. Some of the men and women of Compton who worked the clay formed the Potters Arts Guild and made

pottery—in addition to a few terra-cotta gravestones—that was popular in its day and is now sought after by collectors. And as a new century got under way, Mary Watts wrote that the true meaning of the Carew labyrinth, with its twists and turns and symbols of eternal life, could be found in Robert Browning's poem "Pippa Passes": "God's in his heaven— / All's right with the world."

Eight

THE MOVEMENT

IN THE MODERN FOLKLORE OF LABYRINTHS, nine-thirty in the morning on August 5, 1991, is momentous, something akin—in other contexts—to dawn on D-day or the night jazz moved up the Mississippi from New Orleans. That is the summer morning when Lauren Artress, a young canon at San Francisco's Grace Cathedral with a degree in psychotherapy, led a small delegation from her church into Chartres Cathedral and moved the chairs away to reveal the labyrinth. Then, with the path cleared, they walked it, followed—to their surprise—by a short line of strangers, tourists and perhaps even local parishioners. It was, she has since said, a "golden" moment, as though "someone threw stardust into the air."

Moving the chairs became the dramatic turning point, the crossing of the Rubicon, the nailing of the thesis to the church door in Wittenberg. For the few who knew about it, Chartres's obscured labyrinth was all too symbolic. Out of either Gallic indifference to what was there or a conservative fear of "cultism," cathedral officials kept the labyrinth hidden by chairs, except for a few hours on the summer solstice. Which, in a classic case of self-fulfilling expectations, is the one day of the year guaranteed to attract hordes of what the good fathers probably considered cultists, pagans or deviant Protestants. Just look across the English Channel and see how "Druids" flock to Stonehenge on that day. And then on August 5, 1991, appeared that little band of liberating Californians.

The story is told in a few paragraphs in Artress's 1995 book *Walking a Sacred Path*, but it has become all the richer with retelling. The number of chairs has always been known—there were 256 of them—as have the names of most of the San Francisco delegation. But as with the Gospels, details are somewhat skimpy in the original version. The text, for instance, makes no mention of the police, who are now said to have been called, nor any hint of a comic element of fear. As the dean of Grace Cathedral, Alan Jones, now tells it with mock embarrassment, he did not join the chair movers but timidly waited safely across the street at a sidewalk table of the Serpente Café, a name worthy of medieval allegory. The book version does, however, say that two unnamed members of the group did not take part so they could rescue the others, if need be.

Today, there is a labyrinth in the nave of Grace Cathedral. It is just inside the great western door, a location similar to Chartres's, and another, in stone, is outside, where it can be walked anytime, day or night. At Chartres itself, the labyrinth is now uncovered all day every Friday, the direct result, says François Legaux, a retired canon of the French cathedral, of Lauren Artress's activities. Yet these two achievements, considerable in themselves, are perhaps the least of her achievements. It would be hard to overestimate the effect she has had on the labyrinth's revival at the end of the twentieth century. She has said—in just about every speech since that August morning—that her goal is to "pepper the world" with labyrinths. And a decade has seen a remarkable peppering of North America and the world beyond. Yet labyrinths for her are not an end in themselves. A phrase she uses almost as much as the pepper image is that the labyrinth is "a spiritual tool." She has also called it "a wonderful simplifying principle" and a "journey to God." Most recently she has begun to call it "the blueprint." A tool, a principle, a journey—the labyrinth is useful, however beautiful it may be. Lauren Artress has probably never said so, but the historical labyrinth, even the one at Chartres, probably has a limited interest for her. The important thing is what can be done with it. As she says, "I can teach anything through a labyrinth." She adds, "Anything I care about."

Artress, who grew up in Ohio and earned graduate degrees at Princeton Theological Seminary and Andover Newton Theological School, had walked her first labyrinth only a few months earlier in 1991 at a spiritual conference held off-season at a YMCA camp in upstate New York. That labyrinth was simply made, a Chartres design marked out on the floor of an indoor basketball court, but she knew at once that she wanted to build one at Grace, where she was a canon pastor. In many American cities the social outlook and theology of the neo-Gothic Episcopal cathedral at the top of Nob Hill would be considered fairly liberal, but in San Francisco it had a somewhat conservative reputation. The little raiding party on Chartres was, in fact, less of a research project than a way of drumming up support for a labyrinth among the right people within the congregation. It worked. When they returned to San Francisco, Artress and some others got busy making a portable labyrinth, something that could easily be moved, packed away and rolled out when needed. Using volunteers, they sewed ten-gauge canvas into six seven-by-forty-two-foot panels that could be linked together with Velcro strips. On it, the volunteers painted, in vivid purple, the outline of the medieval labyrinth. After a successful out-of-town tryout at a religious conference in Washington, D.C., the labyrinth was introduced on its home turf on the night before New Year's Eve as part of a twenty-four-hour end-of-the-year observance. Lured only by a brief newspaper story and the usual church-bulletin announcements, a line—which included a good number of the simply curious—formed at six p.m., and an unbroken parade of walkers moved without letup through the purple lines until midnight. That is the legend. In any case, Grace Cathedral and the Reverend Dr. Lauren Artress were now in the labyrinth business.

And that, perhaps more than the moved chairs, was a truly historic moment. After a lapse of some four hundred years, the labyrinth was again playing an active role in the life of a cathedral and its community. At first, the canvas was unrolled and hooked together only twice a month, but by 1994 it had become more than a bit worn and the popularity of walking it justified a permanent installation. It took the form of what the cathedral called a floor tapestry and just about everyone else called a carpet. It is a thirty-six-foot, nine-hundred-pound version of the Chartres design woven in wool and installed near the top of the center aisle. The minor adaptations made by Robert Feather Anderson grew out of the experiences of those two years and are so subtle they have been unquestioned by thousands of contemporary walkers who believe they are following the original Chartres path. The major change—besides a reduction in size from forty-two feet—consists of stretching out the space between the ten back-to-back turns—called the labryses—to allow unobtrusive places for people to step off the path to pause, rest, pray, meditate or simply let the walkers behind pass by.

If the Worldwide Labyrinth Project began as an outreach program, a way of bringing into the cathedral people in the community who might have felt uneasy with traditional dogma, it soon was much more. Lauren Artress's title became canon for special ministries, and the labyrinth became the silent bridge between traditional and untraditional, all the more effective, Artress believes, because it is nonverbal. Words can breed dissension. The "peppering" began almost at once, as the fertile new name for the project suggests. Now it is called Veriditas, a name

Artress says she borrowed from the medieval mystic Hildegard of Bingen, meaning the power of green or greening. Before long Veriditas was spreading the word, preaching the gospel of the labyrinth. Not only were programs and "pilgrimages" scheduled regularly at the cathedral, but there was also what amounted to a traveling road show called the Theater of Enlightenment. Usually including musicians such as harpists or percussionists, the weekend theater programs are always held at conference centers rather than at churches, to bring labyrinths to communities that have never seen them, for two days of walking and meditation. It is, quite frankly, an evangelical operation as well planned as a Billy Graham Crusade. The goal is not to save souls as such but to spread the use of the "spiritual tool" and, perhaps more important, to recruit "facilitators," a knowledgeable and experienced corps of aides to instruct and assist walkers. Veriditas and the people at Grace Cathedral would never use the term, but the facilitators—who must complete a $500 two-day training program—are the missionaries in the field.

Walking a Sacred Path has also played a key role in the labyrinth revival. When it was published in 1995, there were only a few books on the subject. The standard text was then a paperback reissue of W. H. Matthews's *Mazes and Labyrinths*, published in 1922, and for those who could read German, there was Hermann Kern's encyclopedic catalog of labyrinth lore, which had not yet been translated into English. Important as both remain, neither promotes the concept of the spiritual tool. Artress's unintimidating book contains the historic fundamentals but portrays the labyrinth experience as a personal one, both through the author's own meditations and with comments from the everyday people who have been spiritually enriched by walking labyrinths. What is stressed is how unthreatening a labyrinth is, how nonjudgmental, how there is no right or wrong way to walk. Prospective walkers are encouraged to look inward, to simplify and to lose themselves. As with the young girls on a beach in E. E. Cummings's poem "maggie and milly and molly and may," they learn that "whatever we lose (like a you or a me) / it's always ourselves we find in the sea." Or in a labyrinth.

The book also makes two important contributions to what's become accepted labyrinth terminology, the words *lunations* and *labrys*. Artress may actually have coined *lunations* for the 112 teeth, or partial circles, that form the outmost ring of the Chartres labyrinth. She has said the word came to mind after she had talked with the British labyrinth theorist Keith Critchlow about a possible connection between the "teeth" and the lunar calendar, 112 being four twenty-eight-day lunar months. *Labrys*—or *labyrs*, as she spells it—was probably used before as the name for the ten places in the Chartres labyrinth where the path turns back to back to create an image resembling the Cretan double-headed ax. But it remained obscure until popularized along with *lunations* in *Walking a Sacred Path*, and both words have now—in most circles at least—become part of common usage.

The book has sold more than 125,000 copies, and more often than not, is its reader's introduction to both the labyrinth and the pathway as a form of walking meditation. Veriditas estimates it has trained about eleven hundred facilitators over the years and caused as many as eight hundred labyrinths to be built throughout the world. These range from simple Scandinavian-style stone arrangements to portable canvas drop cloths to colorful images painted on playgrounds to huge landscaped monuments costing hundreds of thousands of dollars. The number does not include thousands of temporary labyrinths built to last a day or a weekend. They can be anything from masking-tape outlines on a gymnasium floor to images cut with a lawn mower through high grass to pathways scratched onto a sandy beach or marked out with string or miniature flags or even Christmas tree lights.

Veriditas—now confident enough to call itself "The Voice of the Labyrinth Movement"—sells ready-made labyrinths. A thirty-six-foot canvas replica of the one in the nave in San Francisco, hand painted—the sales brochure says—"in the crypt of Grace Cathedral," sells for about $4,000, while a twenty-four-footer, with seven rather than eleven circuits, costs about $2,500. But a small commercial labyrinth-making industry has also sprung up to satisfy—and encourage—the new market. Three of the principal makers, with very different approaches, tell surprisingly similar stories of finding themselves in an unexpected line of work. Robert Ferré, who might be called the dean of the new maze makers, got into the field through his lifelong interest in the architecture of the cathedral at Chartres, which he has, by his count, visited forty-six times in thirty-five years. It was, though, an interest that until 1995 had never involved looking down at the cathedral's floor. Chartres brought him together with Lauren Artress, who mentioned in passing that her book—published that year—was creating a demand for portable labyrinths with no one to meet it. Ferré, who had just taught himself to draw the design freehand with a compass and a ruler, had been in the construction and real estate business, as well as advertising and travel. He had never actually made a full-sized labyrinth, but he said he could do it. The result was the Missouri-based St. Louis Labyrinth Project (now called Labyrinth Enterprises), which has produced more than 650 labyrinths, all individually drawn and hand painted on canvas and other fabrics. The company has also built and landscaped a number of permanent labyrinths, usually made of concrete, and on New Year's Eve, for a number of years, constructed a ninety-five-foot labyrinth from masking tape that was walked annually by about two thousand St. Louis revelers. The Project is a two-women, one-man operation (Ferré, his wife, Ruth, and a longtime assistant) in what had been the high-windowed gymnasium of a 1920s parochial school.

Their greatest achievement, however, may not be their meticulously produced designs, but the books and pamphlets Ferré has
written instructing others how—using his measurements and
experience—to make their own Chartres labyrinths.

David Tolzmann was in the industrial recycling business
when some women in his church in suburban Baltimore asked if
he could solve some of the technical problems with the labyrinth
they wanted to build. He bought Lauren Artress's book, got some
additional advice and found that he could indeed help. Soon his
recycling operation had a subsidiary called the Labyrinth Company, and he was turning out models (twelve standard designs,
eight basic colors) and custom designs from six to eighty-five feet
in diameter and made of canvas or paving blocks. It wasn't long
before the subsidiary overwhelmed the mother company, and
Tolzmann, who boasts of three thousand hits a day on his sales
Web site, estimates that he has sent more than a thousand
labyrinths out into the world.

Marty Kermeen was what he calls a "patio and driveway man"
who had a paving and stonecutting business in northern Illinois
when—in 1999—someone in North Carolina saw one of his
advertisements and asked if had any experience designing and
building labyrinths. He knew nothing about what he says he
regarded as "a geometric design from hell," but he took this as a
challenge. To learn, he bid on and won a contract to revive a
stalled plan to put a labyrinth in Riverwalk Park in nearby
Naperville, Illinois. It was a hectic three-week rush job of cutting
and fitting paving blocks so exactly they required no concrete. He
lost $3,000 on it, and he never won the North Carolina commis-
sion (no one did), but, he says, the experience changed his and his
family's life. And it produced one of the most admired Chartres-
style labyrinths in the country. What he created at Naperville
was the prototype of the building technique he has been using
ever since: thousands of individually cut blocks fit together as

tightly as a Roman mosaic. Marty Kermeen and his wife, Debbie, and their four-man construction team have become full-time labyrinth builders. They have constructed more than twenty-five stone and brick labyrinths around the country, including ones at the Museum of International Folk Art in Santa Fe and St. John's Episcopal Cathedral in Knoxville, Tennessee. Eighty percent of their customers want a traditional, eleven-circuit Chartres design (a full-size one costs $112,000), but the Kermeens also create their own designs. Recently they made a trip to the abandoned and overgrown limestone quarry near Chartres where the cathedral's building blocks were cut at the turn of the thirteenth century and brought back boxes of stones to include in their projects. They make nothing portable, nothing on canvas, nothing that they believe won't outlive them.

One result of all this at times inspired commerce is that the labyrinth shopper has a surprising number of off-the-shelf choices. David Tolzmann claims that the two variables that usually define what gets picked are the available space and the size of the budget. Even so, the various makers offer a wide variety: many sizes of the eleven-circuit Chartres, of course, but also the Amiens octagon, the long-lost Reims image with its four-corner "bastions," the Ely square, and every imaginable change that can be rung on the classic Cretan design. Want a six-foot design for a nursery school or a mini-labyrinth based on just the center and the five inner rings of the Chartres design, or a *Reader's Digest* seven-circuit condensed model or a gaudy thirteen-foot number sewn from a rainbow of different colored materials? They're all available on different weights of canvas, nylon and parachute fabric and in sizes that range from twenty to forty feet.

The most widely adopted new labyrinth—and one of the first ever to be copyrighted—was designed by Lea Goode-Harris while she was a graduate student living in Santa Rosa, California. Called, logically enough, the Santa Rosa, it looks at first

glance like a miniature but uncluttered Chartres image. But it has only seven circuits, six labryses and an unusually large center where walkers can gather; and its path, in proportion to the size of the entire design, is slightly wider than most labyrinths', making it compatible for wheelchairs. Although her father used a wheelchair, that, Lea Goode-Harris says, was not its intent. The design was inspired, at first in a dream, by what she calls the "Divine Life Force" and was made practical through a combination of research into antique labyrinths and the seasoned advice of contemporary labyrinth workers from America and England. Whatever its source, the Santa Rosa has found a following by suggesting a grander design while being able to fit neatly into the space and budgetary restrictions of hundreds of crowded institutional basements and small gardens.

The matter of the path's width is typical of the problems faced in redesigning and streamlining the labyrinth. On a full-size forty-two-foot Chartres labyrinth, the path is about thirteen inches wide (13¹¹/₁₆ inches, according to Robert Ferré's measurements) and cannot be made much narrower on smaller designs. It can, however, be made wider to create a more open feeling and make two-way traffic on the lanes simpler. Some, Lauren Artress among them, feel that narrow pathways promote deeper personal introspection and encourage a focusing of the mind, while wider ones stimulate a more social, even communal feeling. Indeed, it might be said that a narrow path marks an introvert's labyrinth ("Strait is the gate and narrow is the way," says the Bible), while a wide path is the extrovert's. Others might argue that a narrow path causes intrusive congestion, while a wider one promotes smooth, mind-freeing traffic flow.

Robert Ferré's fascination with the labyrinth seems to be centered on what he would call its sacred geometry, the intersection of the correct measurements with the numbers' symbolic meaning. David Tolzmann seems intrigued by the problems of meeting the needs of a rapidly expanding market. Marty Kermeen has said that what he loves most about his complex stone structures is building them, particularly solving their construction problems. All are unabashed businessmen. It would be hard, however, to know how to define Alex Champion, another labyrinth designer, who is a true believer not embarrassed to use the seemingly contradictory words "magical" and "scientific" to describe what he builds. He has seen angels in them and felt waves of energy few can sense. And he has written numerous books and essays explaining the science behind what he does.

Champion has a Ph.D. in biochemistry from the University of California. In 1972, while he was still at Berkeley, he and a partner bought some land near Philo, in Mendocino County, with the hope of someday planting grapes and starting a vineyard. The vines never got planted. The partnership fell apart. Most of the land was sold off. After twenty years in academia and industry, he turned his back on the laboratory. But he had kept ten acres, and now the rolling hillside is dotted with a unique concentration of earthen labyrinths and mazes. It's a place that could probably exist nowhere else but northern California. Inland from the clapboard-quaint onetime fishing village of Mendocino, the Anderson Valley is in the heart of what's now the pinot noir region of the county's wine country. The hills still have a few low trees and are covered with daffodils and other wildflowers in the spring and are golden in the fall. At least "golden" is how the locals describe the burnt-brown groundcover. Charles Manson once lived down the long dirt road that leads to the main highway, and a Nobel Prize winner has a country place just down the hill from the house Champion and his wife, Joan, an artist, built.

Next to the prizewinner's barn, surrounded by a sagging redwood corral that's seen better days, is a deep-banked labyrinth built by Alex. It's based on a thousand-year-old Viking design, although probably only Champion himself would recognize that.

He discovered labyrinths not through chemistry but through his fascination with the ancient art of dowsing, a practice he calls "applied intuition." Everyone, he says, is familiar with hunches, intuition, an immediate "gut" reaction. Dowsers, he says, simply get to the source of those intuitions. Perhaps it would be more correct to say that he learned about labyrinths through dowsers, many of whom were amateur labyrinth makers. To this day, he will not begin construction on a labyrinth he has designed until he asks for permission from the earth where the image is to be built.

This is done with a dowsing rod, not the bent twig seen in cartoons but an L-shaped piece of heavy wire fit loosely into a tubular handle. Long ago, he established—by asking it—which direction the rod would point when it meant yes, which direction, no. Without any mumbo jumbo he simply asks if he can build (the question needn't be said aloud), and the rod turns. The answer is usually yes, but he has, he says, respected no when he's gotten it. His first labyrinth was one he cut with a lawn mower into the high grass. The first permanent one was a classic seven-circuit Cretan design—sixty-two feet across—carved into the earth just below the thirty-five-foot wooden water tower he built on the hilltop. It is still there, dug far deeper into the ground than any surviving British turf maze, with high mounds between extremely narrow paths. The walker is given every reason to feel he is cutting deeper into the earth as he travels along, every reason to feel he—or she—is moving through something older than Knossos. It is easy to see why Champion claims his earthworks are greatly influenced by the huge, coiling effigy of a snake left behind by ancient mound builders in a southern Ohio river valley.

Other labyrinths followed in Mendocino, including a double spiral (like two entwined snakes) that seems made for running rather than walking and a deeply sculptured, almost knotlike earthwork called a flower wand, 142 feet long, which a Veriditas facilitator would probably say was not a labyrinth at all. Or even a maze. Champion gave his own definition of a labyrinth to a group of volunteer labyrinth builders in Sacramento who were trying to cope with laying out one of his mathematically complex configurations. It went: "It's an easy path through a complex geometric symbol, filled with confusing elements in which there are added complications." The statement is something of a maze in itself, but the key words are "geometric symbol" and "added complications." He believes that the labyrinth itself is an energy force and that the complications increase that energy. He encourages his walkers to soak in the energy by sitting or lying on the earthworks. But not for too long. There can be energy overdoses.

Although there are no easy-to-do Alex Champion labyrinth kits for sale, he is a designer for hire and has created fifty or so original labyrinths or mazes or—as some may prefer to call them—earth sculptures since 1987. A few can be found in private gardens, including one—built on a steep Bay Area hillside—that makes liberal use of steps and stairs. Many are in parks, one next to Lake Merritt in Oakland, and an "earth maze" originally part of an outdoor art exhibition in Richmond is now on permanent display on the grounds of the Huntington Library in San Marino in southern California. But one of his best is the seventy-two-foot-wide Viking Horse Trappings Maze in the Nobel Prize winner's corral.

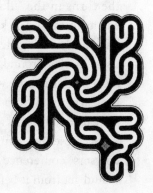

How it came to be built tells a lot about how Alex Champion works. In 1990, he became intrigued with an illustration in

Caerdroia, the British labyrinth magazine, of an abstract design found on a ceremonial Viking horse blanket. Made with thirty-six straight lines, the figure probably represented a horse to its creator. Horses have thirty-six ribs, and thirty-six seems to have been a sacred number, perhaps shorthand for 360, the days—more or less—in a Viking year. There is reason to believe, then, that the horse was a symbol for time, and at the image's center, at the core out of which the design grows, is a swastika. Long before the symbol was hijacked by the Nazis, swastikas appeared in cultures from India to the American Southwest. Its bent-arm, or "fly-foot" (to use an old term from the British Isles), form is basic to the design of the meander and, indeed, the labyrinth itself. Besides which, Champion believes it stands for the passing of time.

The numerology, the symbolism, the antiquity—it became a challenge he could not pass up. Using the thirty-six Viking "bones" as its skeleton, he created a labyrinth. But not a traditional one, of course. For one thing, the path reaches but never enters the center. For another, immediately upon entering, the walker must make a choice to go right or left (as is true in the Hopi mother and child birth labyrinth) and the way not taken becomes the way out. Champion says, "If you take a Cretan labyrinth and straighten out all the turns, you'll get a line. Take out the turns in the Viking maze and you'll get a circle. There's no end to it. You can keep going around forever." The two-and-a-half-foot-wide single path (rather than the two feet he usually uses) circles around a deep hole at the center that may recall ancient Celtic holy wells. The path comes to the hole's edge, the spot where the cross of the swastika would have been, then retreats and returns a total of four times.

He presented a full-size temporary version of the design at a dowsers' conference to see what sort of energy readings others would get from it before asking permission of the land in Mendocino County to begin work. Then he laid out the image, called together his volunteer diggers and—as he always does—said a prayer with them before cutting the often sharply curving path of the earthwork deep into the soil.

Although the individual labyrinth as an energy source has always been an end in itself for Champion, he has recently been promoting a project that is almost as ambitious as Lauren Artress's peppering campaign. One day, looking at an aerial photograph of his property, he realized that three of his labyrinths were in a straight line. This had not been planned, and it got him thinking of England's legendary ley lines, which some people believe are invisible but powerful straight paths of energy along which many ancient monuments appear to be aligned. About the same time, he discovered that his Mendocino labyrinths, the ancient snake effigy in Ohio and a fifty-five-foot nine-pointed labyrinth he had built in Missouri (based on the pavement Michelangelo put atop the Capitoline Hill in Rome) were all located along the same parallel: 39.1 degrees north latitude. And there were other long-established labyrinths there as well. This, he thought, could not be a coincidence. Why not build on this? Why not encourage the creation of a line of labyrinths, called the Art Line, that would run across the United States from the flower-wand earthwork near his water tower to the Atlantic shore of Delaware and southern New Jersey? It could even end with a mirror image of the Mendocino labyrinth, and a dedicated walker could go from coast to coast, moving from labyrinth to labyrinth the way the hero of John Cheever's short story "The Swimmer" swam across Westchester County by following a trail of swimming pools.

Champion, his wife and some fellow enthusiasts formed a committee, put up a Web site in 2000 and the following year presented a slide show on the Art Line at the gathering of the Labyrinth Society in Atlanta. In response came promises of new labyrinths as well as news of other existing ones along the route. Numbering about fifty, they reflect the variety of contemporary labyrinths and their builders. Marty Kermeen will build one of his stone-block installations in Maryland. In the fields outside Sibley, Missouri, is Toby Evans's idiosyncratic seven-circuit circular labyrinth built in 1995. It is huge, 166 feet in diameter, and since it is located in her husband's five-acre prairie-restoration project, the grass is cut into stands six feet tall in the spring. Every fall it is consumed by fire in a controlled burn. Although Evans, a former high school art teacher, believes that she once lived on the site in a former life as a Native American and saw—in a dream—her people's village burned to the ground by federal troops, there is nothing symbolic about the fire. It's all part of prudent prairie land management.

Two labyrinths along the Art Line, in Ohio and Indiana, are on university campuses, and in Manhattan, Kansas, a town made famous by the murders described in Truman Capote's *In Cold Blood*, a new installation has been promised by Jim Buchanan. Buchanan is a Scottish landscape architect who may hold the record for creating the world's biggest labyrinth. It's a three-acre classic seven-circuit Cretan design about four hundred feet wide, with walls at times five feet tall. He built it 1996 on a hilltop in Tapton Park in Chesterfield, in northern England, out of thirty-three hundred tons of landfill discarded from an adjoining munic-ipal building project. It is at once an efficient and economical way of, quite literally, disposing of a construction problem and creat-ing an eye-catching public artwork. A traditional British turf maze grown to monumental proportions, it is so large its com-plete design can be grasped only from hills on the other side of Chesterfield. But since glimpses of portions of its curving walls can be seen in various parts of town, Buchanan paid special atten-tion to the changing shadow patterns they would cast during the course of a day. Historically, the labyrinth image has been flat or low to the ground, but here there are true walls, and the look of the labyrinth as a three-dimensional physical presence became unusually important. Four trees were planted on it, along with thousands of different colored wildflowers: cornflowers and marigolds on the outer ring, with alternating inner rings of whites (daisies, yarrow, cow parsley) and blues (teasels and field scabiosa). But for all this carefully planned color consciousness, the labyrinth may be most popular for reasons totally unexpected. When it snows, as it sometimes does in Chesterfield, young sled riders fill its pathway, careening down and then up the sides of its steep banks.

Caerdroia, the magazine with the article on a Viking horse blanket that inspired Alex Champion, is edited and published in a village in southern England by Jeff Saward, a former industrial chemist who could pass as the retired drummer from a seventies rock band. He has probably amassed—and digested—more information on labyrinths and mazes than anyone else now writing or talking about the subject. His aim, quite simply, is to collect every scrap of information (true or false) that has surfaced over the past twenty years, to personally visit every known, rumored and newly discovered labyrinth site, and to draw and photograph the whole works. An unending project, the goal is to create the world's most complete labyrinth research archive. So far his research has filled two rooms of his and his wife Kimberly's house in Thundersley, but he has yet to make a catalog or index. "I know where everything is," he says. Indeed, in the past few years he has written two books of his own and his research, photographs and drawings have appeared in one way or another—even uncredited—in just about everything published on the subject.

He has also traveled extensively on the trail of obscure labyrinths, to arctic Russia, the American Southwest, Mediterranean Spain and into East Germany at a time when border guards found tales of turf mazes hard to believe. He went into the abandoned quarry near Chartres with Marty Kermeen and his reaction to the limestone used to make the cathedral's labyrinth was typically direct: "It's a weird, weird rock, full of little crystals. It looks like butter when you cut it and then turns a mellow orange."

His interest in labyrinths began when he was a college student attending an astronomy conference in Winchester. There he stumbled, quite literally, upon the turf maze on St. Catherine's Hill. He had never seen anything like it and was puzzled by the fact that there was no puzzle, just a single track leading— eventually—to the center. He began reading and searching for other such curiosities and in 1979, while working as a chemist for an oil company (a job he had for twenty-three years) he published a pamphlet guide to British turf mazes. To his surprise, the first printing of two hundred copies sold out almost immediately, and he began receiving letters with corrections and additional information. He printed them and sent copies to all the letter writers, about thirty of them. That was 1980 and the beginning of a newsletter he named with the Welsh word for labyrinths. In 1989 *Caerdroia* became an annual magazine, and it now has a subscriber list of about five hundred.

Since it is written largely by its readership, most of the familiar names in the labyrinth world contribute articles. There are also essays and photographs by Saward, color photo inserts and numerous line drawing and maps. Its collegial tone combines elements of both an academic journal and one of those chatty form letters old friends mail out at Christmastime. The magazine has made a singular contribution in introducing studies of Scandinavian labyrinths (and the research of John Kraft) to the English-speaking world. Saward is also an enthusiastic debunker of labyrinths that he feels are not what—or as old as—has been assumed. For example, two classic-style carvings in Rocky Valley, near Tintagel in Cornwall, are usually said to date from the Bronze Age, and have even been cited as evidence that ancient Cretan sailors reached the west coast of Britain. But an essay by Jeff's daughter Abegael argues convincingly that they date, at the earliest, from the late eighteenth century. Given less attention in the magazine is what has been called the New Age element, writers on meditation and healing, both physical and spiritual. Saward is interested in the labyrinth as a historical phenomenon. "My mission is to find and get out the information. If you have a theory about labyrinths, that's fine, but be sure you are playing with a full deck." Meaning a full deck of facts. If Lauren Artress can be called the modern labyrinth movement's spiritual godmother, Jeff Saward is its factual godfather.

The major labyrinth association, the Labyrinth Society, was organized in 1998 and is open to all enthusiasts, no matter how many cards in their individual decks. There are about 650 members, primarily—though not exclusively—American and more than half of them women. Once a year they hold a four-day gathering in an American city (Atlanta, Sacramento, Baltimore) and every now and then abroad (Glastonbury, most recently) to hear papers, build and walk temporary labyrinths and generally amuse themselves with others who know the difference between a labyrinth and a maze. The subjects of talks and workshops at a typical gathering range from theories on the origins of the labyrinth and possible derivations of the word *maze* to the use of labyrinths in the care of autistic children, fund-raising and grant-writing techniques, the "Black Virgin" of Chartres, dowsing, dance and the labyrinth, medieval geometry and labyrinths in hospital settings. It seems a most unlikely mixture of medievalists and massage therapists, but they all seem to respect one another—however tacitly—through their respect for what brought them together.

A subject that appears with increasing frequency at the gatherings involves labyrinths and traditional medicine. More and more hospitals and clinics seem to be adding labyrinths. David Tolzmann believes it is the major market of the future. Marty Kermeen has found that he is building a larger percentage of labyrinths at medical facilities, but he thinks this reflects a growing interest in a new area rather than a slacking off in more traditional sites, such as churches and schools. Robert Ferré estimates that there are now fifty to sixty medical labyrinths in America. The trend is away from portable canvas models to permanent installations, which suggests that after a period of probation, labyrinths are finding an increasingly committed acceptance. A possibly more cynical observer, with some experience in the field, suggests that some benefactors prefer paying for labyrinths rather than new MRI machines because they are "prettier and sexier" and far more obvious to the casual passerby. Victoria Stone, a designer-decorator who has installed a labyrinth at the California Pacific Medical Center in San Francisco, believes the appeal of a labyrinth for a secular institution is that it is "spiritual" without being "religious."

And they are being built and used. Both Stone and Tolzmann cite Dr. Herbert Benson of Harvard Medical School, who, although he doesn't mention the word *labyrinth*, does advocate the therapeutic value of what he calls "focused walking" in his book *Timeless Healing*. A volunteer involved in the building and maintenance of a labyrinth at the Westchester Medical Center in suburban New York recalls a major surprise. In the years before it was replaced by a rescue helicopter pad, the labyrinth proved to be most popular not with the patients or their families—as had been expected—but with the staff, not so much doctors and administrators as nurses, orderlies and others whose working hours are often long and grim.

Far outnumbering landscaped garden labyrinths at most hospitals is another kind of labyrinth. Lap-sized and carved out of wood, molded in plastic or simply printed on cloth or paper, these finger labyrinths are used by increasing numbers of bedridden or confined patients who follow the pathway manually. As the well-worn thirteenth-century labyrinth stone at the cathedral door in Lucca shows, it is a practice almost as old as walking the path, and in that repeated ritual, many have found a calming, if not a cure. With some, it is a form of meditation not unlike saying the rosary. Neal Harris, a psychotherapist who has employed labyrinths in many ways, even uses a dual finger labyrinth—two mirror-image labyrinths carved onto a single piece of wood—to begin some of his psychotherapy sessions. Moving at their own speed, analyst and patient face each other, the analyst tracing one pathway, the patient the other. Sometimes the exercise is done in silence; sometimes the analyst asks questions or proposes a subject to think about. As a practice, he has found, it improves the rapport between the two. If nothing else, it encourages a few moments of opening calm as patient and analyst go about their tasks.

Stories are told of seemingly miraculous cures taking place on labyrinths, people who suddenly no longer need their eyeglasses or arthritis patients who all at once start walking with a brisk pace. The question is asked: if the labyrinth is indeed a center of energy—as Alex Champion and all those dowsers say they can demonstrate—why shouldn't that energy heal? But the stories of the cures are almost always secondhand. Someone knows someone who heard about or saw the wonderful event. There is no evidence that could be called scientific. And the answer to the question is that there is a difference in meaning between the words *cure* and *heal*.

The subtitle of Melissa Gayle West's book *Exploring the Labyrinth* begins with the words *A Guide for Healing*. She is a psychotherapist and director of Harvest Hill Cancer Retreat in the state of Washington, and works almost exclusively with the critically ill. She calls the labyrinth "a powerful ally" and the "archetypal map for the healing journey." But she makes the distinction clear. A cure is an end to the illness or affliction, as though, perhaps, it had never happened. Healing is an inner matter, emotional, mental or spiritual, through which a person becomes whole. Curing, she says, is "purely mechanical," while healing is about "attending to the wellness and the entirety of a person with an illness." Healing can be reached no matter how ill the person remains physically. No one has kept count, but this search for wholeness, strength and peace rather than hope for a Lourdes-like cure has probably drawn an unusually large number of women with cancer to the labyrinth.

Lynn Fielder was diagnosed with Parkinson's disease when she was thirty years old. Parkinson's is a progressive degenerative disease in which certain brain cells cease to function. The cause is unknown, and there is no cure. But the symptoms—which include shaking and the refusal of the brain to order the body to perform such ordinary functions as walking—can be partially controlled by medication. Writing ten years after the original diagnoses, Fielder recalls that her first response to Parkinson's was denial, but she adds that walking a labyrinth helped her face up to the reality of her illness.

Since the onset of the disease, she had found it impossible to meditate. The disease simply would not let her sit still for it, but at the Golden Door, near Escondido, California, one of the first health spas in the country to use labyrinths, she walked a concrete replica of the Grace Cathedral design, and found that her brain's craving for movement could, for once, be used as an advantage. Walking the labyrinth one day, she writes, "I was struck by the observation that the twirls and turns of the labyrinth reminded me of the brain, my brain. If I was walking in my brain, I was wholly part of it and it was part of me. Thus my Parkinson's was part of me, not an external 'It' that had a separate life." It was a turning point in her being able to live with her disease. She could now accept Parkinson's as being "as much a part of me as my left arm."

While she was walking a labyrinth one afternoon her medication wore off, and she froze in place, her brain refusing to give the command to keep walking. But like a stutterer who knows he can sing effortlessly when it is impossible to speak, Lynn knows how to trick her body into activity—at least briefly—by running, walking backward or performing some other unexpected motion. That afternoon, she danced, first swinging her arms, then rotating her entire body as she whirled and followed the path to its end. At first, she recalls, she felt self-conscious; there were, after all, other walkers. But later she was told that her dance was an inspiration. "There was freedom and flight there," another walker said. She had freed herself and, however unwittingly, she had returned a health spa's concrete pavement to one of the labyrinth's earliest uses, a dancing floor.

Turning to the labyrinth is hardly a matter of passive submission. Dona Gallagher is a volunteer Christian chaplain in Gatesville, Texas, a town with six prisons and more than eight thousand convicts. In the year 2000 she decided her ministry could benefit from a labyrinth, and circumstances dictated the form it would take. It had to be portable and light enough for her to carry by herself, and since there was no budget, it had to cost next to nothing. So she bought three twelve-dollar rolls of black plastic ground cover, the kind gardeners use to keep weeds from growing, and with eight prisoners in the gym of the Mountain View women's unit (one of them Jewish, another Muslim) cut and sewed the sheets together. Consulting the section in Melissa West's book that tells how to make a labyrinth, they used plumber's chalk to draw the thirty-foot Chartres design (without the 112 lunations) and then, after some erasures and corrections, sprayed on the image with cans of yellow Wal-Mart paint. It all took about two months.

"The yellow's now a bit chipped from use and being folded up in the little black nylon suitcase I carry it in," Gallagher says, "but that just adds character. The plastic's so light that when you walk on it it billows like waves or the wind ahead of you. The pattern is always moving just a little bit."

She lays out her labyrinth from six to ten o'clock on Saturday mornings, and as many as thirty women have walked it at a time. Some of the women will be in prison for only a few years. Many are serving sentences that range from twenty-five years to life. Some walk for the full four hours. Some walk and sit and walk again. A few carry and read Bibles. "Silence is the most noticeable thing," she says. "Prisons are very noisy places. The warden has not been especially enthusiastic about all this, but he is impressed that we keep quiet for so long." She also gives the women paper finger labyrinths to take back to their cells, but she is not sure how much they are actually used.

Gallagher does not make inflated claims. One prisoner told her she walked the labyrinth thinking of her mother, who had just died, and felt that she had come to know her for the first time. She does not cite a catalog of dramatic breakthroughs. "The women come and walk," she says, "and for a few hours it is peaceful. The labyrinth is a wonderful metaphor. There are no rules, no dogma, but only one way. It's not magic, you know. It's just a tool, an instrument." And although she does not say the next words, it is difficult not to think of St. Francis of Assisi's prayer to be made an instrument of peace.

A very different group of volunteers built a very different labyrinth in New York City a year after the September 11 attack on the World Trade Center. Located in Battery Park, on the southern tip of Manhattan, it is a few steps from a Korean War memorial and the War of 1812 circular fort the National Park Service uses as a ticket office for ferries going to the Statue of Liberty and Ellis Island. The labyrinth is set in a grove of young cedars that was

Jerusalem's bicentennial gift to the City of New York, but the harbor is so close you can hear the wake of passing boats lap against the bulkhead. One of the cedar trees stands within the labyrinth. It faces the walker as he or she enters, blocking both the view ahead and of what is being entered. Indeed, to make the first turn into what is revealed to be a circular Cretan design, the walker must duck down a bit. A purist might point out that it is not truly classical. The path is a bit wider than usual. The center is a circle, not generally the case with this design, and it takes up more space than usual. As a labyrinth for a crowded city, the pathway is lined with recycled Belgian paving blocks (courtesy of the Parks Department). The path itself, made of clover, plantain and mugwort, all plants that have been used for healing purposes, is meant to be noticeably softer underfoot than a sidewalk or even the grass in the surrounding park. Only at the very end of the seven circuits of the way in, only when the walker comes to the end of the long back-and-forth sweeps of the pathway and makes a sharp right turn toward the center, does he or she look directly at the view the cedar tree blocked. It is the empty gap in the skyline that the World Trade Center, once only a few thousand feet away, had filled. The significance of what is not seen comes as a dramatic realization.

The labyrinth is sponsored by the Battery Conservancy, a citizens' group that oversees an increasingly crowded park. And there were restrictions governing its design and construction. All the work had to be done by neighborhood volunteers; all nonliving materials had to be recycled; all plants in the adjoining beds (artemisia, lavender, sage, rose hips) had to have traditional healing properties. Its architect—who codified most of these rules—is a young Scot, Ariane Burgess, who calls her one-woman labyrinth design firm Camino de Paz, road of peace.

The Battery Park labyrinth is elegantly understated and fits so unobtrusively into the landscape that some have complained that it is hard to find. Another of her classical Cretan labyrinths lies on the edge of Long Island Sound in the front yard of the Oaks, a nineteenth-century mansion in New Rochelle, New York. The mansion is now used as a healing center, and when Burgess set out to build her variation on a Scandinavian stone labyrinth she put out a call for volunteer workers and fifteen hundred stones. She got both.

The labyrinths that Burgess most likes to talk about, however, are anything but elegant. Since 1999 she has been building labyrinths in a largely Spanish-speaking section of Mott Haven, a neighborhood in the South Bronx that's probably better known for crime statistics and movies such as *Fort Apache, the Bronx*. Perhaps it's more correct to say that she has been encouraging the children of the neighborhood to help her build them—and walk them. She lays out labyrinths in such public places as a city playground, a community garden, a parochial school parking lot and the courtyard of a high-rise housing project. A typical recruitment went this way: a girl looking out of her apartment window saw Burgess and others working away, came downstairs to ask if they were building a crop circle (*Signs* was playing in the local theaters), stayed to help and came back the next time. Burgess's dream is a neighborhood full of labyrinths that would be both objects of local pride and something outsiders would want to come and see. To achieve this, she has had assistance from organizations as obvious as the New York City Parks Department and as unlikely as the U.S. Forestry Service, which is eager to raise its profile in the inner city.

Burgess was at work on her most quirky—and appealing— Mott Haven project at the same time as she was putting her mark on Battery Park. Located on the grounds of the George Hardy Houses, a church-administrated housing project, it is a five-circuit free-spirited variation on the Chartres design that looks as though it might have been drawn by a child. And its walls are made of sections of tree trunks, some full round, some cut in half. She got them from a tree service that was all too happy to dump a truckload at the project rather than haul them out of town. Her helpers ranged in age from an eager three-year-old named Jesse to a few thirteen-year-olds. Most were about nine or ten, and they carried the wood from the pile and placed it along the lines Burgess drew on the ground, some on end, some flat and look-ing—as one of the children said—like the spine of a giant dinosaur curling around the center. The logs in the center are on end and form natural seats where the children sit and talk about every-thing from the dinosaur to some mushrooms that sprang up in the path. Many of the walkers have also discovered that it is more fun to run along the top of the logs than to walk along in the some-times muddy ditch between them.

And that's just fine with Burgess. As the name of her one-woman company suggests, she indeed sees labyrinths as roads of peace, inner peace. But she also sees them as a "useful antidote" to always walking with a destination—this said by someone who gets around the city almost exclusively on foot or by bicycle. She built her first labyrinth in Scotland in 1995 after seeing a lavish picture book of garden mazes. It was in a forest near Edinburgh and was made with bricks from a fallen wall. She was also, she says, intrigued by labyrinths because of her name, which trans-lates to Ariadne in French. "I asked myself, what kind of a laby-rinth would Ariadne build? And I guess I am still finding out."

The popularity of labyrinths in the late 1990s saw the building of some that in their perfection border on the surreal. One in New Harmony, Indiana, the raw Wabash River village where Father Rapp built one of his hedge mazes, is now a picture-postcard model of historical preservation. Rapp's old maze has been reconstructed, although no one knows how the original looked, and there is also a dazzling outdoor reproduction of the Chartres Cathedral labyrinth, which a private foundation built after consulting Robert Ferré and his meticulous measurements of the original. It is rumored to have cost more than a quarter of a million dollars, making it one of the most expensive labyrinths in the world. It is an exact replica of Chartres's, except for the fact that it rises ever so slightly toward the center so rainwater will run off without puddling. It is also made of perfectly fit and polished granite rather than the "weird, weird rock" Jeff Saward saw in the Chartres quarry. The result is a smooth surface as slick and as tidy as a hockey rink after the Zamboni machine has done its job. The chipped yellow paint on Dona Gallagher's plastic ground cloth probably has more in common with the labyrinth on the worn and battered cathedral floor.

Another astonishing new labyrinth is behind an upmarket bed-and-breakfast in Sedona, Arizona. Sixty feet across, part Georgia O'Keeffe, part Salvador Dalí, it is a typical cobblestone-on-the-strand Scandinavian-Cretan labyrinth. Only the sand is the deep burnt red of the northern Arizona desert, the smoothly worn cobbles are rich tan river rocks and the sound in the air is the wind blowing over empty land and not the crash of waves. At the right time of day, in the cloudless desert light, it takes on a sharpness of focus that surely would have astonished those long-gone sailors on the Baltic Sea.

For every showpiece such as New Harmony's Cathedral Labyrinth, the peppering has produced dozens, maybe hundreds of more spontaneous manifestations. Dori and Chuck Bohntinsky's labyrinth is far too personal to be called typical, but the passion that has gone into its planning and creation is not uncommon. Their zeal, perhaps, is. The Bohntinskys live outside Hayward, California, in the hills east of San Francisco Bay, and built their eighty-four-foot interpretation of the Chartres design on a hillside between their house and the road. When they began they didn't know that it was more than twice the usual size or that labyrinths are usually flat and that their paths don't usually curve around trees blocking the way. Chuck, the director of training and development with a large investment company, and Dori (short for Dorothy), a former speech pathologist, had never seen—let alone walked—an actual labyrinth before they built their own.

It came out of grief. When their fourteen-year-old daughter, CJ, a high school freshman, died from an obscure leukemia-like disease in 2000, Dori went searching for a way to cope. She saw a labyrinth on the Internet and knew at once that she had to build one. "That," Dori says, "was before I knew labyrinths were like cats. You don't own them. You just feed them and learn from them."

The Bohntinskys had begun work on their hillside, with its little orchard of apricot, apple and plum trees, when a curious neighbor loaned them Lauren Artress's book. They later bought a copy and, using its drawings of labyrinths more as suggestions than plans, laid out a design with string, skirting trees when necessary. Their first attempt to create a pathway involved spreading ashes from their backyard barbecue pit. Dori says, "In the beginning it was my project and Chuck was just being helpful, but after we laid it out for the first time and he walked it, he became an equal partner, maybe more. The first thing he said was, 'We've got to get a rototiller.' "

Although they say work on it will never be done, two years later, the Bohntinskys had their labyrinth, CJ's memorial, the "tool" (it is the word Dori uses) that healed their grief. It is open seven days a week, twenty-four hours a day, not only for anyone in mourning but for anyone who wants to walk a labyrinth for any reason at all. "Kids always want to run on it," Dori says, "and their parents are always telling them to be careful. I tell them, 'Don't be careful. Use it any way you want.' That's what you do on a labyrinth, you find your way."

The two-foot-wide pathway is covered with shredded bark and moves from time to time up and down steps to adjust to the slope. The space between each circuit is a foot wide, ample room for daffodils, lavender, gladioluses, lemon-scented geraniums (which the local deer don't like), ornamental grasses and the bearded irises that pre-dated the labyrinth. The twelve-foot center, with its six raised-brick Chartres petals, is paved and holds a bench facing east, downhill toward the entrance, and small statues of a boy and girl placed there in memory of Dori's parents, both of whom died while the labyrinth was being built. Near the entrance to the pathway at the bottom of the hill is a full-size sculpture of a cougar, probably the only cougar on a labyrinth anywhere in the world. "CJ loved tigers," Dori says, "and cougars are a good California equivalent. Now I want to find a rabbit sculpture to put next to it and we'll have a California version of the lion and the lamb lying down together."

Not all of the mementos were placed by the builders. "People add things all the time," Dori says. "Stones they've brought, carved inscriptions, even a Power Rangers action figure and a few plastic angels. That's okay with us." Except from two upstairs windows, the Bohntinskys can't see the labyrinth from inside their house, but they can sit on a patio—on which they sometimes place a canvas seven-circuit labyrinth—and watch the walkers. "It's a good sight," Dori says. "Sometimes they wave, but there's no sense that they are visiting *us* or that they should come down and say hello. Every full moon we have a special night walk and there's a whole Labyrinth Day in October, but it's always open. Someday I would love to look up and see a big yellow school bus parked up there and dozens and dozens of kids running through it."

After sundown the Fairview Labyrinth, as they call it, is lit by a hundred solar lamps. "One night," Dori says, "we were sitting out there and I got to looking at all those lights. I said to Chuck, 'You know what? I think we've built one of those UFO landing pads.' He just laughed. Visitors sometimes ask, 'What's the catch?' There's no catch. Just a labyrinth. But maybe that's the catch."

Nine

THE PUZZLE

THERE WAS A TIME WHEN LONGLEAT HOUSE, in Wiltshire, was known for its fine Elizabethan architecture and well-preserved Capability Brown landscaping, its unique library of rare books, and a ghost who, like most ghosts in stately English mansions, was seen walking down a long hallway fairly regularly. Distinguished as all this was, it did not attract many visitors willing to plunk down what was then three shillings and a sixpence to see the place. Then Longleat's successive owners, the sixth marquess of Bath and his son, the seventh marquess, introduced two innovations that made the grand old estate a major tourist attraction: lions and mazes.

Lions came first, in 1966. Along with other African animals, they were installed by the sixth marquess well out of sight of the house itself, in what was called a safari park, the first outside of Africa. Ticket-holding visitors—warned constantly to keep their car windows closed—could drive through at a dignified pace and pretend they were in Kenya. The marquess's son, the current Lord Bath, added the mazes. By the end of the 1970s first one maze, then more, were built close to the great house. "People were spending five minutes in the garden and then leaving having seen it all," the marquess says. "We had to come up with something to keep them longer." Greg Bright, a maze designer, suggested planting the world's largest hedge maze, and Lord Bath said, "Why not?" He claims to have no particular interest in mazes and says he has never actually walked any of his from beginning to end. "Oh, I'll stand at the entrance to lure the tourists in," he says, "but that's about the end of it."

The official name of the 1978 maze is The World's Longest Hedge Maze, and although there have been rivals to the title since then—mazes from Wales to Japan—it is still, with 2.72 kilometers of pathway (about a mile and three-quarters), one of the longest. And just as the Empire State Building has remained a sentimental favorite decades after it ceased being the world's tallest building, the hedge maze at Longleat continues to command recognition. As designed by Greg Bright, with a long spiraling path it combines the unicursal labyrinth with the puzzle maze. More important, by including six bridges (which Lord Bath claims was his idea), it introduces a third dimension and a new level of intricacy. Paths can pass above and below each other without ever crossing. As for statistics (and anything that calls itself The World's Longest requires statistics): its dimensions are 360 by 175 feet, and it contains 160,000 English yew plants. A skillful, or just plain lucky, walker can get though it in an hour; most take more time, many much more time.

But it has its critics. In a *New Yorker* article taking notice of 1991 as the Year of the Maze (a celebration organized by the British tourism industry in honor of what it rather arbitrarily decided was the tricentenary of the Hampton Court maze), the novelist Julian Barnes asked England's best-known maze designer, Adrian Fisher, for an example of a "bad maze." Fisher cited The World's Longest. "It goes on for an hour and a half, and that's not funny," he was quoted as saying. "It doesn't vary its pace, and that's not funny. There's an utter contempt for the market," by which he seems to mean those ticket buyers Lord Bath tries to lure in. But funny or not, Longleat now has about half a million paying customers a year, a figure that has not been ignored by the owners of other stately homes.

The maze may not only have kept the tax man from Lord Bath's door; it also marked the beginning of the late-twentieth-century hedge-maze boom as lords of other manors began commissioning mazes. They had never become extinct, of course. There was always Hampton Court, and a few Victorian mazes were still in existence, such as the laurel maze at Glendurgan in Cornwall. Some new ones had even been built after World War II. At Chatsworth, the duke of Devonshire's estate, the grand old glass conservatory built by Joseph Paxton, architect of London's Crystal Palace of 1851 (and one of that innovative building's prototypes), had years before been torn down and replaced by two tennis courts. By 1962 they had become "unsatisfactory." To quote a member of the Chatsworth staff: "The heating pipes underneath gave way in places causing disruption to the game." The courts were ripped out and replaced by a five-ring circle-in-a-square maze of 1,209 four-year-old yews, with 257 yards of pathway, four entrances (only two of which will get you anywhere) and a single tree at the center. While the east and west entrances are shams, the route from the north entrance is about seventy yards longer than the southern route. The plan was drawn by

Dennis Fisher from an old design he is said to have found in the house's archives, which suggests the new maze might have been a reconstruction of a long-forgotten earlier one on the estate.

The result, with its six-foot-high, slim and curving walls of meticulously clipped yew, may well be the most austerely beautiful maze in England. But its creation was something of a fluke

reflecting a long-gone age. It was a private affair, not open to the public—at least not then. No one else, faulty plumbing under their tennis courts or not, was building mazes in the 1960s and after the stir caused by Lord Bath's marketing innovation in 1978, few new mazes would be built along the classic lines of Chatsworth or even Hampton Court. It is nicely ironic that the revival began at Longleat on grounds laid out by Capability Brown, the eighteenth-century architect renowned—or, in some circles, infamous—for destroying garden labyrinths and mazes to make way for what he believed was a more "natural" landscape.

Over the years the original Longleat maze has been joined by others that reflect the revolution in maze design. There's Graham Burgess's Labyrinth of Love, with yew and dwarf boxwood tracing out hearts and lips and other romantic images (Burgess himself is more than a bit coy about what else is actually depicted there), topped off with thirteen hundred rosebushes. Randoll Coate has provided a brace of mazes that sit side by side: the Sun Maze and the Lunar Labyrinth, with knotlike boxwood designs, pathways of both grass and gravel and patches of mosaic paving. The sun is bursting with symbolic flames and may even seem to be smiling. The moon is an austere crescent. A more recent addition is off in the stables in one of the former carriage houses. Designed by Adrian Fisher and called King Arthur's Mirror Maze, it is a high-tech reworking of an old-fashioned amusement park fun house. Using mirrors, optical devices, computer-generated images, a fog machine and sound effects, its path moves through scenes from the life of King Arthur (the Sword in the Stone, the Round Table and so on) much the way the Versailles labyrinth led its eighteenth-century strollers through the tales of Aesop.

With these new mazes, the simple—or perhaps not so simple—matter of getting to the center and out again is no longer the major interest. The game is in the increasingly complex route along the way, which may contain more riddles and secrets than the walker ever realizes. Indeed, at times the designer may be having a good deal more fun with his private jokes than the walker who passes through them. One of the most witty was designed for a private garden by Randoll Coate in 1975. It is the imprint—outlined in yew—of a giant foot sticking a toe into the Thames at Lechlade, near the uppermost point where the river is navigable. The toe is a tiny island connected to the almost sixty-three-yard-long footprint by a bridge. It is all meant to symbolize the imprint of man upon the earth and contains, we're told, hidden representations of the two sexes, the Trinity, the four elements, the five senses, not to mention the planets and the signs of the zodiac. Also included to entertain any children who might wander in are hidden images of Noah's Ark and thirty—or perhaps more—animals found in the English countryside.

An even more complex, if less humorous, example of this visual riddling was made a few years later for a Swedish baroness's estate at Varmland Saby, again by Randoll Coate. Entitled "Creation," it is in the shape of a fifty-five-by-forty-four-yard egg with a blazing sun as its yolk. Hidden away in the design of the pathways are Adam and Eve, the Tree of Knowledge, twenty-two animals, the Minotaur and Icarus venturing too close to the yolk-sun. Men and women enter the maze by separate entrances and follow different paths, which meet in one of Adam's ribs and then move on together into the Garden of Eden. And, again, the walkers have no idea that they are progressing through such ingeniously symbolic images or that almost all the numbers involved are multiples of eleven, which Coate says is "the cyclic number of the sun."

Complexity carried to enigmatic extremes is one hallmark of the new mazes.

The compulsion to make it into the *Guinness Book of World Records* is another. "The World's Largest Symbolic Hedge Maze" is at Blenheim Palace, in Oxfordshire, close by the spot where legend says Henry II hid his mistress in a maze. The Marlborough Maze, covering dozens of acres, reproduces a stone carving by Grinling Gibbons on the roof of the palace that celebrates the trophies of war. Passing birds and low-flying planes can see a gigantic still life composed of a big-wheeled cannon, pyramid piles of cannonballs, massed flags and military bugles all picked out in hedges. In its way, it is something of a bucolic English equivalent of Peru's Nasca lines, those giant desert images that mysteriously seem to display themselves only to the heavens.

"The World's Largest Brick Pavement Maze" is a giant Tudor rose composed of all or parts of some two hundred thousand bricks in the courtyard of Kentwell Hall, in Suffolk, a moated Elizabethan manor famous for its period brickwork that attracts tourists with reenactments of Tudor life. The symbolic rose maze, designed by Adrian Fisher, has an interesting genealogy. Clearly created for the domestic space it fills, it contains stylistic echoes of an earlier rose designed by Fisher—but never built— that was intended for a cathedral, St. Alban's in Hertfordshire, where it would have been a focus for Christian pilgrimages. The petals in the St. Alban's rose contained fifteen diamonds, symbolic of the Five Joyful, Five Sorrowful and Five Glorious Mysteries of the Gospels. To reach the center (which Fisher labeled "Salvation" on his St. Alban's drawing, reproduced in Hermann Kern's *Through the Labyrinth*), the pilgrim had to visit them all. This design, in turn, was probably inspired by a maze built by one of the visionary pioneers of the modern labyrinth movement, a country vicar in the Cotswolds. Canon Harry Cheales had a mystical dream in 1950 in which a figure, perhaps an angel, stood behind him and instructed him in considerable detail on how to build a religious maze in an overgrown section of his Wyck Rissington churchyard. And the priest did as he was told, creating a yew maze that owed little to Crete or Chartres and a good deal to the rosary and the fifteen Mysteries. Little signs were posted along the path that instructed the walker on how to proceed. At the point that symbolized death, for example, there was a note telling those who believed in an afterlife to take one fork in the path and those who didn't, another.

Sadly, Cheales's successor at Wyck Rissington destroyed the maze, but the church now has a wall mosaic designed by Fisher commemorating the canon's work by reproducing the original design. Fisher had met the canon when he was in his early twenties, about the time he designed his first maze, and he'd walked the labyrinth at Wyck Rissington several times. "It wasn't a pretty maze," Fisher says. "It would have never made it into one of today's garden magazines. But he was one of the holiest men I ever met."

Fisher insists that the plan for St. Alban's was not a first draft of the later design. It is, he says, an entirely different maze. The sacred mysteries do not appear in the petals of the Kentwell rose, but logos of Tudor achievements—such as the Age of Discovery—do. Patrick Phillips, the owner of Kentwell Hall, who commissioned the Tudor rose, has been quoted as saying that what you find in the center of most mazes isn't worth the trouble of getting there. The unusually spacious center of his maze, however, is different. There is no hint of salvation, but it does contain a chessboard large enough for live humans—in Tudor dress, of course—to stand in for the traditional chessmen.

As for the pathways, they are made in three colors of brick—gold, red and brown—which allows them to seemingly cross over and under one another in the style of an Elizabethan knot garden, creating something of a three-dimensional effect. And the walkers are given a choice. The design can be followed as one large puzzle maze or as five shorter unicursal labyrinths.

Another of the contenders for a World's Largest title has actually been around for a long time. Glastonbury Tor in Somerset rises so dramatically on the outskirts of Glastonbury that it almost looks like a child's drawing of a magical hill. It has the ruins of a fourteenth-century tower near its peak and a holy well called the Blood Spring at its foot. Some claim that from its banks they can see spread across the flat fields below a giant jigsaw puzzle of the zodiac. The hill's sides are circled with a narrow spiraling pathway cut into the slope on a series of small terraces. Some say they are cattle paths, some say farm plots (although there is no local medieval tradition of terrace farming), and some that they are the remains of a road dating to the Middle Ages that allowed oxcarts carrying building materials to reach the church site on the summit. And some say it is the winding path of an ancient maze dating back as far as the third millennium B.C., one so large it can take as much as three hours to climb to its center 550 feet above the plain. There was a time when the validity of the maze's existence was supported primarily by the same people who could see the zodiac pattern in the fields below. But in 1979 the respected but frequently controversial Arthurian scholar Geoffrey Ashe, who lived in Glastonbury, wrote an essay arguing that a maze, although perhaps a rather untidy one, was probably there. A map was also published that filled in the spaces where the path was difficult to follow or seemed to double back on itself, and at the International Gathering of the Labyrinth Society in 2002 hundreds walked it. When asked after the Gathering if there really was a Glastonbury Tor maze, Jeff Saward, the editor of *Caerdroia*, gave an answer that was both diplomatic and accurate: "There is now." And so perhaps it does deserve the title as the biggest of them all.

Three names keep turning up in reference to the maze boom: Adrian Fisher, Randoll Coate and Graham Burgess. Fisher was a marketing expert who had been touched as a young man by the example of Canon Cheales and built a maze in his father's garden. Coate was a designer fascinated by symbolism and the layering of symbols on top of one another. The two met in 1979 and later formed Minotour Designs, a rather loosely organized company that called itself "the only professional firm of maze designers in the world." They were joined in 1983 by Burgess, a landscape architect and expert on water lilies who had been associated with Kew Gardens. They went their separate ways at the end of the decade, but for a time it is more than a little tempting to think of the imaginative and inventive trio as the Monty Python's Flying Circus of the labyrinth world.

Besides the Minatour Designs already mentioned—"Imprint" (the giant footprint) and "Creation"—their mazes include the now-destroyed Beatles Maze in Liverpool (Queen Elizabeth II herself was photographed standing stone-faced in the conning tower of the Yellow Submarine at its center), an 1803 steam locomotive (the year is spelled out in hidden Roman numerals, MDCCCIII) in honor of the Lappa Valley Railway in Cornwall, a dragon for the Newquay zoo and an elliptical faux-eighteenth-century design (with a mosaic Gorgon's head at its center) to sit along a riverbank amid the real eighteenth-century architecture of Bath.

After the Minotaurs split up, Adrian Fisher emerged as the major maze maker of his age, the man who has probably built more mazes than anyone in history. The figure seems staggering, but he claims that every year, worldwide, in Europe, the Americas and Australia, three million people walk through an Adrian Fisher maze or labyrinth. And although he has created about twenty-five labyrinths, his heart is clearly in the maze, having built at least five hundred of them. He has said, "I design to tease people with the idea that maximum fun is just around the next corner." Literally, the next corner. He has also said, "I want people to solve the maze just before they've had enough." But only just.

For many years Fisher's company (ten or so employees: three designers besides Fisher, most of the rest in sales and marketing) operated out of Victoria Lodge, a nineteenth-century Portsmith villa with mazes on its wrought iron gates. In 2002, it moved to the country and a Georgian mansion on the Stour River in Dorset surrounded by seven acres just ripe for experimental mazes. Design work is done there almost exclusively on computers, with Fisher frequently consulting with Ed Pegg Jr., an American mathematician who lives in Champaign, Illinois. "I know the craft," Fisher says, "Ed knows the math, and together we can do what neither of us can do alone." Fisher has developed a seven-sided, two-inch-thick ceramic block and a system of combining it with compatible ceramic squares. With it, he says, "We can pave anything." Although there are still customers for pavement mazes in the West, such as a giant shopping mall in Atlanta, Georgia, the fastest-growing market is in private gardens in the Middle East. Fisher says there is a long tradition of both geometric designs and ceramic tiles, but mazes are seen as something new, even trendy.

The true boom market for Fisher's enterprises has been in corn mazes, temporary mazes cut into cornfields as tourist attractions. In 2001, he created eighteen of them. A year later, twenty-nine Fisher designs appeared in fields from Canada to Israel, where one was built on a kibbutz in the Elah Valley, on "the precise spot," Fisher says, where David slew Goliath. Its theme, like the theme of all Fisher maize mazes that year, was the American Southwest.

Fisher's imagination and marketing flair have led him in many directions. He invented color mazes, in which the secret of navigation is based on following different colored paths in a fixed color sequence. The puzzle is in figuring out the sequence. He has created Six-Minute Mazes, overgrown board games played on the floor in which, ideally, he says, the player spends two minutes looking the board over, two minutes in utter confusion bordering on despair and two solving it. He has invented a playing-card maze. He has built a maze of mirrors on a pier jutting into Lake Michigan in Chicago, another in China, and a maze of stepping-stones—and ambushing water jets—in a pond on the grounds of Hever Castle, in Kent. But not all of Fisher's designs are exotic. He still builds hedge mazes. Working with yew bushes is different from working with bricks or seven-sided ceramic tiles or even mirrors, in that time is a factor. Yews should be planted, Fisher says, before they are three feet high, and it will be at the very least three years before they are of a usable height. So for a maze in honor of courtly love commissioned by the Viscount de la Panouse for his château in the south of France for use in 2002, Fisher planted five thousand yew bushes in 1995.

The Hever Castle water maze sits close by the hedge maze William Waldorf Astor, who owned the castle, built there in 1905 to commemorate the spot where Henry VIII supposedly met Anne Boleyn. It was one of the first great traditional hedge mazes of the twentieth century. The yew maze Fisher designed to draw visitors to Leeds Castle—home of the world's only dog-collar museum—was one of the last. It opened in 1988, and in fact is not as traditional as it first seems. The hedge is not purely geometric but forms an image, maybe more than one. The outline of a royal crown is hidden in it, and John Martineau has suggested that the five circular paths and the two squarish ones stand for the week, with its five workdays and two free ones. As at the Villa Pisani, there is a stumpy tower at its center.

But the most important variation is the exit. Unlike the poor souls in *Three Men in a Boat*, the wanderer who gets to the center does not have to plot an escape. As with many Fisher mazes, the way out is much simpler than the way in. Beneath the tower are steps that bring the walker down into a domed mosaic grotto with an underground stream, giant grotesque heads, fantastical seashells and a secret passage that leads to daylight outside the maze. The reason for it may lie in the simple economics of crowd control in a tourist attraction, but by freeing customers from retracing their steps he has allowed the way in to be longer and more ingenious than was previously possible.

Prominently listed among Adrian Fisher's credits is usually a corn maze in Shippensburg, Pennsylvania, a depiction of Sir Francis Drake's *Golden Hinde* ("A ship for Shippensburg"), which was, at least in 1995, listed in *Guinness* as the world's largest corn maze. The man who brought Fisher to a Pennsylvania cornfield is Don Frantz, whose office, fittingly enough, is just off Times Square in a building full of theater producers and agents. A graduate of the Disney organization, he is a showman and he's proud of it. The idea for what is usually recognized as the world's first corn-maze tourist attraction came to him in 1991. The movie *Field of Dreams*, a couple of years before, had made the phrase "If you build it, they will come" part of the vernacular. The British tourist industry was promoting the Year of the Maze, and Don Frantz was a forty-year-old director of musical shows at Disneyland. It was also the year Lauren Artress moved those chairs in Chartres, although Frantz didn't know that then. As he tells it, he was flying from Los Angeles to New York, looking down on all the fields below, thinking of the Kevin Costner movie and British mazes when all the pieces came together. He immediately contacted his old school, Lebanon Valley College, in Pennsylvania, about setting a fund-raiser in a corn maze. And after a local farmer agreed to allow them to use three acres (they had to buy the corn at the going rate of $200 an acre), he began planning for the fall of 1992.

Even the project's now copyrighted name had its show-business roots. Frantz says, "I was having lunch with Stephen Sondheim early in 1992 and had just started telling him about building a maze in a cornfield when without missing a beat he interrupted and said I had to call it the Amazing Maize Maze. So, I did."

Frantz also contacted Adrian Fisher and asked him to design a dinosaur maze that would fill three acres. As Frantz tells it, what happened next was one of those turning points in the history of maze design. Fisher was interested, but said that a maze figure that large was just asking for trouble; the walkers would get bored and frustrated and might even begin attacking the maze itself and try to destroy it. (As, in fact, later happened in some corn mazes, Frantz says, although never at one of his.) Fisher suggested making the dinosaur a complex of three interconnecting mazes, but Frantz insisted on just one. "Americans like big things," he says. "They like adventure. I told Adrian to do the design and I'd find a way to amuse the customers." Maze walking would no longer be a solitary pursuit. Frantz sees the maze itself as the stage set for a much larger production, with music, props, actors and a story. As the concept developed through subsequent projects, walkers in his mazes were never truly alone. They are equipped with group flags (no two designs alike), and an employee with a loudspeaker stationed on the high exit bridge gives a running and always encouraging commentary on the movement of the various banners around the field. Just like a sporting event. A Maze Master high in a tower can be appealed to through strategically placed Talk Stalks (hollow plastic tubes) for riddlelike clues on how to reach the center. The entire network of paths is also color coded with ribbons running along the side that correspond to a color-coded map walkers carry, itself a jigsaw puzzle, the pieces of which are picked up at "mailboxes" placed at regular intervals. Something is always happening, and the walker is never allowed to feel truly lost. Or alone.

One of Frantz's assistants says, "You have to entertain them every three to five minutes." Her boss makes the same point by referring to what he says is one of Adrian Fisher's favorite sayings. Fisher, he says, compares the maze to a chess game between the designer and the walker in which the designer has already made all his moves and left. (Although when Fisher uses the chess conceit, he also says that it is the maze maker's responsibility to include all the means of his own—that is, the maze's—defeat.) Frantz says, "I've put life back into it. People don't want to be told how to solve the puzzle, but they enjoy riddles and games that move them in the right direction. No one, no matter how lost, wants to be given the solution to a maze, but they are happy to be given hints on how to figure it out for themselves." The Fisher-Frantz partnership lasted for about four years, and together they produced eight mazes.

The creation of a corn maze is more than simply cutting a pattern onto a cornfield. Field corn, sometimes called horse corn, is used because its stalks are taller and tougher than sweet corn, and the seed is planted both horizontally and vertically across the field to form a dense, natural grid. The computer design is also done on a grid and marked out on the field in lime. Pathways—nearly six feet wide—are cut before the plants are more than two feet tall. The schedule changes in different climates across the country, although the old Iowa saying that corn is "knee high by the Fourth of July" is rarely accurate. Planting usually takes place in April, the backbreaking job of cutting and pulling sometime in May. If the weather cooperates, the transfer of the design from computer screen to three-acre field can be accomplished in three days. Bridges (for a quick exit from the center) and other decorative features are then added for a late-July opening. Some maze builders have been accused of using herbicides to tidy up the lines. (Frantz says he does not.) And some employ the satellite Global Positioning System (GPS) to correct the giant images, while Frantz simply has his brother, who did aerial intelligence during the Vietnam War, analyze aerial photographs of the fields.

Over the years corn-maze designs have included a giant sun that also passed as the "World's Largest Sundial," numerous trains, a covered wagon (called a "cornestoga wagon"), spaceships, Henry Ford's first workable car, a portrait of Thomas Edison and scenes from both *Oklahoma!* and *The Wizard of Oz*. They are promoted as good family fun. Old people come to be on a farm again. Young families come to see what a farm is like. Companies—and at least one prison for juveniles—have booked special hours for leadership and creativity training. Most autumns find traffic reports in California warning of massive tie-ups on a freeway north of San Francisco that offers a spectacular view of a cornfield maze and pumpkin patch. Most corn mazes close for the season on Halloween.

Press coverage of these mazes comes in two forms. One has to do with the novelty of the application. The other is economic, telling how mazes have saved small family farms from financial ruin. The *Progressive Farmer* ran a story about a farmer in Tennessee making $100,000 from a ten-acre field that normally yielded a $2,000 crop, and he was still able to harvest the corn after the tourist season ended. Frantz recalls an Iowa banker who would grant a loan only if the farmer agreed to put in a maze. And there has been a good deal of notice of a farm in Paradise, Pennsylvania, that was said to pull in a million dollars a season. But not every story is a success story. Some farmers built it and no one—or at least not enough—came. Location is always important, and some mazes—as Fisher had warned—were either too boring, too complex or too simpleminded. Mazes can also be expensive. An Amazing Maize Maze with all the frills can cost the farmer $70,000 ($14,000 plus a commission on ticket sales goes to Frantz), and with the boom in maze construction they are no longer the novelty they were when the *Today* television show did annual gee-whiz-would-you-believe-a-maze-in-a-cornfield? features. In 1999—probably the high-water mark of the maize boom—they even had Frantz build a miniature version right in Rockefeller Center. Maybe the corn maze is no longer a news-worthy curiosity, but even with bridges, towers and built-in sound systems, they are the most ephemeral of mazes, here one month, gone the next, as insubstantial as a corn stalk.

In 2003, Alan Mart, who describes himself as "an artist and an organic farmer," worked with Charles M. McCulloch, a land-scape architect, to build a new variation on the corn maze near the shore of Tomales Bay, on Point Reyes in northern California. It was made of sunflowers, instead of corn, giant sunflowers ten or more feet tall with leaves a foot wide. And rather than being a maze, it was a labyrinth, a quirky redrawing of a classic Cretan design pinched and tucked to fit into an irregular 17,509-square-foot field in a corner of a local winery. A labyrinth with walls is almost unheard of, but the lack of a frustrating puzzle and the wide pathway made walkimg under the nodding sunflower heads more of an aesthetic experience than a challenge. Alan Mart, who successfully battled cancer the year before he built the unique labyrinth, sees it as a celebration.

A far different, but utterly original maze appeared in 1984 as the result of a newspaper competition. The contest, sponsored by the *Sunday Times* of London, was to find "the Great British Maze." Rules stipulated that the walkways must be made of brick and that there be no high walls on either side of them. What was asked for, in effect, was a modern variation on an old-fashioned English turf maze, one that transformed it into a puz-zle maze with all the usual dead ends. What is unusual for a maze is the absence of view-blocking walls. The walker is able to see far ahead and plan a route, just as someone looking at a printed puzzle maze can see—and avoid—obvious wrong turns. The winning entry, by Ian Leitch, came from Aberdeen, Scotland, with a design based on the shape of four rectangular farm gates lying flat on the ground.

Leitch's design was built in an open courtyard at the Breamore Countryside Museum, south of Salisbury, on the same estate as its turf cousin, the ancient hilltop Breamore Mizmaze. No shrubbery is planted along the pathways of the Great British Maze, of course, but at the center is a visual pun, a topiary sheep—a yew ewe.

Probably the most substantial maze of the late twentieth century is hidden away in upstate New York. Its designer, the British sculptor Michael Ayrton, describes it in his essay "The Making of a Maze":

> It lies in a cup in the Catskill Mountains of New York, and it is built of stone and brick—210,000 bricks. It is two hundred feet across, with seven "decision points" spaced through it. Its walls are eight feet high and at the centre of its 1,680 feet of coil there are two chambers: one is inhabited by the Minotaur in bronze, the other by Daedalus himself, who is at work on the making of a maze, and his winged son, who leaps upward to fly from the centre into the sky. They, too, are of bronze and their chamber is lined with bronze mirrors.

From the outside, approached by a dirt road that follows along a mountain stream through a pasture and into a woods, the maze resembles a large, grass-covered burial mound. It fills a forest clearing, and only on entering does the walker see that the mound is roofless and that the interior, with its befuddling choice of red-paved pathways, is made almost entirely of brick. As built, the walls actually rise from eight feet tall at the outside to ten feet at the center, and the maze contains a subtle clue to guide the attentive walker. The almost claustrophobically narrow path between the walls descends slightly as it moves closer to the center, as if saying, "Getting warmer, getting warmer," and uphill, again almost imperceptibly, as it moves away. ("Getting colder, getting colder.")

Ayrton was obsessed by Daedalus, although some might argue that his real obsession was the Minotaur. He retraced many of Daedalus's steps through the ancient world, duplicated some of his feats (such as casting a honeycomb in pure gold) and decorated a London restaurant, the Minotaur, entirely with his paintings and drawings of the monster. He also wrote an impressive novel, *The Maze Maker*, in which he dramatizes some of his conjectures about King Minos's maze and its meaning. He gives it a dual center ("two chambers separated by a maze within a maze") and adds that "these rooms were conceived as symbols of the juxtaposition of the sun and the moon. The maze between them took exactly as long to penetrate as the time when the sun and moon may be seen in the sky together on the day at the center of the year." As for the maze's coiling shape, it was inspired by ancient memories of primitive man's wonder at the entrails that spilled from slaughtered men and animals.

Soon after *The Maze Maker* was published in the United States in 1967, Ayrton received a request from Armand Erpf, a financier and magazine publisher, asking if he could re-create the maze on his estate in rural Arkville, New York. It seems to have been a challenge the sculptor had been preparing for all his life. It was completed in 1969, and when Michael Ayrton died in 1975, the Arkville maze design was reproduced on his gravestone in Hadstock, a village not far from the great turf labyrinth at Saffron

Walden. Although the maze itself
is rarely open to the public, a casting of the Minotaur in the moon
chamber at its center can be seen
near St. Paul's Cathedral in London,
dominating tiny Postman's Park, a
former churchyard where mailmen
used to rest.

A shady path made of black and white pebbles leads away from
the Arkville maze and farther into the woods. Along the way are
overgrown plinths topped by giant urns that would be equally at
home in either the formal gardens at Versailles or a picture book
by Edward Gorey. The path ends at the opening of a small
(twenty-six-foot) black-and-white stone version of the octagonal
labyrinth at St.-Quentin in France. Here, perhaps intended to
serve as a calming antidote to the terrors of the Minotaur's den, it
is called simply the Jerusalem Maze.

It was made at the request—perhaps even the insistence—
of Armand Erpf in 1970. Ayrton was not much interested in
cathedral-floor labyrinths, what he called the "Christian unicursal maze." Indeed, he probably found them a bit dull. In a speech
given at the Detroit Institute of the Arts, Ayrton described the
kind of maze he made, with its many opportunities for taking the
wrong turn, as having "the more ruthless view of chance and
necessity which was general before the birth of Christ." The
Christian labyrinth, while it may lead relentlessly to "redemp-
tion," is, he said, "without risk of error" and "leaves nothing to
chance." He never used the word *unadventurous*, but in context
he didn't have to. Eventually, his patron got the labyrinth he paid
for, but handsome and elegant as it is, it lies almost literally in
the shadow of its more dramatic neighbor.

Other late-twentieth-century mazes and labyrinths have been
less literal than Arkville's, but their creators, like Ayrton, were

usually artists, not professional builders. In 1970, in an alfalfa field in Whitewater, Wisconsin, Dennis Oppenheim used a laboratory rat maze as a model to build a six-hundred-by-one-thousand-foot maze of hay bales and then ran a herd of cows through it. The cows were in search of corn. The artist's stated purpose was to observe "the flow of bodies through an imposed structure" and "the transfer of food from outside to inside animals." The art critic Lucy Lippard saw it as "a kind of perversion" of the funeral games, the old Game of Troy, Virgil describes in *The Aeneid.* Twenty-three years later, in Los Angeles, Robert Irwin, commissioned to design the $8 million center garden of the new Getty Center, used a maze of three interconnecting circles as its focal point. But it is an inaccessible maze no one will ever walk on. The walls are masses of many different varieties of azaleas set into a gigantic metal planter (the garden's real maze), while its "pathways" are filled with the rushing water of a diverted stream. In 2001, on a level spot in the Wave Hill public garden high above the Hudson River in New York City, Willie Cole installed a pathless temporary maze. It was a square composed of rows of fifty white turnstiles inscribed with phrases—different ones on each blade—beginning with the words *everything* and *anything,* such as "Everything you always wanted" and "Anything that makes you blush." There were no marked paths, no routes, no dead ends, no center, but at each junction the walker had the opportunity of four phrases to choose from and follow to the next turnstile.

A curious boom-and-bust maze craze swept through Japan in the late 1980s, with more than two hundred wooden maze structures using wall panels rather than hedges being built and destroyed in less than five years. Competition and the stress of a time limit added pressure to the game, described frequently as a "frenzy." Walkers—more often than not—turned into runners as they rushed to find their way from tower to tower, crossing bridges as they went, getting their "passports" stamped at each new objective, and finding a way out before the time limits were up. The names and times of record breakers were kept posted as a further incentive. To frustrate the home-court advantage of frequent players, the wall panels were shifted from time to time to create new routes.

Several were built in the United States as tourist attractions. One went up in Pigeon Forge, Tennessee, but failed, perhaps not surprisingly, to find an audience there. Another, called the WOOZ, with four towers, six bridges crossing above the maze and a forty-minute time limit, survived briefly in Vacaville, California, where it was visited by Alex Champion in 1989. He writes in his book *Earth Mazes:* "I thought I could get a better view, by going up on those bridges, but the towers and the bridges themselves prevented [that]—a typical maze puzzle trick, a tempting but false shortcut." He and his wife escaped the WOOZ about an hour and a half later.

Jeff Saward has tracked down the history of the phenomenon. It was all the work of an Englishman named Stuart Landsborough, who grew up not far from Hampton Court Palace and settled in New Zealand. In 1973, he built a wood-paneled maze as a tourist attraction at the resort town of Wanaka, the idea being that panels would save the time and expense of hedges. The next few years taught him that a walker's patience usually gave out after about twenty minutes, but in 1982 he added bridges, giving him more use of the same space plus the sense of a third dimension, and then came the towers as an added diversion. He found that his customers were now good for forty minutes, maybe more. The mazes were copied in tourist towns all around New Zealand and Australia, and in 1985 he opened in Japan and found an audience beyond his wildest dreams. He kept designing ever more complex mazes with more bridges and towers. The crowds kept getting larger and larger until 1990 or '91, when suddenly everyone seemed to have had enough. The mazes' forty minutes were up.

Not all mazes can be walked through. The concept of the maze is at the heart of most video games. Dark quests such as Doom, Myst, Castle Wolfenstein and hundreds of other video games are based on the challenge of getting through a web of possibly disastrous choices and dead ends to reach a goal. And puzzle books and magazines have been staples of the publishing business for decades. Robert Abbott, creator of the ingenious Super Mazes (difficult puzzle mazes with built-in rules such as "No left turns"), traces these pen-and-paper mazes to the time of Charles Dodgson, the Oxford mathematician who wrote *Alice in Wonderland* as Lewis Carroll. Carroll included a maddeningly intricate maze, full of over- and underpasses, in *Mischmasch*, a magazine he produced between 1855 and 1862 to entertain his family. Both Abbott and Ed Pegg Jr., the mathematician who sometimes collaborates with Adrian Fisher, note even earlier roots in a vexing puzzle called "The Seven Bridges of Konigsberg." The problem is to cross the seven bridges on a route that takes you over each bridge only once. It is the puzzle world's equivalent of *The Mystery of Edwin Drood*, the murder mystery Charles Dickens began writing but never completed. The eighteenth-century mathematician Leonhard Euler explained why there was no solution to the bridge problem, but for centuries that has not stopped people from trying.

As for the maze of the future? It will probably change physically. Its topiary past will be—perhaps only temporarily—replaced by high-tech gadgetry. But the puzzle will remain at the core of its being. Jim Buchanan, the designer of the huge hilltop labyrinth in Chesterfield, describes himself as an "earth artist," but he has been experimenting not only with earth but also with mazes made solely of beams of light. Lord Bath, of Longleat, pictures making a three-dimensional maze something like a giant Swiss cheese, in which people would crawl through the holes,

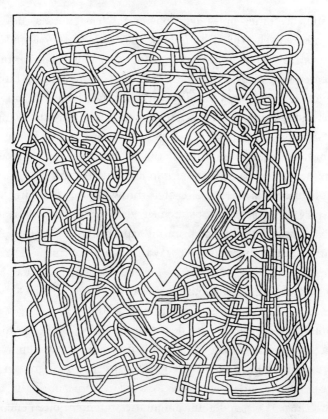

although, he admits, it might become a bit claustrophobic. And Don Frantz, always the showman, has been toying with the idea of a maze surrounded by bleachers filled with a paying audience. The field looks bare except for a few towers and perhaps a winding staircase. As in Willie Cole's maze, there are no marked paths. What the audience is watching are cautious walkers, who, like dogs inside an electronic invisible fence, wear devices that give a mild shock whenever they step outside paths that cannot be seen. The walkers' task is to find and navigate the invisible maze with as few shocks as possible. Or perhaps the future is the world's largest video game.

After all, the best-known modern mazes—the ones people who know little about mazes most often seem to mention when the subject comes up—never existed, at least not as they are remembered. The 1986 film *Labyrinth* is called either a Jim Henson or a David Bowie movie, depending on which faction of its dedicated following is doing the talking. For the Muppet crowd, the picture is Henson's, the director's. For the perhaps older Dungeons and Dragons generation, it's Bowie's, who plays the King of the Goblins. And perhaps there is even a minority who says it belongs to Terry Jones, late of the Monty Python troop, who wrote it. Part *Alice in Wonderland* and part *Wizard of Oz*, with bits of Cinderella and M. C. Escher thrown in for seasoning, it is the story of a conscientious teenage girl who sets out to rescue her baby brother, who has been kidnapped by the Goblins. And finding him means finding her way through a labyrinth—actually a maze—built over the Bog of Eternal Stench. In actual fact, only part of a maze was built—about fifty yards square—at the Pinewood film studio in London, and made to look larger and complete by optical devices designed by Terry Pope. The film's often self-mocking sense of humor is no doubt one reason for its near-cultlike following. At one point a threatening figure in the maze tells the girl, "The way forward is sometimes the way back," the sort of ponderous, enigmatic statement often encountered in labyrinth literature. But here, in this Muppetish world, the sage comment is followed by gales of laughter.

The century's most famous movie maze, however, is no laughing matter. It is the thirteen-foot-tall hedge maze at the Overlook Hotel in Stanley Kubrick's 1980 film *The Shining*, and it, too, is a sound-stage illusion. The movie follows the crack-up of Jack Torrance, an alcoholic, unsuccessful writer, who has signed on, with his family, as winter caretaker of a huge summer hotel. No one forgets the film's climax, the crazed, ax-wielding Torrance (Jack Nicholson, of course) chasing his young son at night through the frozen dead ends of the empty hotel's snow-filled maze. The exterior views of the Overlook were shot in Colorado, according to film historian Thomas Allen Nelson, but the maze—and not a complete maze at that—was built indoors at the Elstree Studios in London. The original screenplay, Nelson says, the one Kubrick and Diane Johnson based on Stephen King's novel (which has no maze), called for a set a hundred yards long. It ended up being much smaller, although, in fact, three mazes appear in the film. Early on, while it is still fall, Torrance's wife and son walk into a sunny hedge maze, passing as they go a signboard with a map— shown very briefly—of what looks like a fairly simple maze. Inside the hotel, Torrance looks at a model of a maze far more complex than the map and has a vision, a "shining," of his wife and son wandering the pathways. The mazes, then, are the "real" one, the map and the model.

In his book *Kubrick: Inside a Film Artist's Maze*, Nelson goes to great lengths to show that the sprawling hotel, with its meander-design hall carpeting, is indeed itself a maze. Just as some geography-minded critics have mapped the Dublin of James Joyce's *Ulysses* to show it is a maze for the novel's Stephen Dedalus to walk and escape, Nelson maps the labyrinthine Overlook to chart Torrance's erratic path to destruction. The exercise may be distinctly academic (Nelson is a professor of English at San Diego State University), but it displays an understanding of the maze that some members of the Labyrinth Society lack: the maze is a learning experience. Anyone in the maze who does not learn from his mistakes is doomed.

To say there is animosity between labyrinth people and maze people is to overstate the situation, but it is safe to say that most people who devote themselves to the labyrinth simply do not take the maze seriously. The labyrinth is seen as the serious, even saintly form, and the maze the buffoon. The public's confusion about the meaning of the words is irksome, and indeed the Labyrinth Society has an organized campaign to get dictionary writers and publishers to stop listing them as synonyms, even though throughout most of their history the words have indeed been just that. The most damning thing a labyrinth devotee can say about an innovative design (and Alex Champion has heard it more than once) is that it is only a maze. Only.

The title character in Vladimir Nabokov's comic novel *Pnin* argues that Salvador Dalí and Norman Rockwell were born twins, but Dalí had been kidnapped by Gypsies. Something similarly irreverent can be said about labyrinths and mazes. They are both attempts at coping with chaos, but the older, unicursal labyrinth went to church and found the way through faith, by believing that the way—no matter how seemingly devious—will reach its goal. The maze, although it perhaps fell in with a bad crowd, is an antic and sometimes frightening celebration of learning and memory. The way may be marred by false starts and dead ends, but the walker can learn from those mistakes and triumph. The labyrinth may be a way to inner peace, quiet and understanding, while the maze delights in conquering puzzlement. And here is something to consider: by choosing one form over the other, are we taking sides on that old theological question of whether we are saved by faith or by works?

Like Rodney Dangerfield, the maze all too often gets no respect, but over the centuries it has given a lot of people a lot of fun. And it may not be as frivolous as it seems.

Ten

THE GOAL

FOX AND GEESE, AS CHILDREN CALL IT, is a winter game that may still be played in some sections of rural North America. It requires space and snow, and the more players the better. But the game has never had an instruction manual or a governing body, and in every case local rules apply. It is always played on a home field. After a heavy snowfall boys and girls spend a good deal of time tramping out what they call a maze with long spirals, lots of twists and turns and dead ends where a fox can trap a hapless goose. There is no set pattern to what they are making, just whatever comes to mind, and the field changes with every new snow. Frequently the game never gets much beyond making the maze (with its accompanying snowball fights), but if it begins, Fox and Geese is like nothing so much as arctic tag. There is one fox, and all the rest are geese that flee along the beaten pathways. And everyone, of course, wants to be the fox. Much like Michael Ayrton's Arkville maze, there are two centers, although they are rarely in the center. One is the fox's den, where captured geese are taken to await being eaten up, and there is the nest, where geese are safe from fox attacks. The geese held in the den can all be freed by any brave or wily goose who outwits the fox and makes it there without being caught.

The family of Mary Jane DeWeese—now a Washington, D.C., lawyer—moved to a rural community outside of Rochester, New York, in the 1970s, and she remembers how she and her brothers were taught Fox and Geese by a local farm family that had been playing it for at least three generations. "It was a very fast game with lots of running," she recalls, "but the person who won was usually the one with the best memory of what paths went where." And when the snow was deep enough, she could crouch down close to the ground and disappear. "It was all white on white and the fox couldn't see a thing." Over the course of a long winter—if there were no major thaws and if everyone didn't become bored with the whole thing—the maze could be expanded until it filled an entire pasture. "The best ones took up acres and acres," DeWeese says. "And you could make spirals off somewhere no one else knew about."

The game of Fox and Geese dramatizes the ancient mystery of the labyrinth with its wandering path to salvation or, at least, to rest. It can be read as a parable, the fox being either the rapacious devil or—in the words of Francis Thompson—the Hound of Heaven pursuing the reluctant believer "down the nights and down the days . . . down the aches of the years . . . down the labyrinthine ways." What is contrary to the spirit of the labyrinth is the chaos of the snowy pathway, its lack of order. Traditionally labyrinths and most mazes, too, have been notable for their "fearful symmetry"—to use the words of another poet. Writing in a different context, the contemporary labyrinth philosopher Sig Lonegren has said, "Labyrinths are, if nothing else, mirrors." Mary Watts, explaining the iconography of her chapel, quoted from the Apocrypha: "All things are double, one against another." Throughout most of its long history one side of the labyrinth has pretty much reflected the other, a perfectly balanced geometric shape. The form with, ironically, a name that has come to become a synonym for confusion and perplexity is in truth a model of perfect order.

The medieval devotion to sacred geometry has been given a lot of credit for this. The world was thought to be have born out of "harmony, heavenly harmony" and, in Saint Augustine's much quoted words, "God made the world in measure, number and weight"—words he found in the Apocrypha, in The Wisdom of Solomon. And wasn't Solomon a man well acquainted with geometry? God was the master mathematician, and all numbers and measurements reflected this and were taken very seriously indeed. At Chartres, as we have seen, numerical and geometric symbolism is all pervasive. The number four and the square are emblematic of mankind and earthly matters. Three and the circle are divine. Combinations of three and four (by addition seven, by multiplication twelve) linking man with his God are the most profound. The labyrinth's circuits number eleven (indicating sinfulness), but with the circle in the center—achieved by reaching the goal—there are twelve rings, the jubilant number of Apostles, months, tribes of Israel, zodiac signs and countless other good things. And the proportions, as indicated in the measurements of Robert Ferré, are full of threes and fours. The center is one-quarter the width of the entire labyrinth. The circles formed by each petal in the center are one-third the diameter of the center. The path width is one-third the diameter of the petals. The lunation teeth on the outer circle are spaced the same distance apart as the width of the path. There are 112 lunation teeth, four twenty-eight-day months on the lunar calendar. And so it goes, everything relentlessly in order.

But this tidiness was not a Christian innovation. Although inexactly drawn, the earliest labyrinths scrawled on tomb walls are just as symmetrical, as are the Knossos coins, the Roman floors, the Pompeii graffiti, the Hopi *tapu'at*, the Mysore *chakra vyuha* and the garden maze at Hampton Court. In one of the earliest eyewitness descriptions of something called a labyrinth, the ancient Greek geographer Strabo noticed that what seems confusing on ground level makes a good deal more sense when looked down on from above.

To Tony Phillips, a modern mathematician with a special interest in mazes, the geometry is not divine at all. The classic Cretan labyrinth is just a simple alternating transit maze—an S.A.T., for short. A transit maze, in his definition, is one that moves—makes the transit—from the outside to the center without branching. Alternating means that at each new circuit, or level, the path reverses direction. The classic Cretan maze is simple because the walker is on each circuit only one time in the course of transiting from the outside in. (The Cretan path sequence of circuits, numbering from the outside in, is 3, 2, 1, 4, 7, 6, 5, 8.) The great arcs sweep uninterrupted from one side of the labyrinth to the other. The Chartres design is not so simple because the image is divided into quarters and there are four places where reversing turns can take place. This means that the walker moving from the outside in is required to visit each circuit not once but four times. Yet, simple or not, the geometric balance is always maintained.

Labyrinth images, as shorthand symbols for doubt and confusion, are so elegant and simple that they attract imitations. But not exact ones. The labyrinth purists' frequent complaints that this or that image is not a *true* labyrinth may become tedious, but they have a lot to complain about. The conception of mazes and labyrinths as tidy symbols of chaos is so appealing that misidentifications are commonplace. That the form attracts so many impostors—no matter how unwitting—is in itself worth noting. At its most mundane a cab driver battling through traffic and a network of one-way streets to reach a midtown train station complains that the city is a maze. But a distinguished scholar can also believe he is seeing archetypal medieval European labyrinths in the spirals decorating a South Pacific tomb. Major companies spend fortunes in legal fees to keep their brand names—such as Scotch Tape, Xerox or Animal Crackers—from going generic, losing their uppercase status and becoming accepted terms for any product resembling theirs. Labyrinths—and mazes, too—have in effect gone generic. Their concept of order in chaos gives comfort. If you call something a maze you can feel reassured that hidden somewhere within it is indeed a solution. Hope for a solution is implied, and—after all—we all live in hope.

Knot gardens, as we've seen, are frequently called labyrinths, as are many garden plantings. Indeed, just about anything in a garden that hints of pathways is called a labyrinth, such as the flower beds laid out in concentric circles that were so popular in the early nineteenth century. A well-preserved one with a magnolia tree growing in its center, probably dating from the 1840s, is in the front yard of Rowan Oak, William Faulkner's house in Oxford, Mississippi. According to a local story, the "labyrinth" was overgrown when the Faulkners bought the place during the first flush of the author's success. Mrs. Faulkner wanted her husband to tidy it up, but he refused, saying, "Only new money would ruin that garden."

Simple spirals are frequently seen as labyrinths, too. The contemporary American sculptor Richard Serra has created giant metalworks often described—but not by him—as labyrinths. His 2003 *Blind Spot* is a weathered steel wall thirteen feet high that makes three circuits turning inward to reach the center. The spiral, however, is pinched together to make four sharp, reversing turns. The naturally oxidized walls curve slightly at the top, creating an illusion. With each turn, the walls above seem to lean in a different direction. The entire work measures fifty-four by thirty-two feet, and at its inaugural exhibit in a warehouse-sized Manhattan art gallery, the more timorous visitors clustered at the sculpture's narrow entrance, afraid to follow the path between the towering walls.

The typical Ye Olde Maze with portable canvas walls found at Renaissance Fairs around the country is not a maze at all but simply a many-forked warren of paths—not unlike Fox and Geese— that leads from an entrance on one side of the ticket booth to an exit on the other. The same is true of a good many homemade cornfield mazes. Crop circles, those geometric designs that have

appeared—perhaps not so mysteriously—in farm fields all over
the world have also been confused with labyrinths. In fact, even
as hoaxes their designs owe much more to knot gardens and so-
called hex signs, which used to be painted on barns for protec-
tion, than to labyrinths.

Many anthropologists would argue that there is no confusion
and no coincidence. Something, perhaps something innate, causes
a nineteenth-century German immigrant farmer in eastern Pennsylvania, an ancient Roman and a Tamil woman in southern India
all to place vaguely similar geometric symbols near their doors
to ward off threats they cannot explain. There is a similarity in
the basic elements of primitive design—the spirals, concentric
circles, dots and zigzags—that seem to be a sign of common hu-
manity. It allows Joseph Campbell to find universal symbols on a
tomb in the New Hebrides Islands, northeast of Australia, and
see designs that—without having pathways or entrances—still
resemble labyrinths at Chartres, Reims (with its "bastion" corners) and Saffron Walden. He describes them as symbols of the
"Journey of the Dead." They also resemble the knotlike carvings
on Celtic crosses, the geometric margin fillers in *The Book of
Kells*, Islamic ceramic tiles and those Tamil doorstep *chakras*. A
thousand years ago in the Caribbean, the now long-gone Taino
culture had clay disks about the size of modern silver dollars
deeply engraved with designs of interrupted concentric circles
that may have been used as ink stamps to apply temporary body
tattoos. All of these reflect the idea of the labyrinth more than
they do the labyrinth itself. Are they, too, pathways of the dead?

Carl Jung found a similar common denominator in the mandala, another image that gets confused with the labyrinth. *Mandala* simply means "circle" in Sanskrit, although the word has
taken on religious and spiritual connotations that could be called
iconic. A circle, often divided into quarters with a dominant figure
in the center, is a familiar art form in Tibetan Buddhism and is a

common sight in Tibet, Nepal, Bhutan and northern India. Very similar circular images—including spirals, snakes and concentric circles—are also found in such diverse settings as scared Navajo sand paintings, the art of such mystics as the twelfth-century Hildegard of Bingen and the nineteenth-century Hilma af Klint and the so-called spirit drawings of the utopian Shakers. The circular, whirling dances of Turkish dervishes can be seen as manifestations of the mandala, as have—pushing the limits a bit—some stained-glass rose windows in Christian churches. Jung had some of his patients—usually schizophrenics—draw mandalas as part of their therapy, and he drew them himself. Studying the images, he saw patterns as old, or older, than human thought, something that seemed to spring from what he called a "collective unconscious" that all mankind shares. The question is, what does it all mean?

Finding similarities among labyrinths, especially the medieval Christian labyrinths, and mandalas is not difficult. They spring at you: the circle itself, the spirals (what is a labyrinth but a combination of a circle and a spiral?), the eye-catching center goal (round or octagonal), the division of the perfect circle into mundane quarters, as though seeking a human quality in the divine. Jung writes:

> We are driven to the conclusion that there must be a transconscious disposition in every individual which is able to produce the same or very similar symbols at all times and at all places. . . . Knowledge of the common origin of these unconsciously performed symbols has been totally lost to us. In order to recover it, we must read old texts and investigate old cultures.

Jung would have us do our homework.

But much of the continuing and immediate appeal of the labyrinth is that it does not require a study of old texts and customs. Its complexity is indeed very simple. It is as basic as a path, and paths were probably one of the earliest marks man made upon the face of the earth. Its design is one of mankind's earliest original artistic creations, a shape not copied from a world anyone saw, not a circle or a square or a zigzag, but an act of the imagination. The walker follows a path utterly unadorned with any image that requires study in ancient texts.

It can be made to seem difficult. Patrick Conty has tried to prove that the basis of the labyrinth is rooted solidly in the same principles as quantum physics. He sees parallels between Ariadne's string and the string theory of physics, the chapter on string theories in Stephen Hawking's *A Brief History of Time* being the point where most of his readers realized they hadn't the slightest idea what Hawking was writing about. But Conty also offers a far simpler explanation. He quotes Chogyam Trungpa, described as a tantric master, who answered the question, "What is a labyrinth?" by saying, "A divine doodle."

That's a cute line, good for a chuckle if not a belly laugh, but it is all wrong. There is nothing divine about it. A labyrinth may be the journey through life, the journey to a holy city either in this world or the world to come. It may follow the whirls of the brain, or the intestines or the birth canal. It may be a system for understanding the calendar. It may be a dance or the signature of master architect. It may be the footprint of a city, that most human of creations. In *The Cable Guy*, the title character played by Jim Carrey even says, "Women are a labyrinth, my friend." Whatever its form, the labyrinth is always utterly human. And if it is a prayer, what could be more human than that? Gods don't pray.

Joseph Campbell, in *The Mythic Image*, interprets labyrinths on megalithic tombs as depictions of the journey that takes place after death. Perhaps he is right. He points to journeys of the soul painted on the walls and ceilings of Egyptian tombs as supporting evidence. Marguerite Young imagined the grotto in the center of the New Harmony labyrinth and saw "a house of wished-for death." Few people in the twentieth century spent more time thinking about labyrinths than the sculptor Michael Ayrton. He drew them, painted them, wrote about them and even built a great maze in a forest. He wrote, "Each man's life is a labyrinth at the center of which is his death." But for many more observers what's depicted is the journey through life, not the journey thereafter. The goal may be death, but the path to it is life itself.

In spite of the labyrinth's very early appearance on a few tombs and some anthropologists' fixation on myths of an afterlife, labyrinths and mazes have traditionally been the property of the living, not the dead. They are in the people's part of the cathedrals, not the priests'. The miracles of the altar were elsewhere, far off but within sight. And labyrinths are venues (or "tools," to use Lauren Artress's word) for doing something, be it seeking peace or winning a race or seducing a stranger. They are fields of action where even quiet contemplation and meditation are accomplished with the rhythmic movement of a slow dance.

"Doing something" is a basic human need. People terrified of sitting alone in a darkened sanctuary find they can walk a labyrinth. Much the same desire to do something that filled Red Cross blood banks in the days after the destruction of the World Trade Center also drew people to labyrinths. A volunteer at St. John's Cathedral in Knoxville, Tennessee, where Marty Kermeen had built an outdoor labyrinth, described the day. A conference of Episcopal women was taking place when word came of what had happened in Manhattan, the Pentagon and in the air over western Pennsylvania.

"It was the most amazing thing I have ever witnessed," she wrote.

The [conference] participants, most of whom had never seen a labyrinth, seemed mesmerized by it. As the ladies slowly began their walk, people from the street passing by came in and joined them. The meetings dissolved, the workday dissolved, classes dissolved, overcome by the need to try to make sense out of what was senseless. This continued throughout the day, collars and business suits, ripped jeans and barefoot, age, color, gender, religion all came to this touchstone, trying to find some healing, swaying, touching, being touched.

They walked.

The same scene, with the same lines trailing down sidewalks and around the block, was played out at labyrinths throughout the country. In Trinity churchyard, within sight of the Trade Center ruins, a labyrinth designed by David Tolzmann was cleared of inches of ash and debris as soon as people were allowed back into the area. And just a few dozen yards from the grave of Alexander Hamilton, as rising smoke still polluted the air, neighborhood workers on their lunch hours began following the ancient path as it had been painted on a now deeply stained sheet of canvas. It was something to do, something besides looking at the empty space in the skyline.

On the wooden ceiling of a room in the fifteenth-century section of the ducal palace in Mantua is a square Roman-style labyrinth that is unusual for the text that is repeated over and over again along its pathway: *Forse che sì, forse che no*. Maybe yes, maybe no. Gabriele D'Annunzio used the phrase as the title for a novel set in the palace. Some think the image and the words have something to do with the captivity of one of the dukes at the hands of the Turks, or perhaps they represent the thoughts of another duke while deciding whether to make a strategically necessary retreat in an important battle. Or perhaps it is all simply an architectural equivalent of pulling petals from a daisy and saying, "Loves me. Loves me not." The phrase is repeated in its entirety, *Forse che sì, forse che no*, ten times before it reaches the center, and then, with a final *Forse che sì*, it enters the goal. Labyrinths are rarely given words to speak, but like Molly Bloom's closing words in another unconventional labyrinth, James Joyce's *Ulysses*, it ends by proclaiming a life-affirming *Yes*. And perhaps that is the silent message of all labyrinths.

APPENDIX: HOW TO DRAW A LABYRINTH

HOW TO DRAW CRETAN LABYRINTHS

FIRST PUT DOWN ON A SHEET OF PAPER what's called the Seed Pattern: a cross with equal-length arms, four dots and as many L-shaped angles as needed. Then, moving either clockwise or counterclockwise around the Seed Pattern, connect the dots and lines with curved lines as shown in the diagrams below.

THE SIMPLEST POSSIBLE LABYRINTH:

THE CLASSIC SEVEN-CIRCUIT LABYRINTH:

ACKNOWLEDGMENTS

Few authors begin a book knowing everything that will appear in its pages. I, certainly, am not one of them. For me, writing this book has been a learning process. I have had many excellent, provocative and astonishingly generous teachers and am probably even more indebted to them than I realize. Members of the Labyrinth Society have been more than willing to talk about their favorite subject. I would especially like to thank Alex and Joan Champion and Jeff and Kimberly Saward. The Champions' hillside in Mendocino County, California, should be preserved as a national labyrinth landmark. Visiting labyrinth sites in Britain with the Sawards was both eye-opening and just plain fun.

No one could write about labyrinths today without several invaluable publications, including the pioneering *Mazes and Labyrinths* by W. H. Matthews, the encyclopedic *Through the Labyrinth* by Hermann Kern and the annual issues of *Caerdroia: The Journal of Mazes and Labyrinths* (53 Thundersley Grove, Essex SS7 3EB, United Kingdom). I also found Nigel Pennick's sometimes quirky *Mazes and Labyrinths* especially informative. A complete bibliography of consulted books and articles appears on page 239.

The following people responded to my perhaps annoying questions, made suggestions that sent me off in one direction or another or were otherwise more helpful than they had any need to be: Nonnie Balcer, Helen Barolini, Polly Berends, Louise Brown, Graham Burgess, Darian Cork, Ross Ferlito, Martin Gardner, Martin Gregory, Jan Gustafson, Peter Heidtmann, David and Carol House, Judith Joyce, Mary Catherine

Kelly, David King, John Kraft, Judith Kroll, Rafil Kroll-Zaidi, Dr. Bernice
Kurchin, Benjamin McCullough, Katherine McCullough, Ann McFar-
lane, Barbara McMannus, Frank Meddens, Jim and Julie Monson, Janet
Murphy, Murial Olsson, Cindy Pavlinac, the Reverend Okke Postma,
Dan Raven, Lucy Rosenthal, T. G. Rosenthal, Kimberly Lowelle Saward,
Le Anne Schreiber, Kirsi and Jukka Seppala, Dick Sheridan, Will Shortz,
Irene Skolnick, Beth and Ray Smith, Sue Smith, W. D. Snodgrass, Gaby
Speyer, Barbara Thompson and Antoine Veray.

I would especially like to thank Hervé Coffignal and Patricia O'Neill
in Normandy, and Mary Clemmey in London. I am indebted to William
Bayer, for so generously sharing his copies of Gustav Palm's mirror-maze
patent papers, and to Lynn Fielder, for permitting me to quote from
her unpublished essay "Insights on the Labyrinth." I also gratefully
acknowledge Sue Erpf Van de Bovenkamp for her permission to visit
Michael Ayrton's Arkville maze.

Those who generously sat still for longer interviews include: Robert
Abbott, Lauren Artress, the marquess of Bath, Dori Bohntinsky, Ariane
Burgess, Alex Champion, Helen Curry, Mary Jane DeWeese, Robert
Ferré, Adrian Fisher, Don Frantz, Dora Gallagher, Robert Goldsack,
Marty Kermeen, Alan Mart, Terry Pope, Warrie Price, Jeff Saward, Ray-
mond V. Shepherd and David Tolzmann.

The indispensable libraries always ready to find the elusive book are
the Hastings-on-Hudson Public Library, the Pierpont-Morgan Library,
the New York Botanical Garden Library, the New York City Public
Library, the New York University Library and the Westchester County
Library System.

The following institutions provided useful help and information: the
Baron Gerard Museum (Bayeux, France), the Battery Conservancy, the
Catskill Center for Conservation and Development, Chatsworth House,
the Office of the Mayor of Chesterfield (England), the Colonial Williamsburg Foundation, the Trustees of the Hastings-on-Hudson Historical
Society, the Labyrinth Society, Labyrinthos, the London Transport Museum, Longleat House, the Museum of Witchcraft (Boscastle, England),
the National Museum of the American Indian, New Harmony State Historical Site (Indiana), the New Harmony Workingmen's Institute, Old
Economy Village (Pennsylvania Historic and Museum Commission),
the University of Mississippi and Veriditas: The Worldwide Labyrinth
Project.

Two editors played major roles. Kathleen Kiernan was there at the beginning, and Alice van Straalen guided it through to the end with a rare mixture of insight and good humor.

And, of course, Fran McCullough is in a category all her own. Without her, this book might not have been written at all.

There is something almost grudging, even legalistic, about the sound of the word *acknowledgments* that I do not intend to suggest. What I'm saying is "Thank you."

BIBLIOGRAPHY

Abbott, Robert. *Super Mazes*. Rocklin, Calif., 1997.

Artress, Lauren. *Walking a Sacred Path*. New York, 1995.

Attali, Jacques. *The Labyrinth in Culture and Society*. Berkeley, Calif., 1999.

Avery, Catherine B., ed. *The New Century Classical Handbook*. New York, 1962.

Ayrton, Michael. *The Maze Maker*. New York, 1967.

———. *The Minotaur*. London, 1970.

———. *The Rudiments of Paradise*. New York, 1971.

Barnes, Julian. "Letter from London." *The New Yorker*, September 30, 1991.

Bayer, William. *Mirror Maze*. New York, 1994.

Benson, Herbert. *Timeless Healing*. New York, 1996.

Berry, Wendell. *The Country of Marriage*. New York, 1973.

Bord, Janet. *Mazes and Labyrinths of the World*. New York, 1975.

Borges, Jorge Luis. *Labyrinths*. New York, 1964.

Brion, Marcel. *Pompeii and Herculaneum*. Translated by John Rosenberg. New York, 1960.

Burgess, Graham. *Labyrinths and Mazes*. Whitechurch, England, 2002.

Campbell, Joseph, *The Hero with a Thousand Faces*. Princeton, 1949.

———. *The Mythic Image*. Princeton, 1974.

Catullus, *Poems*. Translated by Francis W. Cornish. Cambridge, England, 1913.

Champion, Alex. *Earth Mazes*. Philo, Calif., 1990.

———. *Essays on Labyrinths.* Philo, Calif., 2001.

———. *My Involvement with Labyrinths.* Philo, Calif., 2000.

Charpentier, Louis. *The Mysteries of Chartres Cathedral.* Haverhill, England, 1972.

Conty, Patrick. *The Genesis and Geometry of the Labyrinth.* Rochester, Vt., 2002.

Cowell, F. R. *The Garden as a Fine Art.* Boston, 1978.

Cruttwell, Robert W. *Virgil's Mind at Work.* Oxford, England, 1947.

Davill, Timothy, et al. *The Cerne Giant.* Bournemouth, England, 1999.

De Bay, Philip, and James Bottom. *Garden Mania.* New York, 2000.

DeWald, Terry. *The Papago Indians and Their Basketry.* Tucson, 1979.

Doob, Penelope Reed. *The Idea of the Labyrinth.* Ithaca, 1990.

Eliot, T. S. *The Complete Poems and Plays, 1909–1950.* New York, 1952.

Evans, Arthur. *The Palace of Minos at Knossos.* Vol. III. London, 1930.

Ferré, Robert. *Constructing the Chartres Labyinth.* St. Louis, 2001.

Field, Robert, *Mazes.* Norfolk, England, 1999.

Fisher, Adrian, Randoll Coate and Graham Burgess. *A Celebration of Mazes.* St. Albans, England, 1984.

Fisher, Adrian, and Diana Kingham. *Mazes.* Princes Risborough, England, 2000.

Fisher, Adrian, and Howard Loxton. *Secrets of the Maze.* London, 1997.

Frazer, James. *The Golden Bough.* New York, 1996.

Gide, André. *Two Legends: Oedipus and Theseus.* Translated by John Russell. New York, 1950.

Goode, Patrick, and Michael Lanchaster. *The Oxford Companion to Gardens.* Oxford, England, 1986.

Gould, Veronica Franklin. *The Watts Chapel.* Farnham, England, 1993.

Graves, Robert. *The Greek Myths.* New York, 1955.

Gregory of Tours, *The History of the Franks.* Translated by Lewis Thorpe. New York, 1974.

Hadingham, Evan. *Circles and Standing Stones.* New York, 1976.

Harris, Neal. "Therapy Utilizing Finger Labyrinths." *Caerdroia* 32 (2001).

Harvey, P. D. A. *Mappa Mundi.* London, 1996.

Herodotus, *The History.* Translated by Henry Cary. New York, 1873.

Hichin, Francis. *Earth Magic.* New York, 1977.

Hinds, William Alfred. *American Communities.* New York, 1961.

Homer. *The Iliad.* Translated by Robert Fitzgerald. New York, 1975.

Jackson, J. B. *The Necessity of Ruins.* Amherst, Mass., 1980.

James, John. *Chartres: The Masons Who Built a Legend.* London, 1985.

Jung, Karl. *Mandala Symbolism.* Princeton, 1972.

Kern, Hermann. "Image of the Workd and Sacred Realm: Labyrinth Cities and City Labyrinths." *Daidalus* (Berlin), March 1982.

———. *Through the Labyrinth.* Munich, 2000.

Kraft, John. *The Goddess in the Labyrinth.* Abo, Sweden, 1985.

Laishley, Lilan. "The Harmonist Labyrinths." *Caerdroia* 32 (2001).

Lapatin, Kenneth. *Mysteries of the Snake Goddess.* Boston, 2002.

Ling, Roger. *Ancient Mosaics.* Princeton, 1998.

Lippard, Lucy R. *Overlay: Contemporary Art and the Art of Prehistory.* New York, 1983.

Lockridge, Ross E. *The Labyrinth.* New Harmony, Ind., 1941.

Lonegren, Sig. *Labyrinths: Ancient Myths and Modern Uses.* New York, 2001.

Macaulay, Rose. *The Pleasure of Ruins.* London, 1953.

MacGillivray, J. Alexander. *Minotaur: Sir Arthur Evans and the Archaeology of the Minoan Myth.* London, 2001.

Martineau, John. *Mazes and Labyrinths in Great Britain.* Powys, Wales, 1996.

Matthews, W. H. *Mazes and Labyrinths: Their History and Development.* New York, 1970.

McMahon, Bernard. *The American Gardener's Calendar.* Philadelphia, 1806.

Meehan, Aidan. *Maze Patterns.* London, 1993.

Miller, Malcolm. *Chartres Cathedral.* New York, 1996.

Mitchell, John. *Megalithomania.* Ithaca, 1982.

Nelson, Thomas Allen. *Kubrick: Inside a Film Artist's Maze.* Bloomington, Ind., 2000.

Nyenhuis, Jacob E. *Myth and the Creative Process: Michael Ayrton and the Myth of Daedalus the Maze Maker.* Detroit, 2003.

Pennick, Nigel. *Mazes and Labyrinths.* London, 1998.

Pliny the Elder. *Natural History.* Translated by D. E. Eicholz. Cambridge, England, 1962.

Plutarch. *The Rise and Fall of Athens.* Translated by Ian Scott-Kilvert. New York, 1960.

Purce, Jill. *The Mystic Spiral.* London, 1997.

Renfrew, Colin. *Before Civilization.* New York, 1973.

Rogers, Elizabeth Barlow. *Landscape Design.* New York, 2002.

The Royal Commission on the Ancient and Historical Momuments of Scotland. *Argyll.* Vol. 6. Edinburgh, 1999.

Rudofsky, Bernard. *Streets for People.* Garden City, 1964.

Sands, Helen Raphael. *The Healing Labyrinth.* Hauppauge, N.Y., 2001.

Saward, Jeff. *Ancient Labyrinths of the World.* Thundersley, Sussex, England, 1999.

———. *Magical Paths.* London, 2002.

Schaefers, Fons. "A Catalogue of Labyrinths and Mazes in the Netherlands." *Caerdroia* 32 (2001).

Schneider, Michael S. *A Beginner's Guide to Constructing the Universe.* New York, 1995.

Shchimmel, Annemarie. *The Mystery of Numbers.* New York, 1993.

Shields, Carol. *Larry's Party.* New York, 1997.

Spirn, Anne Whiston. *The Language of Landscape.* New Haven, 1998.

Thacker, Christopher. *The History of Gardens.* Berkeley, 1979.

———. "The Long Labyrinth of Darkness: The Landscape Garden and the Maze." *Daidalos* (Berlin), March 1982.

Virgil. *The Aeneid.* Translated by Robert Fitzgerald. New York, 1983.

von Simpson, Otto. *The Gothic Cathedral.* Princeton, 1956.

Walker, Jearl. "The Amateur Scientist." *Scientific American,* June 1986.

Waters, Frank. *The Book of the Hopi.* New York, 1963.

Watts, Mary. *The Word in the Pattern.* London, 1904.

Weschler, Lawrence. *Robert Irwin Getty Garden.* Los Angeles, 2002.

West, Melissa Gayle. *Exploring the Labyrinth.* New York, 2000.

Whalley, Robin, and Anne Jennings. *Knot Gardens and Parterres.* London, 1998.

Wright, Craig. *The Maze and the Warrior.* Cambridge, Mass., 2001.

Young, Marguerite. *Angel in the Forest.* New York, 1966.

ILLUSTRATIONS

INDEX

tria; the turf labyrinth known as Julian's Bower, Alkborough, England; the detail from the *Mappa Mundi* in Hereford Cathedral, Hereford, England; the petroglyph at Arroyo Hondo, near Taos, New Mexico. Copyright © by Jeff Saward/Labyrinthos. Reprinted by permission of Jeff Saward.

Image of the medieval labyrinth, Chartes Cathedral, Chartes, France. Copyright © Cindy A. Pavlinac/Sacred Land Photography. Reprinted by permission of Cindy A. Pavlinac.

Image of 2002 Amazing Maize Maze at Cherry-Crest Farm. Copyright © Cathy Kornfield. Reprinted by permission of Cathy Kornfield.